DAVID EARLE

A Choreographic Biography

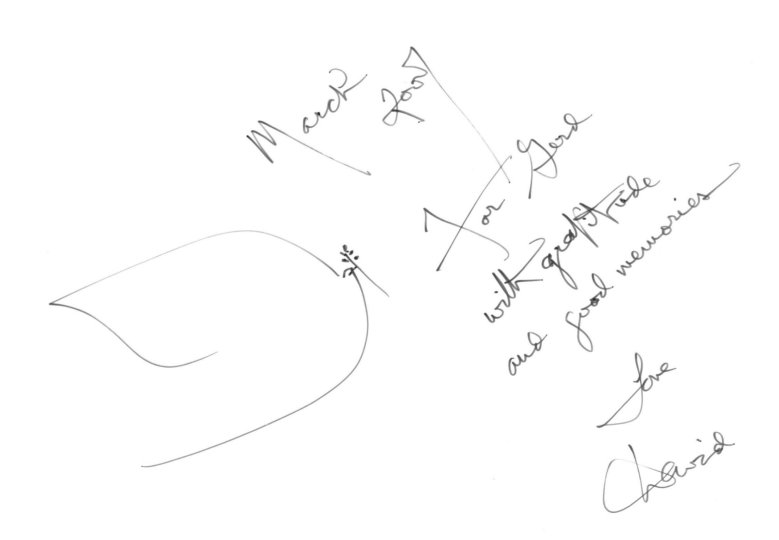

March 2009

For Gord
with gratitude
and good memories

love

David

DAVID EARLE

A Choreographic Biography

by Michele Green

TORONTO, 2006

David Earle: A Choreographic Biography
Copyright © 2006 Michele Green, David Earle, Graham Jackson
Editors/Readers: Miriam Adams, Amy Bowring, Allana Lindgren
Permissions Research: Seika Boye
Book Design: Michael Caplan
Cover Photo: Beatrice De Conti

Published by:
Dance Collection Danse Press/es
145 George Street
Toronto, Ontario Canada M5A 2M6

Library and Archives Canada Cataloguing in Publication

Green, Michele, 1952-
David Earle : a choreographic biography / Michele Green.

ISBN 0-929003-58-6

1. Earle, David--Catalogues raisonnés. I. Title.

GV1785.E27G74 2005   792.8'2'092   C2005-905448-4

Best efforts have been made to identify copyright material contained in this book.
The publisher welcomes any information enabling it to rectify references or credits in
a future edition.

Arts Inter-Media Canada/Dance Collection Danse gratefully acknowledges
organizational support from the Canada Council for the Arts, the Ontario Arts
Council and the City of Toronto through the Toronto Arts Council. Special thanks to
the late Nick Laidlaw.

ISBN 0-929003-58-6   Manufactured in Canada

CONTENTS

ACKNOWLEDGEMENTS

This choreographic biography has benefited from the assistance and resources of many people. I would like to thank Jay Rankin, Bridget Cauthery and Ruth Hoch of the Toronto Dance Theatre and Ken Hernden at the York University Archives and Special Collections for invaluable cataloguing information and photography. Thank you to Deborah Lundmark, Michael deConinck Smith, Richard Rutherford, David Ferguson, Mimi Beck and Mike Moore for filling in the blanks in many of the works. Thanks to Joel Green and Patti Gutierrez for use of electronic equipment and to my husband, Jim, for giving generously of his time, expertise and patience. Special thanks to Michael English for videotaping the interviews and unearthing many elusive names and dates; and to Suzette Sherman without whose massive personal archives and day-by-day help and encouragement this project would have remained only a dream.

And finally, thank you to Miriam Adams and Amy Bowring for pushing this work to its conclusion. I dedicate this book to the memory of Lawrence Adams, who convinced me of its importance and persuaded me to tackle it. The history of modern dance in Canada is a grander stage with a larger audience because of him.

MICHELE GREEN

INTRODUCTION

A book cataloguing 130 choreographic works by an artist whose output spans four decades is, in itself, an astounding volume of information. Compiling the fragments of facts from archives, house programmes, newspaper articles and personal memories proved to be an interesting, often daunting, and occasionally frustrating task. Documenting David Earle's œuvre was, in the opinion of many of us from the dance world, an overdue first step to retrieving an important piece of Canada's modern dance history. The completed file dating from 1963 to 2005 is David Earle's legacy and I felt a sense of accomplishment in being responsible for salvaging these scattered artifacts.

This book offers much more than a catalogue which, indeed, can be dry matter ... names, locations and dates, often with cryptic programme notes and random newspaper reviews ... each entry merely the final compressed statistical data of a long choreographic voyage. Interesting? To a point. Historical? Definitely. But without some understanding of the man responsible for these works or a glimpse at the path of his creativity and his emotional choreographic journey, a catalogue is nothing more than a simple collection of facts. Each of David Earle's works is a process comparable to the birth of a child ... the conception (of an idea); the months of gestational nurturing and growth (the choreographic process); the birth (the premiere); and the emotional turmoil of setting this creation free.

David is, in his own words, a 'visual junkie'. The seeds of his creations often stem from photographs, paintings, sculpture and postcards; or, if music has been the basis for a concept, he will sort through his boxes of images searching for those that connect to the score and inspire the musical imagination. During the choreographic process, David frequently wrote a daily journal. The journals' pages overflow with images – guiding and focussing his progress. The original ideas twist and turn with each entry, veering off in new directions, faltering and falling into place, often gelling only days before the premiere.

Reading the journals was, for me, like opening a time capsule and becoming partner to David's daily struggle for the right direction and implied narrative, the appropriate movement and a meaningful title. I saw, first-hand, his dependency on the dancers' feedback, their willingness to contribute to the process and their enthusiasm or lack thereof. I shared in the exhaustion of dead end roads, the frustration of budget cuts, the concern over sets and costumes, the euphoria of even a few musical bars of progress. And … I felt the ecstasy of creation.

As I delved into the ever-expanding repertoire, the parallels in the works became strikingly evident: David's continuing devotion to religious themes; the works steeped in mythology; the role death plays in life and its consequences to the living; and the attendant theme that love, humanity and the spiritual relationship binding individual to community be held sacred above all else. The more time I spent with David, the more I became aware of his powerful beliefs and his continual struggle to understand the cruelty of humanity. These beliefs and struggles are evident in much of his work: *Sacra Conversazione*'s perfect blend of emotion-charged movement depicting life and death struggle to the Mozart *Requiem* was so powerful and poignant that not only the audience, but the dancers as well, were often moved to tears. David has always despised war – despised it because he believes that humankind refuses to learn from the experience. For many years he rejected anything related to the subject of war, but he later felt the need to portray war and its consequences, often from the viewpoint of those left behind. Midway through David's 1999 journal for the choreographic work *Ex Voto* are scrawled the words, "Every death is the equal of our own – why can we not feel it that way?"

During 2002 and 2003, I videotaped interviews with David. In chronological order he recalled, then reminisced about each choreographic work. Some of the stories were seamless and humorous, honed by years of entertaining dancers during breaks between classes or rehearsals. However, despite an impressive list of awards including the Order of Canada, behind the anecdotes simmered his struggles through four decades as a modern dance artist in Canada – the continuing financial hardships, the lack of appreciation by the mainstream Toronto press and the final painful decision to leave his beloved Toronto Dance Theatre.

My research has given me the unique opportunity to see the man as he was and, simultaneously, the man he is today. With this opportunity comes the onerous responsibility of balancing the past and the present without minimizing or diluting these two equally important and valid viewpoints.

The photographic illustrations speak volumes – suspended moments capturing forever many of Canada's foremost modern dancers. The stage experience is limited to a few hours of intimacy shared in the theatre by dancer and audience. The moment can never be reproduced, neither by aging videotapes nor occasional re-creations, and certainly not in the pages of a book. But what a book of this type can do is remind us of the past, recall that moment of connection – that moment of genius, offer a glimpse of the hours, weeks and months that culminated in the birth of the work. David's musings – both during the choreographic process and through memories – bring a new understanding and dimension to the programme notes. The works take on a new, vital meaning. Even without the benefit of seeing the live performance, his words – aided by the photographs – stir the imagination and the choreography comes alive. At the same time, the catalogue, with its casts of dancers, designers, places and dates, sets the performance scene.

David did not create in a vacuum and readily admits that every aspect of his life has affected the finished work: the weather – noted with each journal entry, the season, books read, food eaten, countries visited, relationships, and his greatest influence – the dancers. He reminisced about many of the dancers, specifically the first company of the Toronto Dance Theatre, the pioneers who set the standard for others to follow. "I was always in love with everyone I worked with, and still am", he told me. The dancer is the vessel of his creativity, as is the musician's instrument or the painter's brush. His dancers have given life to his vision and at times the memory of their talent and beauty rendered him speechless.

Some effort is being made to preserve existing videotapes of David's works, and to remount and videotape selected choreographies. However, it is already too late for works that were performed once or twice in workshop productions at Toronto Dance Theatre's Winchester Street Theatre, or performed as commissioned pieces in church settings. It is almost impossible to retrieve those works that are buried in the archives of other companies worldwide. Little is left of these pieces except the occasional crumpled house programme, David's all important journals, and now his memories preserved in this book. "Dance is the vanishing art form", he has said. Art forms that are self-recording – music, theatre, painting – can wait twenty years for assessment by a different public and that is dance's tragedy. "If the dancer, the choreographer or the work are not recognized and preserved immediately they are forever lost."

Combining a catalogue, photography, personal musings and selected journal entries into book form is, until now, an untried process for the recording of dance in Canada. David Earle is a complex man and this book does not begin to delve into his personal story. Neither does it attempt to give weight to a teaching career that has inspired young dancers for decades. "Don't be satisfied with where you are, the next level is awaiting you," he told students at a recent summer school while – at sixty-four years of age – demonstrating the technique with such skill and devotion that the dancers stood mesmerized. "Dance is one of the best ways to know you are alive."

David's contribution as a teacher and mentor is worthy of another book. This choreographic biography gives life to his prolific creative journey – a journey shared by thousands of modern dancers and tens of thousands of audience members worldwide.

MICHELE GREEN
SEPTEMBER 2005

BIOGRAPHY

DAVID EARLE, C. 1944

In the second half of 1939, Canadians were volunteering to serve in the impending Second World War, the country was reeling from the economic devastation of the Great Depression and, on September 17, Charles David Ronald Earle was born in the city of Toronto. Growing up in a volatile family with an athletic older brother, Douglas, who was deemed to follow his father into the business world, David became the peacekeeper – a role he has continued to play in relationships throughout his life.

Childhood exposure to Humbercrest United Church's 'pseudo-gothic' grandeur cultivated a passion for ecclesiastical architecture, stained glass and stone, as well as a love of liturgical music and poetry.

David's dance training began at the age of five with ballet and tap lessons from Beth Weyms and Fanny Birdsall; he made his dance debut at Eaton Auditorium that same year. His beloved paternal grandmother provided positive reinforcement when he presented his first choreographic attempts for an audience-of-one at her Peterborough farm. "I wanted to be a Greek God. The tunic was one of the many remnants I collected obsessively and stored in my dress-up box. I used to dance all the time for Grandmother and afterwards I would ask, 'Was I good?' – the answer, always, 'Very good.' My best reviews ... from somebody who really mattered."

When he was eight years old, David joined Dorothy Goulding's Toronto Children Players and the lavish productions – four each year – filled his summers with the discipline and creativity of the theatre.

At Eaton Auditorium I moved and spoke on stage in myths and fairy tales until I was nineteen, and then I began to dance. It is movement as communication that has kept me tirelessly challenged and perpetually rewarded. Theatre continues to be a highly conscious aspect of my dance creations and, although I always intend to use props I rarely end up doing so. For my choreographic debut at Toronto's YMHA, I performed *Oiseaux Triste* to music by Ravel. I made two newspaper doves that I intended to scotch tape to my wrists but at the last moment realized they were a bad idea. My costume was a T-shirt that I had sewn between my legs. I did a huge sissonne and the whole thing went up my bum. Realizing I could not face the back of

13

DAVID EARLE AT HIS GRANDMOTHER'S FARM IN PETERBOROUGH, C. 1947

DAVID EARLE AND YOUNG DANCER AT
BETH WEYMS' STUDIO, C. 1945

the stage I was forced to improvise. It was the first time my father had seen me dance and he came backstage and said, 'Well, young man, we saw a good deal more of you tonight than we've seen for many years'. *Oiseaux Triste* was never performed again.

Fleeing the Toronto suburb of Etobicoke after high school, David studied Radio and Television Arts for two years at Ryerson Polytechnical Institute. At the age of twenty, a Bolshoi Ballet performance offered a profound inspiration to dance; he auditioned and was accepted as a scholarship student at the National Ballet School. At the NBS, where he stayed for four years, David met eurhythmics teacher Donald Himes who introduced him to the Laban technique at Yoné Kvietys' studio. David performed for two years with Kvietys' company.

Victoria Reilly summarized an event in a January 27, 1964 article in the *Toronto Daily Star*:

> Yesterday, a specially invited audience had the chance to see what goes on in Yoné Kvietys' "Modern Dance Workshop" – a series of choreographic lessons held on Sunday afternoons at the YM-YWHA. Miss Kvietys' group of young people, consisting of eight girls and two boys clad in black and bare-footed, brought to life, amongst many things, such mundane objects as a typewriter and a washing machine! In her commentary Miss Kvietys stressed that the dancers were not trying to look like either of these objects but rather were finding and interpreting the 'quality' of their 'movements'. A lot of the work was improvised – improvisation being an excellent developer of creative imagination – but there were also studies prearranged by the dancers themselves, many of which were original and fascinating and at times reminiscent of Picasso's twining forms, now on view at the Art Gallery of Toronto. Outstanding among the performers were Donald Himes, David Earle, Vera Davis and Bessie Zavonovich.

In 1963, David studied with Martha Graham, José Limón and Donald McKayle at Connecticut College and spent the next two years on scholarship at Martha Graham's school in New York. Also studying in New York were Donald Himes, Susan Macpherson, Lilian Jarvis, James Cunningham and Patricia Beatty. Peter Randazzo was occasionally class demonstrator for Miss Graham. In 1966, as a member of the José Limón Company, David performed at Connecticut College and the American Dance Festival. At New York City's Harkness Dance Festival he entertained the Central Park

TO DANCE AT HART HOUSE

The Contemporary Dance Company, directed by Yone Kvietys, will present a program of modern dancing at Hart House March 16 and 17, starting at 8.30 p.m. Members here are, from left: George Donnell, Don Himes, David Earle.

GEORGE DONNELL, DONALD HIMES AND DAVID EARLE IN A WORK BY YONÉ KVIETYS, 1962
PHOTO: MARIO GEO, *TORONTO STAR*

crowd as one of the Beatles in *Songs for Young Lovers*. However, with the advent of the Vietnam War, David, a green card holder, had the potential to be drafted.

> During the Vietnam days, I wrote to José Limón explaining why I had to leave the United States. José wrote me a beautiful letter and said, "It's tragic because for centuries, artists had international passports [as goodwill ambassadors] and were welcomed in any country that they would go to. It's a tragic change of values."
>
> – David Earle as quoted in *The New Canadian*, March 16, 1995

David then went to England, accepting a job as dance master from arts philanthropist Robin Howard. He worked with a group of commonwealth dancers assembled for the opening of the Liverpool Christ the King Cathedral and stayed to work with the newly formed London Contemporary Dance Theatre (LCDT) under the artistic direction of Robert Cohan.

In December 1967, David appeared as a guest in Patricia Beatty's New Dance Group of Canada in Toronto, returning to London to direct the LCDT's first London season. He visited Toronto again in March 1968 to stage a concert in collaboration with Peter Randazzo, rehearsing in Patricia Beatty's studio. David then completed his LCDT season, however, his future partnership with Randazzo had been established – Toronto Dance Theatre's (TDT) birth was imminent. Peter and David negotiated with John Sime, founder and principal of the Three Schools of Art, to start their company under his guidance. However, when Patricia offered her school and company as the base for this new venture, the three co-founders formed their unique triumvirate.

Toronto Dance Theatre, a professional company whose dancers trained in the Graham technique, debuted in December 1968 at Toronto Workshop Productions theatre. Nine dancers performed eight pieces, four of the works choreographed by David Earle – *Mirrors* (premiere), *The Recitation*, and *Angelic Visitation #1* and *#2*.

David Earle wrote in his journal in 1973: "I think that when we began to work in Toronto many people were hungry for a more avant-garde oriented theatre experience than it was actually our intention to provide. On the contrary, with uncompromising demands on the technical standard of our dancers, we intend to preserve the classical yet humane dance forms of Martha Graham – so quickly abandoned by some members of her company who founded new, more abstract movements in a city with an unequalled pace in its demand for novelty."

TDT's growth was phenomenal. In 1972 they mounted their first highly successful European tour and for ten years TDT grew despite persistent financial hardships, a second unsuccessful European tour and scathing critical reviews. In the first decade David created thirty-five works.

KENNY PEARL, C. 1983

> Trish and Peter are both enormous universes – both equally unfathomable. They were glamorous, exotic, dark, mysterious, sensual performers and phenomenal charismatic dance artists, and I felt plain beside them. When Peter started choreographing he became one of the first 'macho' bare-chested male modern dancers in Canada who did not hesitate to express anger in his works.
>
> Peter and Trish were the dynamic focus of their choreography and the dancers in their pieces moved on an axis that emanated out from their presence. To dance with either of them on stage was an extraordinary experience because they were so engaged with their performance that it was shocking to encounter – and try to match – their fierce energy.
>
> We were in an arena together where we were creating simultaneously. There was never any conflict or jealousy between us, no miserable altercations or ego fits. We combined works that seemed to fit together in a programme without conscious awareness of whose pieces were chosen because we admired and participated in each other's works.
>
> I feel that one of the problems of this triumvirate was that none of us was more visible than the 'Toronto Dance Theatre'. It became its own power and I began to feel that we were not being understood for our individual identities and gifts. There came a time when 'The Theatre of Peter Randazzo' should have been seen exclusively in one evening and the audience could connect solely with his imagination and genius. While always presenting a mixed programme, we were not able to develop separately or be perceived as distinctly individual dance artists.

In 1979, David originated the School of Toronto Dance Theatre's Professional Training Program. His teaching has taken him to the Université du Québec à Montréal; Les Grands Ballets Canadiens' École Supérieure de la danse du Québec; Southern Methodist University in Dallas, Texas; the Banff Centre; New York University; The Juilliard School; École de Danse du Québec in Quebec City; Ballet British Columbia; Vancouver's Arts Umbrella; and Constantine Darling's former studio in Victoria, the Victoria Arts Collective.

PETER RANDAZZO, C. 1970

PATRICIA BEATTY AND DAVID EARLE IN BEATTY'S
LESSONS IN ANOTHER LANGUAGE, c. 1980
PHOTO: ANDREW OXENHAM

Although David choreographed eighteen works between 1979 and 1982, the workload was overwhelming and, along with escalating financial problems and dancer dissension, the founders knew they needed help. Kenny Pearl, David's first student in Toronto, who later danced with Martha Graham and Alvin Ailey in New York, was appointed artistic director in August 1983. During Pearl's four seasons, David choreographed some of his most renowned works – *Court of Miracles* (1983), *Sacra Conversazione* (1984) and *Sunrise* (1987).

In 1987, David became sole Artistic Director leading the company to its first two triumphant seasons in New York and tours in Europe and Asia. In November 1993, TDT celebrated its twenty-fifth anniversary featuring selected works of the three founders. Despite obvious successes during that period, David was exhausted and defeated by the widening separation between the founders and what had become, to him, an impersonal institution. He handed the artistic reigns to Christopher House in June 1994.

David remained as artist-in-residence until 1996 when he felt he could no longer support the company's direction. Harbouring feelings of resentment and betrayal along with lingering unresolved matters, David presented *Maelstrom* and *Sang* in his final TDT season. He then walked away from twenty-eight years of singularly dedicated work. David had created ninety-five choreographies to that point, many independently, including *Orpheus and Eurydice*, directed by Bill Glassco for the Guelph Spring Festival; *Dido and Aeneas* for the Stratford Music Festival; *Realm*, commissioned by Erik Bruhn for the National Ballet of Canada; *Cape Eternity* for the opening of the Toronto International Festival and *Sacra Conversazione* and *Cloud Garden* for the Banff Festival of the Arts. In collaboration with James Kudelka, he choreographed *Schéhérazade* for Les Grands Ballets Canadiens. For Ballet British Columbia, he created *Architecture for the Poor*; for the Polish Dance Theatre, *Angels and Victories* for the World Music Days Festival in Warsaw and the 1992 Edinburgh Festival; and for Canadian Children's Dance Theatre, *Chichester Psalms*.

In 1996, wanting to establish a permanent vehicle for his work, David launched Dancetheatre David Earle (DtDE) based in Guelph, Ontario to, as David states, "support continuing creation, for the preservation of my repertoire and to serve as a forum for younger artists whose concern is the expression of humanity in dance."

On July 19, 1997 DtDE, a company of twenty dancers, made its debut at the Elora Music Festival. During this time David was also artist-in-residence for

the Canadian Children's Dance Theatre's 1997/98 season. He co-founded Temple Studios in Guelph in 2001 and the following year expanded DtDE to include the third floor of their premises, providing a full-sized studio and chamber performance space. In 2002, the first DtDE summer school of intensive professional training was initiated, attracting students from five provinces.

Over the last two decades the arts community has repeatedly acknowledged and honoured David's work. In 1987 he received the Clifford E. Lee Award from the Banff Festival of the Arts and the Dora Mavor Moore Award for best new choreography for his work, *Sunrise*. Along with Patricia Beatty and Peter Randazzo, in 1988 he received the Toronto Arts Award for Performing Arts. In 1994 he received the Jean A. Chalmers Award for Distinction in Choreography, an award that recognizes a choreographer who has created a substantial body of work of national importance. He received the Order of Canada in 1996 for his contribution to the art of dance; the Muriel Sherrin Award from the Toronto Arts Council Foundation in 1998 and the Canada Council for the Arts Jacqueline Lemieux Prize in 2002. David's work has been presented on film and television in Moze Mossanen's *Dance for Modern Times* and *The Dancemakers*; and he has appeared on City TV's *Originals in Art*. For Rhombus Media he choreographed *La Valse* for a film on the life of Maurice Ravel, and *Romeos and Juliets*, which received a Gemini Award and the Press Award from France's Grand Prix International de vidéo-danse de Sète. In 2003, *Sacra Conversazione* was selected by Canadian dance professionals as one of ten Canadian choreographic masterworks of the twentieth century. In spring 2005, David was awarded a Doctor of Laws by Queen's University in Kingston, Ontario.

Since leaving TDT, David has choreographed thirty-nine works, most of which have been commissioned. DtDE presented works in Waterloo in 1998, 1999 and 2000 for Passchendaele, a collaboration with dancer/choreographer D.A. Hoskins and dancer Mike Moore to honour Remembrance Day. The Company has performed at Spring Rites 2000, the Open Ears Festival, Elora Festival, Numus Concert Series and New Brunswick's Baie de Chaleurs Festival, as well as with the Kitchener-Waterloo Symphony and the vocal ensemble, Tactus. In September 2002, the company presented a full evening of works at the Guelph River Run Centre in collaboration with the Penderecki String Quartet. Extended workshops for young professionals have preceded performances in Vancouver at MainDance, for Ballet British Columbia's Arts Umbrella Mentor Program and for similar programmes in Waterloo, Sudbury and Quebec City.

CHRISTOPHER HOUSE IN HIS WORK, *TOSS QUINTET*, 1980
PHOTO: ANDREW OXENHAM

DAVID EARLE: A CHOREOGRAPHIC BIOGRAPHY

DAVID EARLE IN REHEARSAL FOR HIS WORK *REALM*
AT THE NATIONAL BALLET OF CANADA, 1984
PHOTO: ANDREW OXENHAM, COURTESY THE
NATIONAL BALLET OF CANADA ARCHIVES

David continues to believe in the power of dance, the significance of his choreography and the artistic process that involves nurturing dancers committed to his vision. Although sporadic assistance in the form of awards and grants over the last decade has been forthcoming, it has been difficult to sustain his artistic mission. David regularly presents exhibits of his landscape photography to help subsidize DtDE and has collaborated with Mike Moore and D.A. Hoskins in an organization called Grande Orange – which encourages dance artists to develop secondary creative skills that can yield a better income than dance. "I would like to have a Grande Orange web site that would be open to creating a constructive disturbance culturally and socially and would look for ways to fund the arts outside the control of current established funding bodies."

David has never shied away from complex choreographic themes – death and sensuality, spirituality and community. He would relish having the resources that would allow him to create works for the many senior artists who are part of his legacy. For David Earle the challenges continue into the twenty-first century.

PETER RANDAZZO, PATRICIA BEATTY AND DAVID EARLE
RECEIVING THE TORONTO ARTS AWARD, 1988

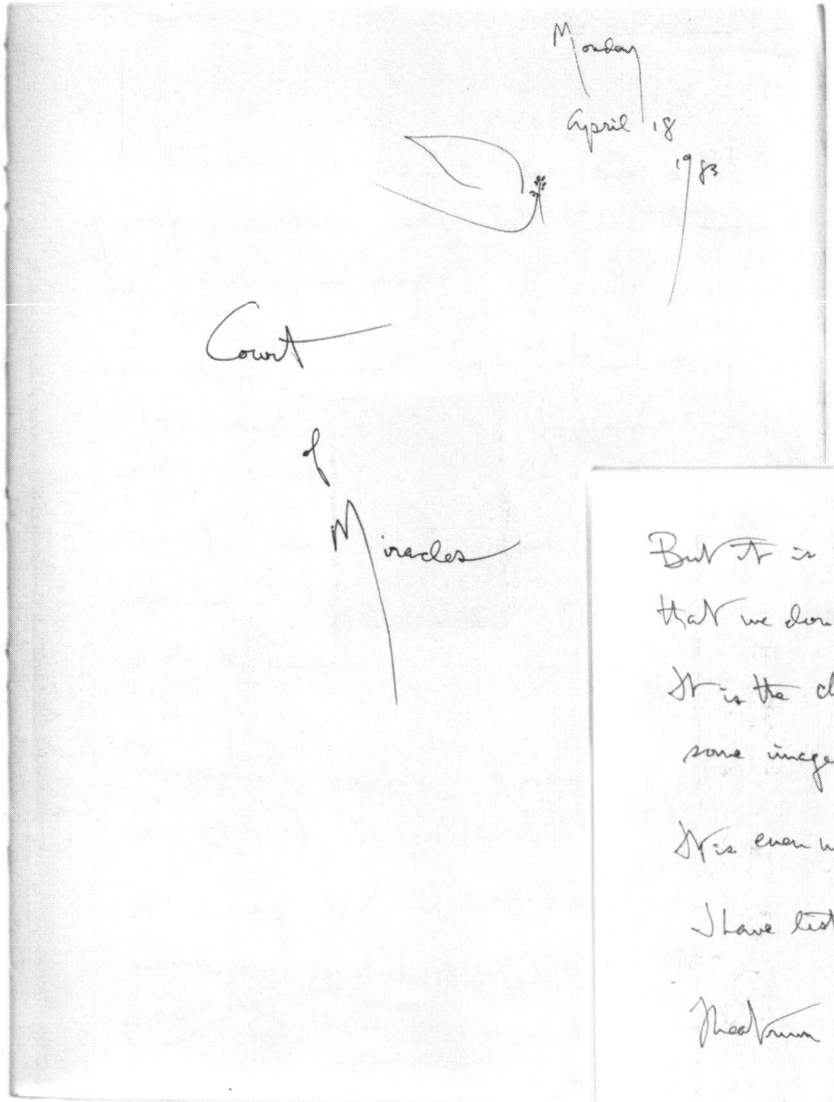

Monday
April 18
1983

Court
of
Miracles

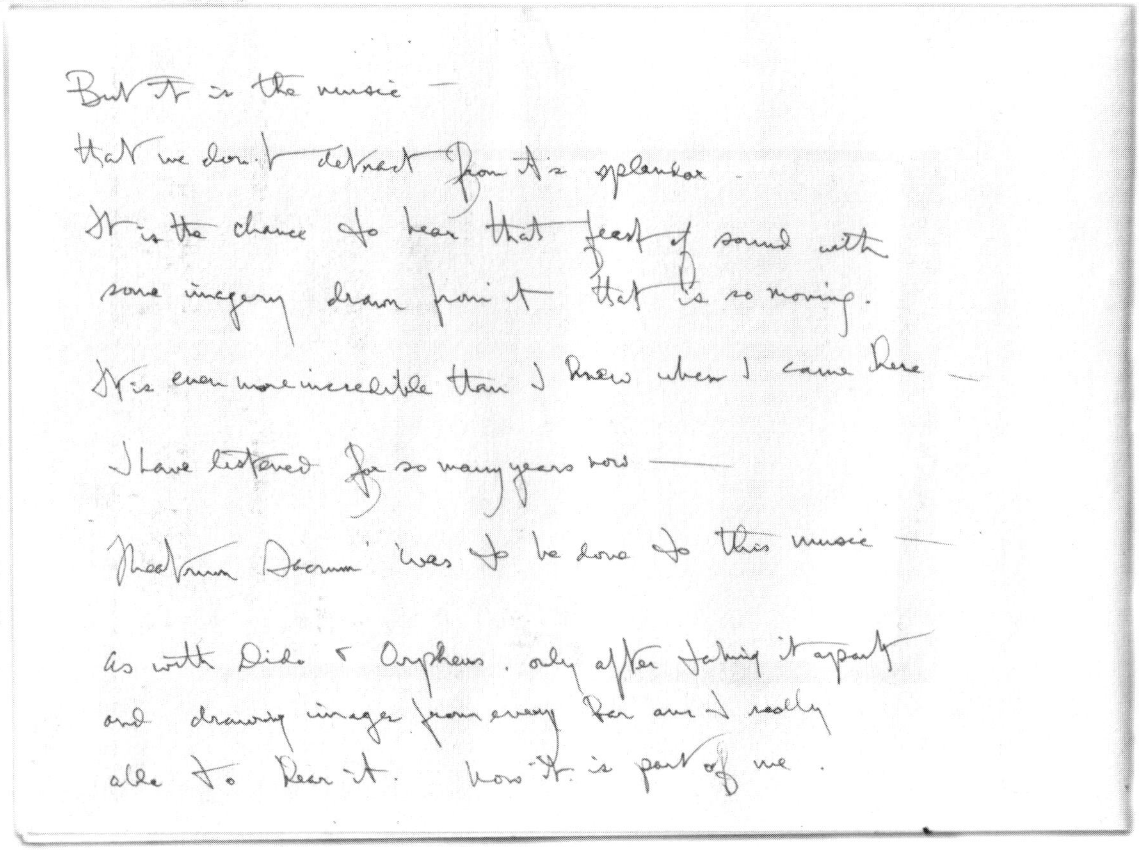

But it is the music —
that we don't detract from its splendor.
It is the chance to hear that feast of sound with
some imagery drawn from it that is so moving.

It is even more incredible than I knew when I came here —

I have listened for so many years now —

Madonna Dacrum was to be done to this music —

As with Dido & Orpheus. only after taking it apart
and drawing images from every bar am I really
able to hear it.   Now it is part of me.

Pages from David Earle's journals for *Court of Miracles*, 1983
and *Sacra Conversazione*, 1984

DAVID EARLE, C. 1968

PIECES OF HEART

By Graham Jackson

It is early September in that year of riots and revolutions, 1968. Here the afternoon light is softer than it has been … golden, almost tender. Autumn is in the air. I am leaving home for an orientation week at Victoria College, just across from the Royal Ontario Museum on the campus of the sprawling university called Toronto. As I put on my jacket, the radio is playing in my parents' kitchen. Janis Joplin is wailing her lungs out, demanding that her unheard lover take another piece of her heart. I'm crazy about this song and in my late adolescent blur of tortured feelings connected almost exclusively to fantasy lovers, I'm convinced I know how she's hurting.

However, this afternoon, I'm feeling mostly nervous, anxious even. I'm joining the big city, a city I've watched from a suburban afar for years with wide-eyed wonder and, lately, with a curiosity tinged with prurience. On the ride "downtown", a ride I've done a hundred times before, I ask myself over and over, will I find my place there? And, more importantly even: will it accept me? An hour later as I climb out of the subway at the Museum stop, a car passes and there's Janis again crying for all she's worth, "Come on, come on, take it! Take another piece of my heart!" But she sounds different than she did in the family storey-and-a-half. Knowing, wise, been-here-before, life's-a-hard-ride different. At the sound of her voice, there on the busy corner, I feel suddenly a thrill of excitement, a sense of having arrived, and an overwhelming desire to have "Life" begin.

Over the previous year or so, I've had several glimpses or previews of this life waiting to begin. Toronto has been changing. Slowly, slowly, of course: Toronto never moves hastily. But some of its sober, good-fellow Presbyterian image has been slipping. There have been riots here, too, or, at least protests and demonstrations – mostly against American involvement in Vietnam and the city is full of angry, committed draft-dodgers, largely professing a vehement left-of-centre, not to say Socialist, position. In the mundane world, Hungarians have established themselves as the aristocracy of the city's café society in haunts like Café de la Paix, Jack and Jill, and the Coffee Mill (still with us after all these years!); and Italians turn up everywhere, on City Council, boards of directors, playing fields, the opera stage and on great, garrulous Sunday promenades along College Street and St. Clair.

JACK MITCHELL
NYC

DAVID EARLE, NEW YORK CITY, C. 1965
PHOTO: JACK MITCHELL

The Central Library Theatre has recently played host to a Canadian-made cause célèbre from New York, John Herbert's homoerotic prison drama, *Fortune and Men's Eyes*, to which available tickets were incredibly scarce. And on the previous July 1, 1967 – in Nathan Phillips Square, that concrete piazza fronting one of the city's bravest and most controversial forays into contemporary architecture, the new twin-towered City Hall – thousands of people actually celebrated! … sang, laughed, shook hands, hugged, ate and soft-drank their way into the 101st year of Canada's history! Near the Hall, the old Bohemian Village on Elm Street clings somewhat forlornly to its "rags-and-feathers-from-Salvation-army-counters" reputation, while further north, in the new-old village of Yorkville the crowds are flocking in from all the bungalowed outposts to gawk at the hippies and "flower children", at the go-go dancers and folk singers who not only give the picaresque warren of streets their colour and vitality, but also their *raison d'être*.

It's in this variegated atmosphere, perfumed with sandalwood incense and patchouli oil, that a fledgling dance company called Toronto Dance Theatre has set up a studio in which to teach the passionate movement language of the great American pioneer of modern dance, Martha Graham. And not only her movement language but also her commitment to dance as the stirring and soulful medium of Eros. I'm not aware of this that day in front of Victoria College as I embrace Life in the great metropolis, but just less than three months later Toronto Dance Theatre has had its première at Toronto Workshop Productions and its star is sparkling brilliantly in the sparsely tenanted firmament of Toronto's cultural life.

I don't actually pay formal court to TDT (as it came to be known by everyone) until the steamy summer of 1970 when the company presented a summer season at the new municipal theatre, the St. Lawrence Centre. I had heard stories about the directors and their dancers. People who fancied themselves insiders referred to them as a special breed, demigods almost, physically stunning, sexually ambivalent, impossibly creative. And I saw them with my own eyes, flowing into the Yorkville Public Library where I worked summers to pay for the following school year's bedsit: long-haired boys and girls who looked to me like creatures from another planet, muscular, limber, scantily clad – one of the young men (Barry Smith, I later learned) a veritable Apollonian giant. Under the guidance of one of their leaders they came often looking for inspiration from the poets, painters and legends of another era. Those who followed them, too, the groupies, the fans, the devotees – and in those days these were numerous – did their best

BARRY SMITH IN PETER RANDAZZO'S *DARK OF MOON*, 1971
PHOTO: PETER SLOMAN

to emulate this exoticism, aiming for as un-Toronto a look as they could devise: cape-wearing men, foreign-looking women with great ruffs of dark hair and kohl-lined eyes, svelte boys in tight sky-blue T-shirts and red bandanas, fiercely earnest sinewy girls who wanted to dance more than anything and did jewellery or Tarot on the side while they watched for their opportunity. They were all in the lobby that summer night, when I caught my first glimpse of what really made TDT newsworthy.

Works from all three of the company's artistic directors were danced that evening. From Bennington-and-Graham-trained Patricia Beatty, there was the haunting solo, *First Music*, set to Charles Ives' *The Unanswered Question*, as well as *Hot and Cold Heroes*, a quirky group piece inspired by media guru Marshall McLuhan's playful and provocative enquiries into medium and message. Peter Randazzo, New York-born-and-raised protégé of the great Martha – he had danced with her for several seasons and had important roles in some of her late masterworks like *Circe* – offered a furious male duet based on the Cain and Abel story, *I Had Two Sons*. And from the creative genius of the third, a Torontonian of Anglo-Protestant stock, David Earle, came two dances: a witty frolic called *Operetta* which spoofed the manners and morals of the silly medium that gave the piece its name and, in quite a different vein, a sombre, melancholic meditation on the experience of legend's most famous whore, Mary Magdalene. Entitled *A Thread of Sand*, it featured actress Jackie Burroughs as the aging Magdalene recalling Christ and his Passion with tender sorrow while dancers around her carved out her memories in remarkable sequences of movement, as sensual as they were spiritual. It was this piece that struck me most forcibly that evening, this piece that turned me into a TDT devotee. I remember feeling, when the lights dimmed on *Thread of Sand*, as if I'd just witnessed something absolutely unexpected, unknown, mysterious, "other", and dazedly I wondered where I was. Was this Toronto? Or the moon? Or ...? I went home that night, back to the suburbs where I was again living temporarily with my parents, trying to make some connection between those bland streets and the misty, otherworldly landscape through which I had just been led. And I felt an indescribable longing to get back as soon as I could to the place of beauty David Earle had offered us.

Among TDT's founding directors, David Earle was the one most influenced by Toronto. Not in the way his colleague Peter Randazzo was influenced by *his* hometown. With Randazzo, the lean, mean, angular, street-smart edginess of New York found its way into his movement phrases

PETER RANDAZZO AND DAVID EARLE IN RANDAZZO'S *I HAD TWO SONS*, 1969
PHOTO: ERIC DZENIS

DAVID EARLE: A CHOREOGRAPHIC BIOGRAPHY

KEITH URBAN, BARRY SMITH, MERLE SALSBERG AND SUSAN MACPHERSON IN DAVID EARLE'S *OPERETTA*, 1970

and choreographic patterns. No, Earle was never touched by the spare grid work of Toronto's streets or the stubborn stolidity of its architecture in that way. But he was touched by Toronto nonetheless, as his long-standing rebellion against everything it has stood for demonstrates: its slow-wittedness, its smug cultural provincialism, its "stupid money" (a term I heard him use more than once twenty years ago), its coldness, its indifference to art and the aesthetic, its conservatism, its pinched soul. In fact, his hatred of the puritanical foundation on which Toronto was built could be said to be one of the most significant goads to his prolific choreographic creativity. Into the face of those who managed this Upper Canadian bastion of Goodness, he repeatedly flung vibrant, luscious, feeling-weighted dance images, inspired by his study of Martha Graham's dance idiom, of course, but also by his reading and travelling and his immersion in the art, music and poetry of other times and places. Ancient cultures; lost civilizations; the Renaissance; Catholic Europe including Italy, Poland, and most especially *la France* in her many variations – Valois, Bourbon, *belle époque*, *fin de siècle*, Parisian between the wars. And in later days the Far East, particularly the stillness, the sense of ritual, the creative balance between sensual and spiritual demonstrated by Japanese culture. These were all part of the "other side" Earle fought for more than twenty-five years to get the good fathers of Toronto to take in. "Come on, come on, come on, and take it!" – they could have been David Earle's words.

Not that Earle didn't find beauty in Toronto. He did. In fact, he was always remarkably open and sensitive to those unsuspected corners of Toronto that to him revealed magic, beauty, mystery, tension, eros. And when he discovered such, he shared his findings generously. Light-dappled parks, stray sculptures caught peeking incongruously out from between unlikely buildings, cafés that breathed out a European air, the Old Masters rooms at the Art Gallery of Ontario or the Chinese fresco galleries at the Royal Ontario Museum, even indisputably WASP corners that somehow managed to transcend their WASPishness – places like Philosopher's Walk or Metropolitan United Church or the neo-Gothic Great Hall of Hart House on the University of Toronto campus. He sought these places out time and again, rhapsodized over them in his journals and photographs and image-collages and publicized them passionately to friends, colleagues, students – even to Torontonians. You could learn a lot about the beauty of this city from David Earle. Many did, for he was an untiring educator and mentor.

To me this all seemed to be part of a greater mission which I would

DAVID EARLE, C. 1970
PHOTO: KEN MIMURA

define now as the unflagging pursuit of recognition for passion, beauty and feeling from those contrary forces of reason, usefulness and thinking that have too long held the upper hand in Western, especially North American, culture. The terms eros and logos best capture the exact nature of this set of opposites, eros referring, of course, to the connective power of heart and body, logos to the more abstract power of word and head. This pursuit for recognition of eros I would say dominated all spheres of David Earle's activity: personal, collective, creative. Though it could occasionally take on a defensive and/or simplistic character, it produced an extraordinary choreographic œuvre that will appeal to us as long as the pursuit is still relevant.

The perennial conflict between eros and logos was frequently the actual "subject" of Earle's dances. Although he never really resorted to the narrative strategies of the storybook ballets, there's no denying that several of his works contained characters, settings, hints of a plot. The most obvious of these was *Courtyard* which looked at the mainly passionate entanglements of a pair of families occupying the same Italian courtyard several centuries apart. The contrasting attitudes of acceptance and rejection, pleasure and horror vis à vis sexual dalliance and erotic love comprised the dramatic device that kept the dance moving.

In *Courtyard* and works like *Field of Dreams*, *Mythos*, *Emozioni* and *Dreamsend*, inspired by one of Earle's favourite writers, Jean Cocteau, evidence of Earle's early theatrical training is perhaps clearest: they are highly theatrical works evoking the proscenium and the heavy red curtain. However, unlike *Courtyard*, the other choreographies are much more allusive, kaleidoscopic, even dreamlike in their pursuit of his favourite themes. Even *Mythos*, which is very closely modelled on the *Phaedra* of Euripides, that shocking play in which a young man is destroyed for daring to reject passion, is more painterly and atmospheric in its dramatic unfolding than strictly speaking narrative. One could almost say that *Mythos* was a kind of dream of the play *Phaedra* and that it points out the importance that the dream landscape, with its merging of conscious and unconscious elements, has always had for the choreographer, beginning with *The Recitation* in 1968 and continuing right up to the present. This merging has allowed Earle the opportunity to show both the persona and shadowy aspects of his themes.

The shadowy aspects of eros define certain of Earle's dances, dances as different as *Quartet* from the mid-seventies and *Furniture* or *Untitled Monument* from the late nineties. Something tormenting – is it mutual loathing? sexual ennui? frustrated passion? – binds the dancers of *Quartet*

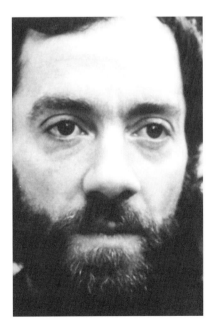

DAVID EARLE, C. 1971
PHOTO: COURTESY GERMAINE SALSBERG

Pieces of Heart

DENNIS (RENÉ) HIGHWAY, CLAUDIA MOORE,
SUSAN MACPHERSON AND CHARLES FLANDERS
IN DAVID EARLE'S *MYTHOS*, 1977
PHOTO: RUDI CHRISTL

together. A length of rope which they manipulate among them symbolizes their captivity. When they drop the rope and begin to experiment with freedom, they come to recognize, like Sartrean existential heroes, how much better off they were when confined by their former torment. At this dawning of "bad faith", one of the men uncoils the rope again and hurls it into their midst, a sinister and serpent-like lifeline.

Both *Furniture* and *Untitled Monument* depict eros as a kind of grotesque carnival clown of an energy that obsesses and addicts those who play with it: perversity is the name of its game. The image of Andrew Giday as a kind of grimacing midnight cowboy posturing with toy guns around a sadsack, threadbare sofa will never be forgotten by anyone who witnessed *Furniture*: his manic efforts to impress, to startle, to titillate recall not only Jon Voight in the celebrated film *Midnight Cowboy* but also American cinematic anti-heroes whose posturing so easily tips over into a genuinely frightening craziness – the De Niro figure in *Taxi Driver*, for example. This is the eros of a maddened, driven society, a narcissistic eros confused with power, looking for victims to provide the quick release.

But eros is also celebrated in Earle's work – more often than it's unmasked. Its radiant side is more often visible than its dark. Most of the time indeed, Earle could be interpreted as following the enthusiastically urgent dictum of E.M. Forster, the English author of *Passage to India*, *Howard's End* and *Maurice*: "Connect – only connect." The sheer bliss of connection is featured in many of the dramatic works already mentioned, even a work as troubled as *Quartet*. It's also present in some of the sombre, elegiac works, like *Exit, Nightfall*, the penultimate section of which, the Miserere, is a paean to the necessity of connection. *Sang*, an in memoriam to friends, lovers and colleagues lost in the great plague, AIDS, features several breathtaking and hopeful moments of coming together that offset the sense of loss that permeates the work.

Where Earle's celebration of eros is at its most fluid, however, is in the works free of programme or dramatic intention, works like the glorious *Baroque Suite*, or the pastoral, French-garden inspired *Courances*, or even the spectral *Diving for the Moon*, in which scarlet-clad dancers sweep like the last of autumn leaves through a penumbral landscape composed of water and mist. Here, in these dances, the drive for connection emerges from the musical moments as if this were the whole point of the music; Earle's deft and tender hearing of music makes it impossible to imagine, in fact, that it had any other purpose than the one he intends. The *Mirrors* section of

Baroque Suite, for instance, in which two couples circle around each other in a polite, quasi-formal style develops into one of the most intimate exchanges of trust and caring I've ever seen on the dance stage. For me, it culminates in a quietly ecstatic moment where each of the women uses her partner's thigh as ground to facilitate a fleeting Icarus-like brush with the ether; at the same moment, the subdued passion at the heart of Bach is released into the atmosphere and we – I, at least – gasp.

Speaking of Bach, the passion and eros that Earle makes the centre-piece of so much of his work very frequently takes on religious overtones. I've already mentioned *Exit, Nightfall*, a work composed in 1981 at a moment when Toronto Dance Theatre was undergoing serious administrative upheavals. Earle was experiencing a deep despondency as he set about choreographing. What emerged from his almost trance-like engagement with the dancers and music (ranging from Xenakis to Allegri) was a work that started in spiritual blackness and ended in glimmers of hope for mankind. But *Exit, Nightfall* was by no means the first of Earle's "religious" dances, nor the first to overlap the spiritual with passion or eros. From the very beginning of his career, he put the two together, proclaiming their relationship to be close and fruitful. The two *Angelic Visitations* of 1968 are the earliest I have seen. In the first, one of the most moving dance duets I have ever experienced, a dozing Virgin Mary rises partially from her couch, certain she has heard something stirring. She looks around, sees nothing, lies back down to try to sleep again. Again a stirring something. Again she rises. Again she wonders and returns to her bed. This is once more repeated until finally she awakens to the awareness that her couch is actually the back of the angel Gabriel. What follows is an intense and passionate dialogue in which he announces to her that she will bear The Child and she, fearfully, humbly and, at the same time, exultantly, accepts her terrible fate.

The relationship between spirit and eros which Earle identified in the *Angelic Visitations* has been the focus of many of his works over the past thirty-five years; one could conceivably argue that it's been the focus – more or less – of all his works. Several of these have taken the shape of liturgical dances, an idiom Earle has continued to explore. *The Fauré Requiem* began life in 1977 as such. Others, notably *Sacra Conversazione*, one of Earle's best loved and most frequently performed dances set to Mozart's crowning glory of a *Requiem*, are unequivocally theatrical in their intentions, but make the same links between spirit and passion, wonder and eros, fury and tenderness, soul and body that the other more formally liturgical dances do.

In *Sacra*, he also underlined another of what I would call major Earle themes: the redemptive quality of spirit + eros to which the dispossessed, here baldly characterized by huddling masses of dancers, have a closer connection than those possessing fortune and fame. Suffering, sacrifice, deprivation, humility … not gold … pave the road leading to rebirth, Earle seems to be suggesting. It's the Sermon on the Mount's message: "Blessed are the meek, for they shall inherit the earth." His 1987 *Sunrise*, which utilizes for its score a movement from one of Brahms' symphonies, depicts, I feel, the dawning of that very day when the meek triumphantly receive their due and they exchange their black and grey garb for the rainbow hues of heaven.

Much of Earle's "religious" work carries the sensibility of Catholic Europe, a kind of ultramontane Catholicism, Baroque in its lushness and sensuality, full of allusions to beautiful angels, languishing saints and larger-than-life holy virgins. Such works – and they're not necessarily big works, they could be as small as a duet to Palestrina – resemble a cathedral ceiling of clouds and constellations dazzling the faithful below. But the religious mood or character of other works is much simpler, quieter, more direct, but never Protestant. It has an Asian feel, almost Zen-like in its spareness, but nonetheless sensual – in some ways more sensual, because it's less decorated or disguised, than its Catholic counterparts. Works like *Frost Watch* and *Cloud Garden* come to mind.

In *Frost Watch*, the spiritual and the erotic meet at the bier of a young man who has recently and quite unexpectedly died – an accidental drowning, it's implied. This sort of meeting is another of Earle's particular takes on the very nature of human interconnection: its evanescent quality. This evanescence, he shows us again and again, goes hand in hand with loss, sorrow, despair, painful memory, and a bittersweet longing to escape the burden of feeling. His dances play frequently in these keys. Most often, as in *Frost Watch*, it's unexpected death which bears the blame for the blasting of earthly joys – cold, pitiless death. However, Earle does not always see death as a neutral phenomenon; rather, he frequently implies, it often turns out to be an ally of those forces in society that would crush the passions as subversive or anarchic. In short, he views death as the terrible parent or implacable god that punishes mortals' efforts to recover their lost divinity through love.

When death is the outcome of war and disease, its role as society's right-hand man is exaggerated that much more. Earle has many times in

MERLE SALSBERG AND KEITH URBAN
IN *ANGELIC VISITATION #1*, 1968

recent years explored this theme: in works like *Maelstrom* (antiwar) and *Sang* (part-AIDS protest), or in the more intimate and yet somewhat more harrowing dances which comprise Passchendaele, named after the horrific battlefield in World War I in which soldiers drowned in a noxious mixture of their own blood and the waist-deep mud of No Man's Land. But Earle has been dealing with this theme since at least 1972 when he made *Boat, River, Moon*, and pitted three archetypal figures representing love, art and spirit against a fourth, a warrior, representing a primitive death-dealing fury. *A Field of Dreams*, my favourite of Earle's works, took the dreams of women whose men had gone off to an unnamed war (vaguely resembling World War I) and fleshed them out in all their archaic, perverse and beautiful imagery ... imagery threaded through with the imminence, the fear, of both death and loss.

A Field of Dreams, in the boldness of its design, its collage-like structure, in its erotic playfulness, its refreshing sentiment, bears a strong resemblance to several other pieces by Earle, works like *The Ray Charles Suite*, *Atlantis* and the extremely popular Christmas festivity known as *Court of Miracles*. All of these works revel in the magic of theatre, in its endless possibilities, and all of them are fascinated by the possibilities of eros. In the dance inspired by the legends of the lost continent Atlantis, those erotic possibilities – hetero-, homo-, initiatory, conjugal – comprise some of the most vivid moments. Again, they are linked with religious ritual. In *The Ray Charles Suite*, the erotic possibilities within bourgeois North American society of the sixties are seen through a comic lens, but one duet, by an evening-clothed pair to the old tune, *Ruby*, turns out to be an aching tribute to old-fashioned desire. And *Court of Miracles*, for all the gypsies and tightrope-walkers and vagabonds that crowd its variegated canvas, has for its heart a wedding ceremony featuring another tender duet paying tribute to committed love. It's *A Field of Dreams* that goes furthest in its exploration of erotic possibilities, however, with its women cavorting with fauns and dabbling in sword-wielding magic, and ends with one of the most extraordinarily lush images Earle ever contrived for a choreography: a mountain of naked dead youth spread, like the figures in one of Gustave Moreau's most famous symbolist paintings, at the feet of an enormous winged creature representing a cross between Lucifer and Death. Through this field of lost youth trips one of the work's dreaming women, a blissfully guileless Persephone plucking flowers at the gates of the underworld.

This image reflects another of David Earle's fascinations, of course –

MODERN DANCING
and **IMMODEST DRESS STIR SEX DESIRE: leading to**
Lustful Flirting, Fornication, Adultery, Divorce, Disease, Destruction and Judgment.

Toronto Dance Theatre

WORKSHOP

CHOREOGRAPHED by MEMBERS of the COMPANY
PERFORMED by the SCHOOL and COMPANY

A T

T.W.P. THEATRE

12 ALEXANDER ST.

THURSDAY JULY 23 8:30pm

FRIDAY JULY 24 8:30 pm

TICKETS $1.00

ADVANCE TICKETS 22 CUMBERLAD ST. 923-6264

FILM NIGHT TUESDAY JULY 21 8:30 pm

Toronto Dance Theatre

the beauty of men and the eros possible between them. Even in the early days, when this theme was not played out as boldly as it was later, it was apparent nonetheless. Inspired by the physical presence of some of his male dancers and by the works of artists and sculptors, he created images – of the angel Gabriel in *Angelic Visitation #1*, for instance – that bore witness to his determination to name this beauty, to have it uncovered, revealed, celebrated in all its potency and all its vulnerability. Though he never took either a philosophical or "activist" approach to this material, as choreographer Danny Grossman has done on occasion, his unveiling of the dual nature of masculine eros proved unsettling to some. Both *Atlantis* and *A Field of Dreams* gained power from such imagery, as did *Legend*, *Mythos*, *Frost Watch*, *Dreamsend* and many, many others right up to the eerie *night/Summer*. In this last work, against a star-spangled sky, a trio of beautiful Fates – danced in the premiere by three of Earle's most radiant femmes inspiratrices, Helen Jones, Grace Miyagawa and Suzette Sherman – meets and, it seems, condemns a beautiful athletic blond youth to death.

In 1978 when England's infamous cabaret troupe directed by Lindsay Kemp came to Toronto, ostensibly for a limited run of his two most famous works, *Flowers* and *Salomé*, and ended up staying for months, people gushed endlessly about the theatrical vision of his work and the dazzling beauty of some of his male performers, particularly David Haughton who acquired near mythic status here as the red-lipped, silver-winged, cigarette-lighting angel. Everyone, straight and gay, was turned on. Torontonians talked then as if this were something absolutely new, as if they'd never seen anything like it before. In fact, David Earle, who befriended the Kemp troupe that season, had been making similar images for years, but amid all the hype surrounding the Kemp performances, Earle's imagery was forgotten or, at least, overlooked.

Overlooked and undervalued. With the disastrous reception given Toronto Dance Theatre on its visit to London, England in 1974, the company's hometown groupies fell away in droves and the Toronto critics turned nasty, as if to show their London counterparts that they, too, could write snotty, dismissive criticism. The company was crushed and Earle in particular felt the reactions as a betrayal. I remember writing a review of a 1976 performance of his *Baroque Suite* at Toronto Workshop Productions – the evening one of the company's greatest dancers, Helen Jones, left TDT for New York – in which I referred to the dance in unflattering terms as sugary sweet. It was a throwaway comment and that was the problem. Too much

PETER RANDAZZO, C. 1975

away, and, in that sense, has exemplified the embarrassingly insensitive and
arrogant Upper Canadian attitude to all those values Toronto Dance
Theatre under David Earle sought to express, to all those themes that he rig-
orously explored for years. His long-lasting bitterness against critics who, he
felt, invariably took refuge from real life under the protective awning of
establishment values, has been more than occasionally justified.

Adding to the company and Earle's change of fortunes was the peculiar
mood of Toronto in the seventies. When, in the late sixties, Toronto woke
up from its deep sleep, the hunger of the undernourished aficionados of the
art scene was huge and they began devouring – indiscriminately it turned
out – all the fads and fancies that they imagined they needed to satiate their
craving. Within less than a decade, they gobbled up, in separate gulps, fifty
years of modern dance, disposing of Graham, Limón, Cunningham,
Douglas Dunn, Judson Church, Twlya Tharp, Lar Lubovitch, performance
art, minimalism, video installations. While on its first appearance Toronto
Dance Theatre's debt to Graham, Limón and Pearl Lang was enthusiastically cited by the "in-crowd" as a sign of the company's maturity and
sophistication, by 1980 it was being labelled by the same people as a chain,
a restriction, a blast from the past. TDT was definitely yesterday's news.

Of the three founding directors, Earle was easily the most articulate in
acknowledging that aforementioned indebtedness to Graham. He pointed
out again and again the archetypal nature of Graham's dance idiom, with
its emphasis on the transforming breath, on the deep relationship of pelvis
to spine, on the importance of eros and feeling as the motor of movement,
on the revelation of an "interior landscape". But while many in the contemporary dance scene, particularly students who often found his way of
working in dance "numinous" or "awe-inspiring", continued to stay connected with that artistic vision – and I numbered myself among them –
many others drifted off to join the camp where they did "pure movement".
This is a term I have never understood very well. After all, how can anything
that a human being performs by way of a movement be "pure" – except perhaps "purely human"? That, I think, was precisely Graham's point, and the
point of all those who were inspired by her, including David Earle.

But in 1980/81, perhaps partly in response to this shift in values or taste,
the three directors invited a very differently reared young choreographer to
join them on their voyage. This choreographer was Christopher House,
who proved to be bright and quick as Hermes, incredibly talented, tirelessly

DAVID EARLE: A CHOREOGRAPHIC BIOGRAPHY

TORONTO DANCE THEATRE MEMBERS, 1972. PETER RANDAZZO, PATRICIA BEATTY, DAVID EARLE, SUSAN MACPHERSON, BARRY SMITH, AMELIA ITCUSH, KEITH URBAN, KATHY WILDBERGER, MERLE SALSBERG, HELEN JONES, DAVID WOOD, NORREY DRUMMOND, DONALD HIMES, ANN SOUTHAM, JIM PLAXTON

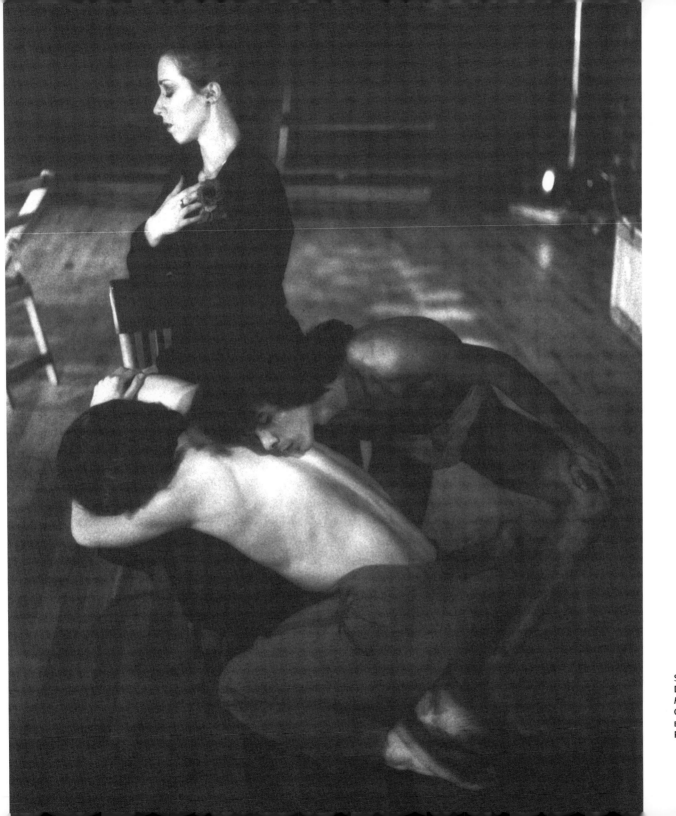

SUSAN MACPHERSON, WILLIAM DOUGLAS AND
DENNIS (RENÉ) HIGHWAY IN *TIME IN A DARK
ROOM*, A PLAY FOR DANCERS WRITTEN BY
GRAHAM JACKSON AND CHOREOGRAPHED
BY DAVID EARLE, 1979
PHOTO: FRANK RICHARDS

energetic, brittle, sharp, and his cooler, more analytical vision of dance couldn't have been further from his seniors' if it had been designed as such. So different was his perspective from that of the directors, and particularly of Beatty and Earle, that, eventually, they ceded their place to him – not altogether willingly or graciously either. Since 1994, he has led Toronto Dance Theatre at its Winchester Street home.

With his departure from Toronto Dance Theatre, David Earle didn't become either a gypsy or a curmudgeon. Taking up with young dancers and choreographers of like mind, he settled down in the jewel-box town of Elora. With its millstream, its stone buildings, its stained glass-makers and its Anglican choristers, the city on certain days and in certain lights evokes his beloved Europe and, for some reason – perhaps the pre-eminence of its waterways – Bruges. There, he dreamed up a new collective showcase, initially called Grande Orange, for his creative efforts and those of his collaborators. For those who had witnessed the changing of the guard at TDT, Grande Orange looked like a slap in the face of all the cool, dispassionate work House and others were crafting in Toronto and elsewhere. Earle was devoting himself to the pursuit of themes that have haunted him all his choreographic life. This he does now not only in Elora and environs, but also in Guelph where he was offered studios and the chance to teach regularly, on Canada's West Coast and even occasionally in Toronto.

Old works are revived – Danny Grossman's company tackled the Cocteau piece, *Dreamsend*, as part of its revival mandate; and for Christmas 2003, in collaboration with local musicians, Dancetheatre David Earle (Grande Orange's public face) took *Court of Miracles* out of the vault. But, I'm certain, it's the desire to continue creating new works where spirit and eros join forces against the philistine that keeps Earle going; that and his right-hand woman, of course, his "wife-muse", as he puts it, Suzette Sherman, who has never in more than twenty-five years ceased supporting his vision.

That David Earle no longer lives or works in Toronto is Toronto's loss. But then would his ceaseless pioneering on behalf of eros find an appreciative audience there today? For one brief shining hour in the late sixties and early seventies, as the love-crazy Janis Joplin was giving away her heart in little pieces and Yorkville was ablaze with colour and music, there were people who understood, who recognized the important role Earle's work played in the foment that defined those times, who were even seduced by its shimmering vistas of what dancer/choreographer Bill Coleman once

designated as "heartland". Now, would theatregoers only find it alien, fantastic or beside-the-point? There's no denying that the narcissism and instant need for gratification that characterizes the current cultural climate has no patience for the sort of artistic vision Earle's work has always propounded. And yet, I know, there are many in this teeming city of Toronto who would be touched to encounter the passionate imagery of his work, many who are hungry for a view of something not built to sell or to garner a profit – something fluid, deep, resonant. From their vantage point – and mine, too – David Earle's lifelong fight seems more than ever a fight for the life of the soul.

CATALOGUE OF WORKS

Accompanying this catalogue of 130 choreographic works are selections from oral history interviews with David Earle which I conducted during the compilation of this book, excerpts from David's journals in which he recorded his thoughts and summarized creative processes over many years of his choreographic life, condensed interviews recorded with some of David's colleagues, author's notes, and edited extracts from articles and reviews.

Existence is miraculous.

We're spinning around upside down in the middle of nowhere – we don't know what we are, why we are, or where we are – but we might learn who we are. How then could anyone have an ordinary moment?

The arts are about identity – the identity of the artist and the heightened sense of self that an art form offers. If we witness a moment of truth, whether we like it or not, we learn something about ourselves.

Character is everything. It is the essential element that makes every life not a book, but a ten-volume set! The arts nourish character, invite expression of the uniqueness we each possess.

When I'm at the theatre I don't think of myself as the audience; I am my singular self with my own memories, my own fears, my own dreams. I am alive in the experience and I have the courage to be there because many other unique individuals are around me.

There is not one appropriate response to a Dancetheatre David Earle performance. Each person will enter into the experience to the degree they are able in the moment. There is nothing to 'get'. What you see and how it makes you feel is everything.

The performers feel deeply about the significance of your presence. They too come alone with their memories, fears and dreams to give substance to this miracle we all share.

RIVER RUN CENTRE PROGRAMME, SEPTEMBER 19, 2002

1

RECITATIVE AND ARIA

(1963)

Composer: Michael Kearns
Premiere Date: 1963. The Contemporary
Dance Company
Premiere Location: Young Men's Hebrew
Association, Toronto
Cast: David Earle, Sheila Pennington

SUMMARY NOTE

David Earle choreographed *Recitative
and Aria* while a student at the National
Ballet School. It was performed by one
of the first modern dance companies in
Canada, The Contemporary Dance
Company, directed by Yoné Kvietys.

MICHAEL KEARN'S SCORE
FOR *RECITATIVE AND ARIA*

2

WITNESS OF INNOCENCE

(1967)

Composer: Grazyna Bacevitchz
Premiere Date: October 1967. London
Contemporary Dance Theatre
Premiere Location: Dame Adeline Genée
Theatre, East Grinstead, Sussex, England

SUMMARY NOTE

Witness of Innocence, based on the life of
Lady Jane Grey, was created on Patricia
Beatty's dance company, The New
Dance Group of Canada. The title was
inspired by a letter Lady Jane Grey
wrote to Mary Tudor that included the
line "These things I say in witness of
my innocence". This work was later set
on and performed by the London
Contemporary Dance Theatre.

DAVID EARLE, IRENE DILKS, XENIA HRIBAR
IN *WITNESS OF INNOCENCE*

ANGELIC VISITATION #1

(1968)

…What was unexpected and very exciting was to see a very promising first work by a young Canadian dancer, David Earle. This told a complicated story of Jane Grey, John Dudley and Mary Tudor with remarkable economy and simplicity, making its effects with stiff, frontal groups (as in a tapestry of the period) and slow, mannered, ritualistic walks: the sense of period shown by Earle was impressive, and even more impressive was the way he produced his dancers, all of whom (apart from himself) were from the school. In some strange way he made the slow, stilted movements and frozen facial expressions dramatically effective, with admirably subtle differences between the performers establishing the various characters – and all the artists looked completely assured in their roles. One might well think that the work was a little too static, lacking the expansion to be found in the great solos of a comparable work like [Martha] Graham's *Seraphic Dialogue* – but such solos might well have been too difficult for dancers who – splendid though they actually looked – were in fact inexperienced. The costumes, by Diane Marly, were executed in beautiful velvets, managing to suggest the style of the period while at the same time permitting free movement – an admirable achievement.

– "Contemporary Dance Group East Grinstead", unidentified publication

Duration: 5 minutes, 15 seconds
Composer: Frank Martin
Music Title: Prelude #7 for Piano
Costume Designer: Susan Macpherson
Set Designer: Norberto Chiesa
Lighting Designer: Ron Snippe after Norberto Chiesa
Premiere Date: March 18, 1968
Premiere Location: Toronto Workshop Productions theatre
Cast: Amelia Itcush, Barry Smith

SUMMARY NOTE

Angelic Visitation #1 was created on Patricia Beatty's company, the New Dance Group of Canada, at her Cumberland Street studio in 1967.

PROGRAMME NOTE

In Christian tradition the Annunciation is the visitation of the Angel Gabriel to the Virgin Mary to announce to her God's desire that she should bear his son on Earth. This duet opens with Mary sleeping on the angel's back. She sits up several times as if she hears her name. Suddenly, the angel discloses his presence and they dance in awe of the import of this moment. At the climax, the angel holds Mary oft in cruciform position in which she seems to accept her son's destiny and in a moment is asleep again on his back, her hand involuntarily falling on her womb – as if a dream revealed the first stirring of new life.

REMARKS

The set was interwoven tubes of gold metal that made a Gothic pavilion intended to imitate paintings of the Madonna in a protective environment.

INTERVIEW: JULY 22, 2002

Intuition is one of those curious things that happens early in your career as a choreographer when you are working with a great well of expression that hasn't yet been tapped … when creation of the movement is mostly instinct. There's purity to that. I feel the piece was inspired by Martha Graham's film *A Dancer's World*. There was something very archetypal and yet humane about that film's images, specifically the duets.

The movement in *Angelic Visitation* suggests that when both our masculine and feminine sides are joined together in love, we become creative beings. This idea represents the overall concept of the piece – it was how I wanted to interpret the Annunciation. Mary's angel was inside of her – all our angels are inside of us. And desire is an essential part of all creation.

Amelia Itcush and Artis (Barry) Smith were the original cast for *Angelic Visitation #1*. Amelia was a technical phenomenon and a tremendous asset. She had absolute commitment to the emotion of every piece. Germaine (Merle) Salsberg and Keith Urban also performed *Angelic Visitation #1*. Germaine was incredibly musical. She was a compact mover, jumper and turner and had a gift for comedy. She possessed 'psychic density' – a term we used for many of our most exciting and charismatic dancers.

AMELIA ITCUSH IN *ANGELIC VISITATION #1*
PHOTO: ERIC DZENIS

ANGELIC VISITATION #2

(1968)

Duration: 5 minutes
Composers: Ned Rorem, Donald Himes
Music Title: Barcarolle
Music performed by: Donald Himes –
piano
Costume Designer: Susan Macpherson
Lighting Designer: Frank Masi
Premiere Date: March 18, 1968
Premiere Location: Toronto Workshop
Productions theatre
Cast: The Angel – Noemi Lapzeson;
The Man – David Earle

SUMMARY NOTE

Angelic Visitation #2 was choreographed
at the Graham Studio in New York.
The duet is a complement to the first
'Angel Duet' although they are often
performed separately. The first is a
portentous message of life and the
second, as a contrast, is a flirtatious
message of death. The roles are
reversed with the girl being the Angel
in the second duet. The mood is
warm and playful, the ending like a
welcome sleep.

KATHY WILDBERGER AND KEITH URBAN IN *ANGELIC VISITATION #2*
PHOTO: ERIC DZENIS

THE RECITATION

(1968)

Duration: 15 minutes
Composer: Ann Southam
Music performed by: Ann Southam – taped piano music; Donald Himes – live piano (Chopin)
Narrator: Joan Fee – voice on tape (later recorded by Jackie Burroughs) reading Archibald Lampman's poem "The Passing of Spring"
Costume Designer: Susan Macpherson
Lighting Designer: Frank Masi
Premiere Date: March 18, 1968
Premiere Location: Toronto Workshop Productions theatre
Cast: Nadia Pavlychenko, Susan Macpherson

SUMMARY NOTE

Based on a painting, *The Recitation*, by Thomas W. Dewing. The characters are two women – the speaker and the listener. The work is in two contrasting parts. The first is a late afternoon in a Victorian garden when two young women are reciting poems to each other; the suppressed elation of the speaker and the boredom of the listener. The second part is night – in an ambiguous setting. The two women are either older or younger, either dead or asleep, but all the warmth has gone and the ease and surface pleasantness have fled. Fear is left, and loneliness, and finally resignation.

PROGRAMME NOTE

The Recitation deals with time – time slipping away and too much time and not enough time.

INTERVIEW: JUNE 28, 2003

I first saw a black and white reproduction of Thomas W. Dewing's *The Recitation* in an exhibition catalogue of American painting. In the picture, one woman was seated, the other stood facing her and they appeared to be in mysterious surroundings. It intrigued me as a possibility for beginning the dance with something very realistic, like the two figures, and then extending the imagery around them into the fantastical. In the conception of the piece I decided on two opposing sections – the first half beautiful and positive in a lush daytime setting and the second half stark and colourless with the women dressed in white in a nighttime setting. Many years later I was in Detroit and saw the painting in its actual size and colour. The painting was remarkable, but most remarkable was that on the wall in the gallery beside *The Recitation* was a painting of two women in white at night. It was one of those rare instances when I had to recognize that there are unpredictable and unexplainable mysteries in this lifetime.

Susan Macpherson was a friend long before Toronto Dance Theatre (TDT) days. We had danced together in Yoné Kvietys' Toronto-based modern dance

JACKIE BURROUGHS IN *THE RECITATION*

MIRRORS

(1968)

Duration: 7 minutes
Composer: J.S. Bach
Music Title: Concerto for violin, oboe
and string in C minor – Adagio
Costume Designer: Susan Macpherson
Lighting Designer: Chuck Renault
Premiere Date: December 2, 1968.
Toronto Dance Theatre
Premiere Location: Toronto Workshop
Productions theatre
Cast: Susan Macpherson, David Earle,
Barry Smith, Irene Dilks (guest artist from
London Contemporary Dance Theatre)

SUMMARY NOTE

The premiere of this work was also the
first performance by the newly formed
Toronto Dance Theatre. *Mirrors* was
later included in *Baroque Suite*, which
premiered in October 1972.

REVIEW BY WENDY MICHENER

Earle works with two couples whose
movements echo each other, and
sometimes catch each other up, or cross
paths, as the themes do in the music.
Formally he is exploring time and motion
in a similar vein to Norman McLaren's
[film] *Pas de Deux.* The smooth swirling
motions of *Mirrors* were perfectly in
tune with the music.

– *The Globe and Mail,*
Tuesday, December 3, 1968

company, at Martha Graham's school in
New York and with England's London
Contemporary Dance Theatre (LCDT).
Susan danced in *Witness of Innocence* for
LCDT and Peter Randazzo, Trish
Beatty and I were anxious to have her
return to Toronto to be part of the
creation of TDT. Susan had a very non-
balletic body; she had a shapely figure
and was very much my kind of physical
ideal. Susan was the perfect protagonist
for my early choreographic vision. I have
always felt very comfortable with my
feminine side and my first protagonists
were women. *The Recitation* was a piece
that ideally suited Susan's innate
elegant graciousness. More than
anyone else in that first period of my
work, she was my muse and I found
her flawlessly beautiful and sculptural.

JEAN-LOUIS MORIN, HELEN JONES,
CHARLES FLANDERS, SUSAN MACPHERSON
IN *MIRRORS*
PHOTO: RUDI CHRISTL

INTERVIEW: JULY 22, 2002
Mirrors is the only dance that I recall
choreographing in collaboration with a
pianist. The Bach music is put together
like a puzzle and pianist Michael Kearns
explained to me what was happening in
the score note by note. In the piece, the
dancers revolved in the same circle for
seven minutes. There's a point in the
middle of absolute stillness when the
couples go to the floor and sit together
as lovers, listening to the next section of
music before they rise to resume their
circular passage. Finally, they join
together at the centre and then separate
to return to their original places at the
circle's edge.

LOVERS

(1969)

Composer: Ned Rorem
Music Title: Lover's Suite
Conductor: Milton Barnes
Costume Designer: Susan Macpherson
Lighting Designer: Chuck Renault
Premiere Date: February 28, 1969.
Toronto Dance Theatre
Premiere Location: Hart House Theatre,
University of Toronto
Cast: Barry Smith, David Earle, Peter
Randazzo, Keith Urban, Patricia Beatty,
Susan Macpherson, Amelia Itcush,
Kevin McGarrigle

REVIEW BY RALPH HICKLIN

Earle's other work, *Lovers*, to a score
by Ned Rorem, is more complex. He
explores the establishment of relations
between – and among – four men
and four women. The relations vary
from love to hate, in varying levels
of intensity. When I say they are
reminiscent of ballets as various as
Lilac Garden, *Age of Anxiety*, and *Jeux*,
I don't suggest that there is any lack of
originality. Rather, I mean that Earle has
been evocative in the best possible way.

– *Toronto Telegram*, May 2, 1969

INTERVIEW: JUNE 2003

Barry (Artis) Smith was an extraordinary
looking being – six feet tall, rake thin,
with golden curls. He moved in
completely his own way and was a
beautiful contrast on stage to the
smaller-framed Peter Randazzo and
Keith Urban.

I've always been a bit of a threat to
men in that I try encouraging them to
submit emotionally to an experience. I
want them to drop their guard and be
vulnerable, while they wish to defend
themselves and stay in control. I think
Artis and I had that kind of tension in
our relationship.

BARRY SMITH AND SUSAN MACPHERSON IN REHEARSAL FOR *LOVERS*

FIRE IN THE EYE OF GOD

(1969)

Duration: 7 minutes
Composer: Dudley James
Set Designer: David Earle
Lighting Designer: Chuck Renault
Premiere Date: February 28, 1969.
Toronto Dance Theatre
Premiere Location: Hart House Theatre,
University of Toronto
Cast: David Earle

SUMMARY NOTE

A monk is stalking through the corridors, pacing out a cross on the floor, pausing to kneel or prostrate himself at regular intervals. He hears a summons – goes to his cell and removes his robe. He climbs into his bed between four suspended cubes and lies outstretched, his fingers gripped in prayer. Finally, the temptation overwhelms him and he begins to touch his body until he flings himself to the floor with a scream of guilt and frustration. He flagellates himself to the point of collapse. When he revives he tries to resume his pacing, but the summons draws him back to the ominous structure from which he fell. He begins to feel a curiosity to climb to the top the structure and then he finds himself stranded, unable to go farther up or back down. He is left hanging in the space between the cubes, his eyes turned upwards in an eternal questioning.

DAVID EARLE IN *FIRE IN THE EYE OF GOD*

REMARKS

The set, designed by David Earle, was inspired by Salvador Dali's *Crucifixion* and consisted of four black cubes suspended in space.

In 1967, David participated in the International Company of Commonwealth Dancers for the opening of Christ the King Cathedral in Liverpool, England. The company was comprised of thirty ballet and thirty modern dancers who rehearsed together for two months. The post-war poverty in Liverpool appalled David and his fellow dancers and they protested the extravagant spending for the Cathedral and its opening ceremonies. The Archbishop forbade the company from wearing form-fitting costumes and dancers fainted from heat prostration in the resulting 'plastic-bubble tunics'. All this combined to make David angry with the Catholic Church. David returned to Canada with a piece of music by British composer Dudley James; the resultant work, *Fire in the Eye of God*, voiced David's discontent.

INTERVIEW: JULY 22, 2002

I thought that I had undone the Catholic Church single-handedly but three days after the performance I received a letter from Father Peter Sheehan of the St. Thomas Aquinas Chapel in Toronto. He found this work profoundly moving and asked if I would consider performing it in his church on Good Friday. I said yes. Father Sheehan continued to support TDT, having us dance at many services over the years. We started a foundation in his name, now administered by Hart House, to give grants to people who had projects related to the arts and worship.

David's many discussions with Peter Sheehan regarding Christ's love life led to the creation of his next piece, A Thread of Sand.

A THREAD OF SAND

(1969)

Duration: 50 minutes
Composer: Ann Southam
Text written by: David Earle
Costume Designer: Susan Macpherson
Set Designer: Aiko Suzuki
Lighting Designer: Frank Masi
Premiere Date: December 19, 1969.
Toronto Dance Theatre
Premiere Location: MacMillan Theatre, Edward Johnson Building, University of Toronto
Cast: The Older Mary Magdalene – Jackie Burroughs; Her Younger Self – Amelia Itcush; Jesus the Christ – Keith Urban; Judas Iscariot – Barry Smith; Mary, the Mother of Jesus – Susan Macpherson; Angels, Saints, Apostles and Friends of Mary Magdalene – Helen Jones, Kathy Wildberger, Merle Salsberg, Susan Urban, Patricia Beatty, Clifford Duck, David Wood, Ricardo Abreut

SUMMARY NOTE

The title *A Thread of Sand* refers to an hourglass. The piece is divided into two sections: (1) Introit and Kyrie – The Desert and (2) The Journey to the Past. The Journey to the Past is further sub-divided into six sections: Sanctus – Song of Innocence; Offertoire – Discovery of Selfishness; Communion – The Dinner; Dies Irae – The Crucifixion; Libre Me – Hell; In Paradisum – The Coronation of St. Mary Magdalene. This work is based more on the representation of the figures in this drama in Medieval and Renaissance Art, than on the New Testament.

PROGRAMME NOTE

A Thread of Sand is a ritual narrative of the memories of St. Mary Magdalene. Alone in the desert, aged, she refuses to give up her spirit until she feels secure that she is not mad, that her memories of Christ, as her own totally human lover, are not deceptions and he will be known by some as being greatest for having been a man such as all men could be. She fears the trappings of mythology will separate him from those he died such a terrible death to reach across time. She imagines she is granted a review of her life and finds it as she remembered it, as beautiful, as terrible. She even believes that she went to hell Orpheus-like, to bring Christ back to Earth – and in a sense she had. She too had to pay the price for looking back and after a vision of herself accepted into Heaven as Christ's bride, she lies down in the sand and one by one all the people in her drama recede, leaving her alone in the centre of the labyrinth of her own quest.

BARRY SMITH IN *A THREAD OF SAND*
PHOTO: ERIC DZENIS

REMARKS

The set consisted of three raked platforms that became a pyramid, panels, a bed or a table. The 'thread of sand' was a very long piece of brown gauze. In the concluding moments the fabric was wound around the stage in a spiral with Mary Magdalene at the centre. The dancers laid the cloth on the ground and exited over the waves of material leaving Mary Magdalene alone in the 'sand'.

INTERVIEW: JULY 22, 2002

I was well aware that portraying Christ as a 'real' person wasn't a popular idea and there was a strong audience reaction – in Sudbury I believe – where someone thought I should be put in prison for suggesting this. But it seemed to me that if He wasn't real, His whole existence was meaningless. So I decided to take the view that Christ had to deal with the same challenges in life that we all do. And why not have love in it? … since love is the reward of existence.

As a young company, we were fortunate to find a dancer like Keith Urban, and we greatly benefitted from his decision to leave the United States at that time. He was handsome, strong and a very fine, clear, unmannered dancer – the person who can portray a simple, masculine presence in a true and beautiful way. Keith had hair down to his waist and an interest in religion; he was the perfect Christ figure in *A Thread of Sand*. His humanity showed in every gesture.

DAVID EARLE: A CHOREOGRAPHIC BIOGRAPHY

Martha Graham is now woven as a central figure into the fabric of my faith … a saint and martyr in her lifetime. She gave her body and her spirit to the forces of mystery and gave birth to a series of physical truths that are some of the most beautiful, sculptured questions that the human body has ever posed.

And where is the dance in all this? The dance you dance, the dance I dance, the dance of our fathers, of the first men who achieved the vertical – this dance is everywhere … in the gesture, too, that feels good for its own sake. And of course the dance of dances – the act of love. Physical attraction leads us to embrace, touch, hug, shake hands. Mothers dance with their children. And animals and birds dance – their energy makes movement instantly. The gap between movement and dance is narrow and highly charged with possibilities.

At the extreme end of dance is dance for its pleasure alone: folk dance, social dance, dance that unites communities, dance that unites two people, the act of dance when no words can match the moment.

DAVID EARLE JOURNAL, 1970S

SUSAN MACPHERSON AND DANNY GROSSMAN IN *OPERETTA*

OPERETTA

(1970)

Duration: 18 minutes
Composer: Ludwig von Beethoven
Music Title: Duet for Clarinet and Bassoon
Costume Designer: Ken Mimura
Set Designer: Ken Mimura
Lighting Designer: Frank Masi
Premiere Date: May 9, 1970.
Toronto Dance Theatre
Premiere Location: Ross Hall, University
of Guelph
Cast: Count Rodolfo – Barry Smith;
Graziella – Merle Salsberg; The Duke
of Savoy – Keith Urban; The Duchess –
Susan Macpherson

SUMMARY NOTE

This work, commissioned by the Guelph
Spring Festival for Beethoven's bi-
centenary, was described by Earle as "a
mixed-media piece of a satirical nature"

REVIEW BY KEN WINTER

… a cheerful and casual mixture of
insouciant designs by Ken Mimura,
some anonymous recorded music with
voices, a live performed duet for
clarinet and bassoon by Beethoven, a
short 'nudie' movie, and a slender
minimum of comic dance. It was all a
bit pixie for me but it set Guelph rolling
in the aisles, affronting the elders and
delighting the juniors.

– *Toronto Telegram*, Monday, May 11, 1970

REVIEW BY HERBERT WHITTAKER

… With the inevitability of fashion,
nudity hit the Guelph Spring Festival on
Saturday but it was so gentle, discreet
and pastoral that the audience could
only be enchanted. Earle's work,
Operetta, was … high spirited and
inventive. It was also multi-media.
It started off with a wobbly film of
rococo design, in which the four
dancers appeared as cardboard singers.
They represented archetypes of
operetta, the duke and countess, the
maid and soldier enjoying affairs
decoeur. The operetta within *Operetta*
over, and bows taken, the sound track
went from applause to dressing room
babble, and the dancers-singers
prepared to disrobe. A blackout
followed and onto the screen their
nude cinema images were projected in
a sylvan setting. The audience widened
its eyes, squinted, then laughed as the
dancers went skittering into the spring
foliage in a keystone romp.

– *The Globe and Mail*, May 1970

For this Guelph Spring Festival commission I went to a music store and asked if an opera so horrible existed that no one would take offense if we made fun of it. I was given *La Favorita* by Donizetti. The bows evolved into almost a separate piece. Peter Randazzo, Trish Beatty and I, and later Claudia Moore, Robert Desrosiers and Danny Grossman – none of whom were actually in the piece – appeared in elegant costumes for the bows. Dressed in the splendour of a court jester, I feigned a heart attack and was dragged off under the curtain. Plants in the audience yelled "Amateurs!" and threw vegetables at the unfortunate dancers.

PORTRAIT

(1970)

Duration: 25 minutes
Composer: Baroque music arranged by Ann Southam
Costume Designers: Susan Macpherson, David Earle
Set Designer: Jim Plaxton
Lighting Designer: Frank Masi
Premiere Date: October 14, 1970.
Toronto Dance Theatre
Premiere Location: Toronto Workshop Productions theatre
Cast: Susan Macpherson; with Patricia Beatty, Norrey Drummond

PROGRAMME NOTE

In France, in the age of magnificence, a beautiful woman, declared to be the mistress of the king, could become the ruling power. Adored by the court, patronized by the queen, she was likened to the goddesses of ancient Greece by artists and poets. She might, on occasion, act the role of a classical heroine in a tragedy written to display her before the embassies of Europe. When she fell from favour, all was lost in an instant, like a fairy-tale in reverse, and she retired to obscurity.

Portrait was inspired by my love of the French Renaissance and today 'renaissance' is my favourite word, that period in history my favourite memory. In the banquet of sensations that those times represent, small painted or sculpted details are my chief delight. I have one essential wish (to me, a wish being a pagan prayer), and that is to wish people the courage to be free. I believe that every extreme indicates its opposite – hate & love, ugliness & beauty. The field of energy in those polar gaps is the world of theatre, of art, of a life thoroughly lived. So when I speak of freedom, of finding yourself, I speak also of being lost, of fear, and of submission to the mysteries.

Existing in an age of the intellect and the written word, I believe we have witnessed the decline of religion and worship in their institutionalized forms. But now their essence is emerging again. Prose has failed to carry the ancient power of mystery, and in fact, I think we can now see that we do not want an answer. An answer is an end – and we want to go on. I think the voyage, the journey, is the point. Rather than an answer, what we want is the question to be meaningfully re-phrased in our time. I believe this is the role of the arts, and dance seems to me the most essential art. Dance has no need of any secondary instrument and is not limited by language – it is the act you see.

The freedom I have mentioned is at the same time bondage, as you become tied to fate. If fate lifts us then perhaps the journey takes less effort. I spent five summers in France searching – the fourth summer in the garden of the Fontainebleau. I felt for an instant that I had found a place I'd known long, long before. I came back a changed person. But, what happens when you begin to reject the confines that your family, friends and culture have devised and you find that small waiting child who was not allowed to grow up? It frightens you; it alarms your family. You lose friends, but your life is your own and you become sacred because you are unique.

DIANE DE POITIERS BY AN ANONYMOUS PAINTER; INSPIRATION FOR *PORTRAIT*

12

PIE JESU

(1970)

Composer: Lili Boulanger
Premiere Date: December 15, 1970
Premiere Location: Metropolitan United
Church, Toronto
Cast: Kathryn Brown

Summary Note

Pie Jesu was commissioned by the
Metropolitan United Church, Toronto.

13

BALLETO AL MIO BEL SUON

(1971)

Composer: Claudio Monteverdi
Music Title: Balleto al Mio Bel Suon
Conductor: Choir conducted by
Charles Wilson
Costume Designer: Susan Macpherson
Lighting Designer: Jim Plaxton
Premiere Date: May 10, 1971. School of
Toronto Dance Theatre
Premiere Location: Guelph Spring
Festival
Cast: Mary Newberry, Colleen May,
Merle Salsberg, Larry McKinnon,
Norrey Drummond, Kathy Phillips

Summary Note

Balleto al Mio Bel Suon was commissioned
by the Guelph Spring Festival.

Remarks

A bit 'tongue-in-cheek'. Something to
do with a beautiful, shy princess and
four ladies in waiting who aren't quite
on top of the ceremony.   – D.E.

Interview: July 22, 2002

I remember the choir standing in the
hall in their tuxedos and black dresses
waiting to enter. When it was time to
summon the dancers from the dressing
room under the stage, I opened their
door and a huge cloud of pot smoke
came out, filling the hallway. The choir
started coughing. It was a horrible shock
for me because I had hoped that this,
our second visit to the Guelph Spring
Festival, would be faultless and we would
be invited back again … but, it was 1971
and you couldn't control everything.
They danced beautifully all the same.

MARY NEWBERRY, COLLEEN MAY,
MERLE SALSBERG, LARRY McKINNON,
NORREY DRUMMOND, KATHY PHILLIPS
IN *BALLETO AL MIO BEL SUON*
PHOTO: PETER SLOMAN

14

LEGEND

(1971)

Duration: 30 minutes, 20 seconds
Composer: Ann Southam
Costume Designer: Susan Macpherson
Set Designer: Ralph Smith
Lighting Designer: Jim Plaxton
Premiere Date: May 12, 1971.
Toronto Dance Theatre
Premiere Location: St. Lawrence Centre, Toronto
Cast: Indian Boy – Keith Urban; The Snake – Barry Smith; The Deer – David Earle; The Bird – David Wood; Spirit of the Snake – Kathy Wildberger; Spirit of the Deer – Helen Jones; Spirit of the Bird – Merle Salsberg; Members of the Community – Ricardo Abreut, Steven Oliver

SUMMARY NOTE

Legend was originally created out of a series of workshops with the dancers. It is intended to communicate the spirit of our heritage from our native people.

REVIEW BY DAVE BILLINGTON

[*Legend*] portrays an Indian boy undergoing his manhood ritual, consisting of remaining in the forest alone for days until he has reached a communion of spirit with the forest gods. In the course of this he is confronted by a snake, a deer and a bird and their spirits. As a test of endurance alone, the role would tax the stamina of a marathon runner. But through it all [Keith] Urban combines power with grace and energy with subtlety right to the climactic moment when he returns to his village with the musical instruments given him by the animals.

– *Toronto Telegram*, May 13, 1971

PROGRAMME NOTE, JUNE 1984

There are many legends told by the native peoples of North America that confer a sacred character on all living things and offer powerful and imaginative explanations for the nature of our existence. This legend describes the origin of music. An Indian boy, reaching the end of childhood, is compelled to live for a time alone in the forest, fasting. He prays to the spirits of the forest to inspire him with a way to bring happiness to his people. In watching the animals and discovering their nature in himself, he is brought to his first experience of manhood – and in the brief clarity of that moment he understands the gift which each animal has offered him.

REMARKS

The set, designed by Ralph Smith, was a semi-circle of hanging fibre on which were tied little pieces of lamb's wool to make a huge diamond-shaped pattern. The light filtered through it, resembling light through a forest. The cast sat beyond this semi-circle playing diverse instruments to accompany the dancing.

Legend is one of my works that I care about most. It was created from my memories of a play, *He Who Makes Music*, in which I appeared as a child with the Toronto Children Players. The work is based on a First Nations legend about the origin of music coming from listening to animals and imitating their sounds. I felt the theme should be the sexual awakening of an adolescent boy. I'm sure it was politically incorrect for me to have made up a First Nations legend but I believe that we should use global culture as inspiration.

When René Highway was in the company, we had a true native artist and he, of course, was perfect in the role of the boy. Like many modern-trained dancers, René was intimidated by dancers with a strong ballet background and he stressed himself out so much about technique, when in fact he was always unbelievably beautiful and powerful.

Dennis (René) Highway in *Legend*
Photo: Andrew Oxenham

DAVID EARLE: A CHOREOGRAPHIC BIOGRAPHY

15

THE SILENT FEAST

(1971)

Duration: 35 minutes
Composer: Robert Daigneault
Costume Designer: Susan Macpherson
Set Designer: Jim Plaxton
Lighting Designer: Jim Plaxton
Premiere Date: October 19, 1971.
Toronto Dance Theatre
Premiere Location: Toronto Workshop
Productions theatre
Cast: Herod – David Earle; Herodias –
Patricia Beatty; Salome – Merle Salsberg;
John the Baptist – Barry Smith; Chorus
– Amelia Itcush, Susan Macpherson,
Norrey Drummond, Jackie Burroughs,
Colleen May, Mary Newberry,
Kathryn Brown, Sam Chaiton, Dawn
Thompson, Jane Foster, Pat Miner,
Alice Frost, Steven Oliver, Peggy Florin

SUMMARY NOTE

The chorus of dancers was under the
direction of Keith Urban.

REVIEW BY WILLIAM LITTLER

… But instead of putting these
characters through conventional
narrative paces, Earle has chosen to
abstract the drama of their lives and
imbue it with a heavy weight of
symbolism. Indeed, they become much
more like archetypal figures in a Greek
chorus which not only witnesses and
comments upon the action but actually
takes part in it, meting punishment
upon all of Herod's family. And what a
chorus! Its members wear rags, climb
through and over walls, break into
barbaric dances and generally behave in
the manner of furies. The stage often
explodes in movement, as the chorus
shoves around the modular elements of
Jim Plaxton's set, now turning them
into a barrier to be broached, now a
jury box, now a bier. The dancing itself
incorporates a rich vocabulary of
movements, some reminiscent of
African tribal dances, some redolent of
the East, some as severely ritualistic as
others are abandoned. And as a
constant confederate of what is going
on there is Robert Daigneault's score,
a powerfully atmospheric synthesis of
sinister electronic growls; quasi-oriental
percussion and, in the case of Salome's
dance, a harpsichord that proves the
equal of a Straussian orchestra in
portraying mounting frenzy.

– *Toronto Star*, Wednesday, October 20, 1971

PATRICIA BEATTY IN DRESS REHEARSAL
FOR *THE SILENT FEAST*

The Silent Feast was performed only one season and no videotape exists. It is a work that I wish wasn't lost. The set of moveable, triangular platforms could be positioned on end to form a mock balcony where Herodias and Salome stood watching John the Baptist being led out of his prison – a raked platform created a wonderful illusion of him in a pit when he was actually on floor level. One of the raked platforms had a hole cut in it that was covered with a swath of black fabric forming an iris over the hole. Salome, covering the hole with her skirt, was able to reach down and pull the head of John the Baptist into her lap; the body of the dancer portraying John the Baptist was cleverly hidden under the platform. It was a very eerie sight.

I played the role of Herod. My head was shaved and I was painted white and covered with blue veins. A huge robe concealed all except my head and hands. I stood on a massive set with the entrance beneath me, the robe extending my influence to every corner of the stage. Following the deaths of Herodias and Salome, I dropped from the platform to the ground. After my dance I leapt up into the hole in the platform, pulled myself up and put my hands back through the robe. The final scene was everyone rolling away from that image. It was a very dark and evil vision.

toronto dance theatre

Artistic Directors

Peter Randazzo	Patricia Beatty	David Earle

The Company

Peter Randozzo	Barry Smith	Kathy Wildberger*
Patricia Beatty	Amelia Itcush	Helen Jones
David Earle	Keith Urban*	David Wood
Susan Macpherson	Merle Salsberg	Norrey Drummond

* leave of absence

at the St. Lawrence Centre
October 3 - 14, 1972

PROGRAMME COVER FOR THE PREMIERE OF *BAROQUE SUITE*

DAVID EARLE: A CHOREOGRAPHIC BIOGRAPHY

BAROQUE SUITE

A visual statement of the spirit of the Baroque – the high clean flights, the formal patterns, the intricacy. *Baroque Suite* evokes an aura of the mellow candle-glow on deep colours, scroll work, patterns and the seventeenth-century formality.

Baroque Suite consists of *Lyrical Solo* (1972), *Baroque Suite Duet* (1973), *Mirrors* (1968), *Lament* (1973) and *Finale* (1973). See more information under individual titles. The name *Baroque Suite* was used from 1972. Later *Lyrical Solo* and *Lament* were dropped and *Baroque Suite* became a sixteen-minute piece consisting of *Duet*, *Mirrors* and *Finale*. Because of the *Baroque Suite's* broad audience appeal it became the most performed work in Toronto Dance Theatre's repertoire.

On May 28, 1981, eight prominent dance companies from across Canada performed in the Canadian Dance Spectacular gala organized by the Canadian Association of Professional Dance Organizations (CAPDO) and held at the National Arts Centre in Ottawa. Toronto Dance Theatre was asked to open the evening with *Baroque Suite*. It was a triumphant performance for the Toronto Dance Theatre and for David Earle.

PROGRAMME NOTE FROM CANADIAN DANCE SPECTACULAR

In the course of its twelve-and-a-half-year history, *Baroque Suite* has been interpreted by many outstanding dancers including Peggy Baker, Patricia Beatty, Kathryn Brown, Danny Grossman, Helen Jones, Kenneth Lipitz, Merle Salsberg, Barry Smith and, of course, Earle himself. Of all Earle's works for Toronto Dance Theatre, *Baroque Suite* perhaps best exemplifies the choreographer's debt to the lyrical humanism of American dance titan, José Limón, with whom he danced. In fact, David Earle describes his dance as "un hommage à Limón".

REVIEW BY ALINA GILDINER

… a work of filigree detail so elegantly wrought that the music rushes like air through the large spirals and slow sweeps of the movement … no matter how often it is performed, *Baroque Suite* continues to display new moments.

– *The Globe and Mail*, February 1983

INTERVIEW: JULY 22, 2002

Baroque Suite is one of those problematic pieces that changed form all through my life.

LYRICAL SOLO

(1972)

Composer: Johann Pachelbel
Music Title: Canon
Premiere Date: March 20, 1972.
Toronto Dance Theatre
Premiere Location: Brock University, St. Catharines
Cast: David Earle

SUMMARY NOTE

Lyrical Solo premiered in St. Catharines in March 1972 and was later presented as part of the *Baroque Suite* at its Toronto premiere in October 1972.

INTERVIEW: JULY 22, 2002

I had performed the *Lyrical Solo* in March of 1972 and felt good dancing it. When *Baroque Suite* premiered in October of that year at the St. Lawrence Centre, the solo opened the programme and I wanted to enjoy being alone on that large stage. In the last week of rehearsal for that season, one of the dancers in the company recommended that I straighten my legs and point my feet occasionally. I went into complete shock. I suddenly felt I really couldn't dance it … and it was programmed for five performances. It was the closest I have ever come to a nervous breakdown. I stood alone on the stage waiting for the curtain to open, my nerves completely shot, praying it would be over soon. I performed it those five times and never did it again. Twenty years later I met a woman I hadn't seen in years on the street. She said, "Not a day goes by when I don't think of that solo you did". At first I thought she was referring to my solo, Yesterday, from *Ray Charles Suite*, which I performed hundreds of times. But, no, it was the Pachelbel solo from *Baroque Suite*! It was a big shock. I learned that you can never say "Oh, I was terrible!" As dance performers we have to believe that the audience saw something worthwhile, and that what we are sharing might touch them in a multitude of unique ways.

BAROQUE SUITE DUET

(1972)

Composer: Arcangelo Corelli
Music Title: Concerto Grosso No. 8
in G Minor – Vivace
Costume Designer: Denis Joffre after
Audrey Vanderstoop after Astrid Janson
Lighting Designer: Ron Snippe after
John Hughes
Premiere Date: October 3, 1972.
Toronto Dance Theatre
Premiere Location: St. Lawrence Centre,
Toronto
Cast: Amelia Itcush, Barry Smith

LAMENT

(1972)

Composer: Johann Pachelbel
Costume Designer: Denis Joffre after
Audrey Vanderstoop
Lighting Designer: Ron Snippe after
John Hughes
Premiere Date: October 3, 1972.
Toronto Dance Theatre
Premiere Location: St. Lawrence Centre,
Toronto
Cast: Merle Salsberg, Patricia Beatty,
Helen Jones, Kathryn Brown,
Norrey Drummond, Pat Miner

BARRY SMITH AND SUSAN MACPHERSON IN *BAROQUE SUITE DUET*
PHOTO: DAVE DAVIS

Critics often wrote that we worked 'in the shadow of Martha Graham's achievement'. Why wasn't it 'in the light' of her achievement? Why is it considered negative to have been inspired by another artist? Biographies of artists over the last thousand years confirm that imitating the masters of their time was the accepted form until each eventually found his or her own style. Acknowledging inspiration from another artist does not make one any less an artist oneself. It's heartbreaking that there has been such a tiny consciousness around modern dance in this country. In my opinion, there have been only a few critics with enough knowledge and respect for modern dance to review it fairly.

INTERVIEW: JULY 22, 2002

BOAT, RIVER, MOON

(1972)

Duration: 24 minutes
Composer: Ann Southam
Costume Designer: Astrid Janson
Set Designer: Ken Mimura
Lighting Designer: Ron Snippe after
John Hughes
Premiere Date: October 3, 1972.
Toronto Dance Theatre
Premiere Location: St. Lawrence Centre,
Toronto
Cast: Boatman – David Earle; Warrior –
Barry Smith; Priest – Amelia Itcush;
Woman – Helen Jones

SUMMARY NOTE

With film sequences by Ken Mimura,
this work was conceived in collaboration
with Mimura. An allegorical folk tale
for four dancers in a Japanese style.
The Boatman represents Fate and the
other three characters represent the
three aspects of each man; the warrior
is the mind, the woman is the emotions
and the priest the spirit.

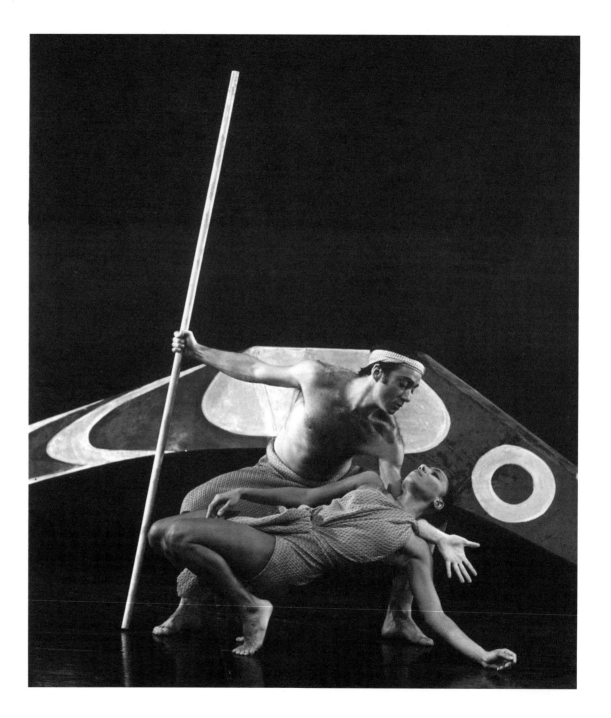

DAVID EARLE AND KATHRYN BROWN
IN *BOAT, RIVER, MOON*
PHOTO: ANDREW OXENHAM

Review by Canadian Press

Major opening night number was *Boat, River, Moon*, choreographed by Earle to electronic music composed by Ann Southam and brought to life at the electronic studio of the Royal Conservatory of Music in Toronto. Played before and behind a plastic curtain on which shadowy swirls are projected, the dance is a moving saga of life, death and resurrection not easily explained. It might have been a primordial rite of spring, the river Styx, or Hiroshima.

– *The Globe and Mail*, November 17, 1972

Remarks

Boat, River, Moon was part of Toronto Dance Theatre's 25th Anniversary Repertoire for its 1993/94 season. The decision to include this work is stated in the programme as follows: *Boat, River, Moon* is the symbolic Earle and this piece is his first turning of consciousness to the East and the rituals of Japan, a subject matter which has increasingly dominated his later works. "I call this my classic because I managed to say the most by the most economical means. It's a large theme and a small cast and I polished the movement until every shape and every detail was perfect. What makes the piece particularly satisfying is that I made up my own myth about the boatman and his three passengers. Long after the fact, though, I realized that the seed of *Boat, River, Moon* was inspired by Kurosawa's film *Rashomon* and its depiction of differing perceptions."

Interview: July 22, 2002

Boat, River, Moon is the first myth I had written. I thought originally of doing the piece with a cast of men as in traditional Japanese theatre, but I'm glad I didn't because Helen Jones was fabulous and contributed a great deal to the creation of her role as The Woman. She was electrifying on stage. I work occasionally with Helen today. She has a genius and a phenomenal instrument – which is still evident. She has always been a highly inventive and passionate dancer and was one of the first 'stars' in TDT to have her own following.

Boat, River, Moon: The Story

Through a spiralling image the boat advances as if from infinity, with three passengers and the Boatman with his pole. The Boatman disembarks and dances a solo describing the three characters that his passengers will assume. A tremendous crash, the boat capsizes and then darkness. When the light returns, bodies litter the stage around the boat as though all were killed. One by one they resurrect, each with a solo that defines his or her character. The Warrior – heroic. The Woman – narcissistic and sensuous. The Priest – a neutral figure.

When The Woman lures The Warrior behind the boat, The Priest begins to tease and annoy them. A fight ensues between The Warrior and The Priest. To assist The Warrior, The Woman gives him The Boatman's pole. The Warrior hits The Priest in the eyes, blinding and, perchance, killing him. The Woman and The Warrior sneak away and go to sleep.

In the next scene the boat has been overturned into the shape of a bridge. The Woman wakes convinced that The Priest is after them. She runs to the bridge but is distracted by her comely image in the water beneath. The image is, in reality, The Boatman who has been ostensibly dead since the shipwreck and he imitates her movements. Entranced by her image, The Woman leans toward the water and The Boatman pulls her into the river where she drowns. The Boatman then turns on the unarmed Warrior, overpowering and murdering him with an invisible pole. Each character dies in the definition of his or her weakness – The Warrior by cruelty and power, The Woman through her vanity. The Boatman now turns his attention to the blind Priest who is using the pole to guide his way. Sensing The Boatman behind him, The Priest turns. The Boatman grabs the end of the pole, pulling The Priest toward him, step by step. The Priest, realizing that The Boatman is actually death, embraces him, dying in The Boatman's arms. The Boatman rocks him lovingly, gently, and lowers him to the ground; then, lifting the pole heavenward he causes the dead characters to rise up. Together they return to the boat and disappear into eternity where they will have another chance – another opportunity – to mend the warring parts of themselves and come to a place where they are whole and at peace.

very great dance artists — √ some for

25 years, some for

Grace, Auzette,

Danielle, Svadne, Barb, Michael

Jean, Graham, Gerald

Although I demonstrate the forms, I have always allowed dancers to adapt those forms to their bodies. A different dancer would mean a different form – to some degree. Our idiom, right from the beginning of every class, has to do with trying to begin to dance from a place in yourself that's true. I would willingly adjust any movement to suit the artist if they give it back to me transformed by their feelings. They have to feel good because it has to feel true for them in order to look clear and powerful. Many of my pieces have parts that have been danced by both men and women and the changes a dancer makes are often essential to the power and validity of their physical statement.

Interview: July 22, 2002

CLAUDIA MOORE AND CHARLES FLANDERS IN THE "RUBY" SECTION OF *RAY CHARLES SUITE*
PHOTO: FRANK RICHARDS

RAY CHARLES SUITE

(1973)

Duration: 25 minutes
Composers: Ray Charles, The Beatles
Music Titles: Collage including
Eleanor Rigby, Ruby, Yesterday,
Hit the Road Jack
Costume Designer: Astrid Janson
Lighting Designer: Ron Snippe
Premiere Date: March 1, 1973.
Toronto Dance Theatre
Premiere Location: Hart House Theatre,
University of Toronto
Cast: Opening – Susan Macpherson,
Amelia Itcush, Helen Jones, Barry
Smith, David Wood; High School
Dance – The Company; Eleanor Rigby
– The Company; Maybe – Merle
Salsburg; Ruby – Helen Jones, Barry
Smith; Yesterday – David Earle; Hit the
Road Jack – Amelia Itcush, Merle
Salsberg, Helen Jones, Kathryn Brown,
David Earle, Barry Smith, David Wood,
Howard Marcus; The Last Dance –
The Company

SUMMARY NOTE

Rhythm and blues hits of American
soul singer-composer Ray Charles is
the background for a satiric romp in
the '50s. From bored sexuality of tired
strippers in what passed for a sinful
environment in these less frank days,
through the adolescent discomfort of
a sock-hop to a lovely duet in the style
of Ginger Rogers and Fred Astaire.

REVIEW BY WILLIAM LITTLER

… extended, satiric romp … this is
almost pure nostalgia. The dancers
move as if the calendar really had
turned back. It is time that provides
the giggle, the punch line.

– *Toronto Star*, undated

I used to go to rock and roll shows at Maple Leaf Gardens and buy seats in the front row to see Black artists from the southern United States. I was completely devoted to Black rhythm and blues in my adolescence and so I found Ray Charles (whose voice always struck me as a kind of open wound) to be an incredibly moving singer. In the *Ray Charles Suite*, I was being nostalgic about, and trying to come to terms with, the painful high school period of my life where I was the odd-man-out.

Dancer and accompanist Ricardo Abreut taught the partnering for the jitterbug and jive dancing in the work – a completely different routine for each couple. It was divine; it was wonderful, wonderful material. Ricardo was the great soul of the Toronto Dance Theatre and when he died on July 12, 1995, I think that was when TDT died for me.

Audiences in Canada loved the *Ray Charles Suite*. They recognized the popular music; they related to and embraced the nostalgic images of the high school dance scene and the naughty, tacky strippers. But when we performed it in London, England in 1974 it was a completely different story★. My North American high school experiences were of no interest to them theatrically; one critic severely labelled *Ray Charles Suite* 'the nadir of tastelessness'. Our problems were partially due to the fact that TDT performed at the Sadler's Wells Theatre, which was entrenched in the tradition of the ballet. The critics and audience of ballet fans held an aesthetic far from parallel to our own. Performing in a venue where I found that elitism and excellence were the foundation for acceptance, we could not do well. Modern dance is a socialist field. It's not about exclusivity or 'excellence' … a very good word for athletics, and often ballet. If it's not careful, ballet has the potential to fail to be the poetry it should be. Excellence presupposes a perfection that everyone can recognize … but any self-reflecting artist finds this impossible to attain.

★ *The scathing English reviews were distributed to Canadian Press. David, Trish and Peter shouldered both the artistic and the financial blame for this disastrous tour.*

BAROQUE SUITE FINALE

(1973)

Composer: Antonio Vivaldi
Music Title: Concerto for 4 Violins in B Minor, Op. 3
Costume Designer: Denis Joffre after Audrey Vanderstoop
Lighting Designer: Ron Snippe after John Hughes
Premiere Date: May 1, 1973. Toronto Dance Theatre
Premiere Location: Toronto

SUMMARY NOTE

Baroque Suite Finale was presented in May 1973 with *Mirrors* and *Duet* as part of *Baroque Suite*. This version of the suite was given to Winnipeg Contemporary Dancers in 1975. A new finale was choreographed in 1979 and performed by Toronto Dance Theatre in September 1980.

CHRISTOPHER HOUSE, MICHAEL MOORE, MERLE HOLLOMAN, SUZETTE SHERMAN, SHERRY LANIER, JULIAN LITTLEFORD, KAREN DUPLISEA, CHARLES FLANDERS, SARA PETTITT, PHYLLIS WHYTE IN *BAROQUE SUITE FINALE* (1980)
PHOTO: ANDREW OXENHAM

ATLANTIS

(1973)

Duration: 30 minutes
Composer: Robert Diagneault
Music performed by: Ann Southam – synthesizer; Mary Morrison, Patricia Rideout, Albert Greer, Roger Hobbs – voice; Dr. Melville Cook – organ
Costume Designer: Astrid Janson
Set Designer: Ron Snippe
Lighting Designer: Ron Snippe
Premiere Date: September 25, 1973. Toronto Dance Theatre
Premiere Location: MacMillan Theatre, Edward Johnson Building, University of Toronto
Cast: Patricia Beatty, Barry Smith, Susan Macpherson, Daniel (Williams) Grossman, Helen Jones, David Wood, Merle Salsberg, John Preston, Norrey Drummond, Jacques du Plessis, Kathryn Brown, Sara Pettitt, Peggy Baker, Donald Himes, Patricia Miner

SUMMARY NOTE

Atlantis is divided into six parts: City Beneath the Sea, Games, Love Duets, The Hunt, the Temple of the Moon and The Rising of Atlantis.

PROGRAMME NOTE

Perhaps the sadness of the music of the peoples bordering on the Mediterranean is a nostalgia for Atlantis.

REVIEW BY JOHN FRASER

… [*Atlantis*] has all the hallmarks of a classic creation; here the constituent parts of movement, music, drama, sets and costumes conspire to produce a completeness and unity that is depressingly rare in any of the arts … *Atlantis* dazzles and inspires as it takes your breath away in its beauty both visually and conceptually.

– *The Globe and Mail*, undated

REVIEW BY DUBARRY CAMPEAU

Robert Daigneault's music is stunning, yet perfectly integrated into the overall scheme, sometimes underlying the dancers' movements, other times seeming to inspire them, always suggesting an otherworldliness without trickiness.

– *Toronto Sun*, Friday, September 28, 1973

I decided to create a myth that the city of Atlantis survived under water and people adapted to aquatic life. The set was six massive hanging panels of white transparent fabric that undulated and breathed with every movement. The piece began with the dancers on the floor under another mass of fabric attached to spiral metal poles. Inspired by Minoan art, I based the costumes on a bare-breasted ivory statue in the Royal Ontario Museum (ROM) called *Our Lady of Sport*. I wanted a unisex look with white loincloths, a roll of fabric around their waists, and bare tops, so asked the company women if they would consider being bare-breasted. It was a lot to ask and I suggested that we might try it privately. It was a curious thing because, after the first half-hour, it stopped being an issue. The lighting for the piece was magical – everything was white and silver. The skin looked incredibly beautiful and the audience admired and appreciated the aesthetic that was presented. We made white, transparent hanging tops for the women to use if, on tour, I felt the audience or situation merited it.

In the final section, The Rising of Atlantis, I reversed the traditional myth so that the rising of the sun destroyed Atlantis and the under-sea community. The huge sun – a silver disk that projected mega-lights onto the stage – blinded and killed all except one performer, who protected his eyes.

When everyone was dead, he picked up the bodies, arranging them into life-sized statues as if he were an artist making memorials to his lost race. As the lights dimmed he continued creating sculpture after sculpture. My ending was to suggest that, although we have lost Minoa and Crete, we have salvaged the images that they made of themselves, including the beautiful statue in the ROM.

NORREY DRUMMOND, PATRICIA BEATTY, SUSAN MACPHERSON, PEGGY BAKER, MERLE SALSBERG IN *ATLANTIS*
PHOTO: DAVE DAVIS

BUGS

(1974)

Duration: 10 minutes
Composer: Robert Daigneault
Costume Designer: Denis Joffre after
Carol Crawley
Lighting Designer: Ron Snippe
Premiere Date: May 10, 1974.
Toronto Dance Theatre
Premiere Location: Ross Hall, University
of Guelph
Cast: (1) Merle Salsberg, Patricia Beatty,
Helen Jones, Norrey Drummond,
Susan Macpherson, Kathryn Brown;
(2) Merle Salsberg, Barry Smith;
(3) Barry Smith, Daniel (Williams)
Grossman; (4) Patricia Beatty,
David Earle, Peter Randazzo,
Susan Macpherson, Barry Smith,
Merle Salsberg, Helen Jones,
Norrey Drummond, David Wood,
Kathryn Brown, Daniel (Williams)
Grossman, John Preston,
Ricardo Abreut, Peggy Baker,
Cornelius Fischer-Credo, Sara Pettitt,
Patricia Miner

SUMMARY NOTE

Bugs was a Guelph Spring Festival commission. The dancers wore longjohns dyed bright colours and Robert Daigneault's score, created on player piano rolls, was played on a Charlestonesque player piano. *Bugs* was divided into four sections:
(1) Ladybugs; (2) Bug Rape Scene;
(3) Bug Fight; (4) Bug Orgy (finale).

PROGRAMME NOTE

A biological survey of behaviourism found in certain species of insects revealing patterns not unfamiliar to certain animals.

INTERVIEW: JULY 23, 2002

When *Bugs* was performed as a finale for the 1976 Toronto Dance Festival at Toronto Workshop Productions theatre, everyone involved in the evening's performances was invited to be in the last section – the Bug Orgy – including Lola, choreographer Danny Grossman's dog. I contributed by streaking naked across the back of the stage doing low runs. I wore a ski mask but everyone recognized me. Danny's charismatic presence on stage was always a great asset. His persona was incredibly dark and sensual and yet he was perfect in *Bugs*. His bug fight with Artis (Barry) Smith was hysterical. *Bugs* was a big gift to have because it tickled people enormously and the company enjoyed performing it. It was short and nutty and a great way to make the audience relax in performances where the majority of the work was serious.

MERLE SALSBERG AND BARRY SMITH IN *BUGS*
PHOTO: DAVE DAVIS

LA BELLE ÉPOQUE À PARIS

La Belle Époque à Paris was a presentation that included the pieces *Parade, Waltz Suite, Deux Épigraphes Antiques, L'Hôtel Splendide* and *Vignette*.

PARADE

(1974)

Duration: 15 minutes, 45 seconds
Composer: Erik Satie (from an idea by Jean Cocteau)
Music performed by: Gary Arbour, Donald Himes – piano
Costume Designer: Carol Crawley
Lighting Designer: Ron Snippe
Premiere Date: November 14, 1974. Toronto Dance Theatre
Premiere Location: Toronto

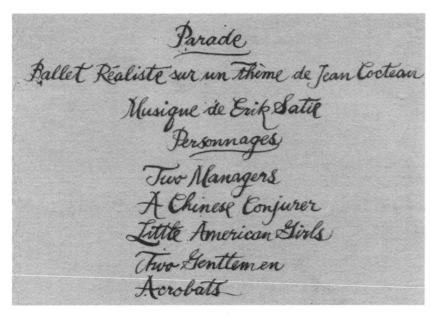

A PORTION OF THE HOUSE PROGRAMME FOR *PARADE*

Cast: Original cast – David Earle, Patricia Beatty, Peggy Baker, Patricia Miner, Cornelius Fischer-Credo, Gary Goodwin, Sara Pettitt, Douglas Hamburg, Grant McDaniel, Roland Woliaski. A later cast included: Chinese Conjurer – David Wood; Two Managers and Two Gentlemen – Jean-Louis Morin, Michael Quaintance; Little American Girls – Helen Jones, Nancy Ferguson; Acrobats – Sara Pettitt, Douglas Hamburgh, Dale Woodland

SUMMARY NOTE

Parade was a ballet first performed in Paris in 1917, the result of collaboration between Pablo Picasso, Jean Cocteau, Leonide Massine and Erik Satie under the direction of Serge Diaghilev.

WALTZ SUITE

(1975)

Composer: Franz Schubert
Music performed by: James Campbell and the Camerata Chamber Ensemble
Premiere Date: January 16, 1975. Toronto Dance Theatre
Premiere Location: St. Lawrence Hall, Toronto
Cast: Susan Macpherson, David Wood, Helen Jones, Nancy Ferguson, Jean-Louis Morin, Sara Pettitt, Michael Quaintance, Anna Blewchamp, Douglas Hamburgh, Dennis (René) Highway, Lilian Jarvis, Neil Clifford

SUSAN MACPHERSON AND BARRY SMITH IN *LA BELLE ÉPOQUE À PARIS*

DEUX ÉPIGRAPHES ANTIQUES

(1975)

Composer: Claude Debussy
Music performed by: Gary Arbour,
Donald Himes – piano
Premiere Date: January 16, 1975.
Toronto Dance Theatre
Premiere Location: St. Lawrence Hall,
Toronto
Cast: Patricia Beatty, David Wood,
Susan Macpherson, Helen Jones,
Nancy Ferguson, Sara Pettitt,
Anna Blewchamp, Jan Messer

SUMMARY NOTE

Deux Épigraphes Antiques is divided
into two parts: (1) Pour invoquer Pan,
dieu du vent d'été; (2) Pour un
tombeau sans nom.

L'HÔTEL SPLENDIDE

(1975)

Composer: Gabriel Fauré
Music performed by: James Campbell and
the Camerata Chamber Ensemble
Premiere Date: January 16, 1975.
Toronto Dance Theatre
Premiere Location: St. Lawrence Hall,
Toronto
Cast: (1) The Invalid – Ricardo Abreut;
The Devoted Daughter – Nancy
Ferguson; (2) The Proud Father –
Dale Woodland; The Doting Mother –
Anna Blewchamp; The Darling Little
Boy – Neil Clifford; The Adorable
Little Girl – Helen Jones; (3) The Recent
Widow – Susan Macpherson; The
Persistent Young Man – Jean-Louis
Morin; (4) The Sweet Sixteen – Sara
Pettitt; Her Best Friend – David Wood;
(5) The Lady Going Back to Paris –
Lilian Jarvis; Three Bellboys – Michael
Quaintance, Douglas Hamburgh,
Dennis Burdon-Murphy

SUMMARY NOTE

L'Hôtel Splendide is divided into 'Cinq
Vignettes'.

DAVID EARLE AND NORREY DRUMMOND IN *L'HÔTEL SPLENDIDE*

VIGNETTE

(1975)

Composer: Erik Satie
Music performed by: Gary Arbour – piano
Premiere Date: January 16, 1975.
Toronto Dance Theatre
Premiere Location: St. Lawrence Hall,
Toronto
Cast: Patricia Beatty, David Earle

INTERVIEW: JULY 23, 2002

For this show at the St. Lawrence Hall, the senior male TDT students wore tuxedos and served cheese and wine. Advance publicity notices invited the audience to wear period costumes and waltz between numbers. Critic William Littler, the self-styled Jack Benny of Canadian dance, came to the show alone (with his pad of paper). He didn't eat cheese, didn't drink wine, didn't dance, and didn't wear period clothes. In his review he wrote, "I didn't have a good time".

It is painful for me to know that many people unquestioningly believe and give validity to newspaper reviews. I was being written about very cruelly at that time and my father, who was dying of cancer, read many of those scathing reviews. His last words to me were, "When are you going to find some work you are really suited to?" Many critics did a terrible disservice to the art form. It was impossible for us to raise money and find support because the reviews biased so many people. Peter, Trish and I might have gone our separate ways after ten years if we hadn't been bound together by our enemies.

We invited National Ballet principal dancer Lilian Jarvis to participate in our presentation of *L'Hôtel Splendide*, a section of *La Belle*. Lilian was at the Martha Graham school in New York the same time I was there in the 1960s and has always been one of the deities in my Olympus. She was unbelievably beautiful and powerful on stage and to have her come into our world of modern dance and perform with us was a great honour.

PATRICIA BEATTY IN *VIGNETTE*

FIELD OF DREAMS

(1975)

Duration: 25 minutes
Composer: Robert Daigneault
Narrator: Sonnets (included in score) written by Edna St. Vincent Millay and read by Jackie Burroughs
Costume Designer: Carol Crawley
Lighting Designer: Ron Snippe
Premiere Date: February 18, 1975. Toronto Dance Theatre
Premiere Location: MacMillan Theatre, Edward Johnson Building, University of Toronto
Cast: Patricia Beatty, David Earle, Merle Salsberg, Susan Macpherson, David Wood, Barry Smith, Peggy Baker, Helen Jones, Sara Pettitt, Patricia Miner, Grant McDaniel, Gary Goodwin, Anna Blewchamp, Cornelius Fischer-Credo

SUMMARY NOTE

Field of Dreams previewed in Ottawa at The National Arts Centre on February 4 and 5, 1975.

SUSAN MACPHERSON, PEGGY BAKER,
PATRICIA BEATTY, CORNELIUS FISCHER-CREDO
IN *FIELD OF DREAMS*
PHOTO: ANDREW OXENHAM

PROGRAMME NOTE

In the absence of their men, in wartime, women must struggle to contain their fears and desires. But in sleep, when reason no longer rules, may not their souls set out to celebrate ancient and terrible mysteries?

REMARKS

The set was a multi-patterned fabric (appliquéd by Earle, Peter Randazzo and Patricia Beatty) that covered the floor and cyclorama. In front of that hung other layers of patterned material that the dancers could walk between as if walking amid trees. The illusion and magic were created by The Bros. Crack Stage Illusions. "It was so optically rich that you could barely look at it." – D.E.

INTERVIEW: JULY 23, 2002

This was my 'symbolist' piece, influenced by an AGO symbolist show of mysterious, otherworldly paintings that were powerful and dark and exactly the kind of poetry TDT was trying to make. We premiered *Field of Dreams* in Ottawa and the work was very controversial because of the nudity, and the nervy concept that a man could understand what women do, or do not, feel. But I've always felt much more able to identify with women than with men.

The idea originated in the poetry of Edna St. Vincent Millay. Poems like "What lips my lips have kissed, and where, and why, / I have forgotten, and what arms have lain / Under my head till morning; but the rain / Is full of ghosts tonight, that tap and sigh / Upon the glass and listen for reply, / And in my heart there stirs a quiet pain / For unremembered lads that not again / Will turn to me at midnight with a cry…." and "I think I should have loved you presently,…" which includes the image "A ghost in marble of a girl you knew…" and "I too beneath your moon, almighty Sex, / Go forth at nightfall crying like a cat, / Leaving the lofty tower I laboured at…"

Not only do these thoughts and feelings find a chord of identity in me, but the idea of a woman of my mother's time so beautifully realizing her sensuality seems startling to me.

The *Field of Dreams* theme connected the sentiments of the poems to symbolist paintings – and also with a very erotic image of death. The exaggeration of the female sexual imagination seemed to me most likely manifested in the absence of men – and so I began to think of women during the world wars who, in their loneliness experienced troubled erotic dreams – allied with violence and death. They would have no control over that and it could be a very potent part of a woman's wartime experiences. The female liberation that began in that period is also part of the theme – the right to full expression of sexual tastes and the revelation of fantasies. The final image was a battlefield of naked, dead soldiers littering the stage. Flowers stemmed from all the openings in their bodies, the cycle of nature continuing beyond their deaths.

QUARTET

(1976)

Duration: 14 minutes, 42 seconds
Composer: Michael Conway Baker
Music Title: String Quartet #1
Music performed by: Diane Tait – 1st violin; Christine Haarvig – 2nd violin; Carol Rowe – viola; David Miller – cello
Costume Designer: Carol Crawley
Lighting Designer: Ron Snippe
Premiere Date: April 9, 1976.
Toronto Dance Theatre
Premiere Location: London, Ontario
Cast: Susan Macpherson, Helen Jones, David Wood, Jean-Louis Morin

SUMMARY NOTE

Quartet is divided into three sections:
(1) The Bonds of Circumstance;
(2) The Bonds of Desire;
(3) The Ties Acknowledged.

REVIEW BY LAWRENCE O'TOOLE

Two couples, physically bonded by a piece of rope, become emotionally entwined as well; the physical ties and tangents become literal representations of an abstraction of a developing, reticular set of relationships.

– *The Globe and Mail,* July 19, 1976

NANCY FERGUSON AND CHARLES FLANDERS IN *QUARTET*
PHOTO: ANDREW OXENHAM

BARBARA PALLOMINA AND DARRYL HOSKINS IN REHEARSAL FOR A LATER VERSION OF *FAURÉ REQUIEM*
PHOTO: DAVID EARLE

FAURÉ REQUIEM

(1977)

Duration: 36 minutes
Composer: Gabriel Fauré
Music Title: Requiem, Op. 48
Conductor: Elmer Iseler
Music performed by: Festival Singers
Costume Designer: Carol Crawley
Lighting Designer: Ron Snippe
Premiere Date: October 21, 1977
Premiere Location: Metropolitan United Church, Toronto
Cast: Eric Bobrow, Wendy Chiles, Robert Desrosiers, David Earle, Nancy Ferguson, Charles Flanders, Judith Hendin, Dennis (René) Highway, Susan Macpherson, Judith Miller, Claudia Moore, Keith Urban

SUMMARY NOTE

Fauré Requiem was commissioned by the Festival Singers, Elmer Iseler, Conductor, and was dedicated to the memory of David Earle's father. *Requiem* is divided into seven sections: Introit and Kyrie, Offertoire, Sanctus, Pie Jesu, Agnus Dei, Libera Me, In Paradisum. It is performed predominantly in religious settings.

INTERVIEW: JULY 23, 2002

I believe I was introduced to *Fauré's Requiem* by Donald Himes who was teaching Dalcroze Eurhythmics at the National Ballet School when I was a student there. He was ten years my senior and introduced me to many of the elements of artistic life that would become the most important to me – one was an introduction to contemporary composers.

I had said, at one time, to choir conductor Elmer Iseler that the *Requiem* was a piece I would like to choreograph to. Later, when he approached me with a commission, I listened to the music again and told him that it was a daunting prospect to put dance to that piece of sacred music. My father had recently died and I hadn't choreographed for a year, but Iseler said, "Just do it", which was exactly what I needed to hear. So I did.

The stage at Toronto's Metropolitan United Church was slightly raked; at the opening of the dance there was a very long sustained parallel relevé and we found ourselves bourrée-ing down the shallow slope towards the precipice – it was impossible not to under those bright lights.

Parts of the *Fauré Requiem* have been performed at dancers' family funerals, ecumenical masses and many sacred occasions – it has had a large life.

MYTHOS

(1977)

Duration: 33 minutes, 45 seconds
Composer: David Akal Jaggs
Costume Designer: Carol Crawley
Set Designer: Dave Davis. Set pieces designed and built by Wayne Lum
Lighting Designer: Ron Snippe
Premiere Date: December 14, 1977. Toronto Dance Theatre
Premiere Location: MacMillan Theatre, Edward Johnson Building, University of Toronto
Cast: Phaedra – Claudia Moore; Theseus (her husband) – Charles Flanders; Hippolytus (her stepson) – Dennis (René) Highway; Nurse/Chorus – Susan Macpherson

SUMMARY NOTE

The whole play is an expression in mythological terms of the truth that to reject a stirring and terrible power of life is to court inevitable disaster involving the innocent and the guilty alike.
— Ian Fletcher and D.S. Carne-Ross, translators of Euripides' *Hippolytus*

This retelling of a story that is known seems valid to me because the characters will be evaluated differently in every age ... a woman in 1979 will feel very differently about Phaedra's plight and history's judgements of her. Phaedra's crime is her choice of lovers – being considered incestuous, although they are not blood relatives – and because he is sworn to chastity.... Her sorrow is lust, which even today can seem, and has to me, to be a trick of fate – a joke the Gods can play on us – the insatiable physical longing for someone who does not love us ... cannot love us. Also, I think, her crime is in being a woman and confessing to physical passion. Times are changing, women can now confess to such strong needs without demeaning their characters. It is time to reconsider Phaedra.
— D.E.

CLAUDIA MOORE IN *MYTHOS*
PAINTING: JOHN FRASER

The set for *Mythos* was based on photographs of ancient Greek furniture and was painted a terracotta color. As always, we had little money for production expenses, so we cut a hula-hoop in half and spray-painted it silver. It made two perfect bows, and presented the ideal parallel shapes when Theseus and Hippolytus were hunting.

I remember Professor John Powell showing me a room lined in copper at the University of Guelph kinetics labs. Copper being the most containing metal, it would make a good theme for the set – unwittingly surrounding oneself with metal as ornament, or consciously as armour – but trapping the passion in. Set designer Dave Davis created a spectacular spider web in copper pipe, which was concealed by a blue curtain until the end of the piece. The floor of Phaedra's room was made of Plexiglas, spray-painted underneath to mimic sheets of copper. We presented the entire piece behind a scrim.

I particularly liked the opening. Susan Macpherson, representing the chorus, stood on a pedestal with her arms crossed behind her torso and her head thrown so far back that, with the light coming straight down, she looked like a headless, armless sculpture. On the first chord of the music her head came up and on the second chord her arms came out. She looked like The Winged Victory, one of my favourite sculptures.

I wanted to make Phaedra's case sympathetic because I could identify with her active humanity. She seemed caught between the unfeeling lover and the man of feeling who could not love, victimized yet determined to be honest no matter what the price. I wanted Theseus to appear so pompous and foolishly masculine, unable to feel or to love, that she looked to the younger man, Hippolytus (her stepson), because he was – in his youthfulness – a little androgynous, sensitive and able to consider her capacity for feeling love. But, dedicated to Diana, the Goddess of Chastity, Hippolytus refuses her advances. Grief-stricken, Phaedra tells her husband that Hippolytus has raped her. So, at the beginning Theseus and Hippolytus were hunting together and at the end Theseus is hunting Hippolytus. In the last image, Theseus shoots Hippolytus with an arrow and as he dies he pulls away the fabric covering the back wall of pipes. Phaedra is exposed, hanging by her red scarf from the copper web. Theseus realizes that she has lied and, fearing his wrath, has killed herself. In a single moment he has lost everything.

Claudia Moore's amazing technical skills and great beauty were always an asset to TDT and in the role of Phaedra she portrayed the exact fragile vulnerability the role demanded.

DENNIS (RENÉ) HIGHWAY, CLIVE THOMPSON, CLAUDIA MOORE
IN *MYTHOS*
PHOTO: ANDREW OXENHAM

Earle … is a more intellectual dancer than Randazzo, though, unlike Beatty, he is not so easy to pinpoint in movement terms. He has only rarely created dances to showcase his own talents as performer and this probably accounts in part for the detachment one senses in many of his works. He claimed once to be "very concerned with love generally and oriented to the past" and certainly his œuvre has borne this out, many times combining his preoccupation with love and sex with his fascination for historical and mythical persons and places.

Atlantis is probably one of his most popular illustrations of this "marriage". With the aid of Astrid Janson's gorgeous white costumes and a gauzy, white panelled backdrop (of Earle's own design), he captures the especial mystery of that submerged continent. Its people, a race of physically beautiful athletes, dancers, priestesses and hunters, enact their ancient games, courtships and temple rites. The section entitled Love Duets shows three couples (one male-female, one male-male and one female-female) each engaged in a slow, sensuous mating ritual that by its extreme tranquillity and gentleness brings out a spiritual side of sex. By contrast, the young man's sexual initiation, which represents the climax of the temple rites in the next section, seems almost brutally graphic; still it, too, makes a clear connection between spirit and sexuality.

Atlantis' popularity aside, the most famous of the dances celebrating sexuality in an historical context was *A Thread of Sand*. "Dance depicts Christ's sexuality", *The Globe* headline proclaimed when the work was first performed in 1969, though in Earle's words what *Thread* really portrayed was "Christ's humanity" recalled by an aging, blind Mary Magdalene as

exquisite blandishment. *Thread* was an unusual theatrical event, employing an actress, Jackie Burroughs, to play the old Magdalene and a dancer, Amelia Itcush, the young.

In terms of controversy engendered, only *Field of Dreams* has rivalled *A Thread of Sand*. Taking for its subject the dream life of women whose men are away at war, *Field* was a cornucopia of sexual imagery: a woman flirting with a faun, another woman encased in a magician's cabinet while swords are run through her, and yet another strolling through a field of naked men dominated by a Lucifer-like creature with huge wings. Although the length of *Field* was somewhat daunting and the transitions from dream to dream somewhat confusing, it was a great work. *Field of Dreams* prompted that reviewer who had branded Randazzo's early works "heavies" to remark that only Earle's psychiatrist would know for sure what was going on. Earle couldn't turn from the surfacey brilliance of *Baroque Suite* to the shenanigans of *Bugs* to the dark, allusive world of the subconscious without being considered too "over-serious".

Just what does this epithet "over-serious" mean anyway? Following in Martha Graham's humanist tradition, TDT has consistently tried to say something important about the way we are, the way we feel, the way we see. If trying to say something important is to be guilty of "over-seriousness" then TDT is definitely guilty. But it has never pretended to be just decorative or easy to grasp. On its own terms, TDT has built an amazing repertoire.

EXTRACT FROM "TORONTO DANCE THEATRE", BY GRAHAM JACKSON ON THE 10TH ANNIVERSARY OF TDT, *CENTRE STAGE* MAGAZINE, JUNE 1978

COURANCES

(1978)

Duration: 15 minutes
Composer: Michael Conway Baker
Music Title: Flute Concerto
Conductor: Milton Barnes
Music performed by: Nicholas Fiori –
soloist; Jerard Kantarjian –
concertmaster
Costume Designer: Carol Crawley
Lighting Designer: Ron Snippe
Premiere Date: August 15, 1978.
Toronto Dance Theatre
Premiere Location: Royal Alexandra
Theatre, Toronto
Cast: Peter Sparling (guest artist),
Susan Macpherson and The Company.
The Company consisted of Peter
Randazzo, Claudia Moore,
Nancy Ferguson, Wendy Chiles,
Dennis (René) Highway, Charles
Flanders, Keith Urban, David Wood,
Suzette Sherman, Sherry Lanier,
Karen Duplisea, Jeannie Teillet,
Grace Miyagawa, Mitchell Kirsch,
Christopher House. Sparling's role
was later danced by David Earle.

Summary Note

Courances premiered at Toronto Dance
Theatre's 10th anniversary performances.

Programme Note

Courances is a domain in the Île de
France. Its name, from the French verb
courir, to run, is inspired by its clear
running waters from a thousand pure
springs. The classical deities that inhabit
the park are animated by moving
patterns of light reflected off fountains,
pools and waterfalls.

Interview: July 23, 2002

Courances was choreographed for
TDT's tenth anniversary season at the
Royal Alexandra Theatre where we
were honoured to share a week with
Merce Cunningham's company. There
was a very technically demanding solo
in *Courances* originally danced by Peter
Sparling and later by Chuck Flanders.
Both of them had more difficulty with
the piece than I would have expected.
When we performed *Courances* in
Ottawa, I danced the solo. The lights
were so glaringly bright I couldn't see a
thing, and could not sense which
direction was front. I'm sure I gave the
worst performance of my life. I had no
idea they had been trying to dance in
such impossible circumstances. Since
that experience I always remember to
ask the dancers at dress rehearsal if the
lighting will negatively impact on their
performance.

SUSAN MACPHERSON IN *COURANCES*
PHOTO: FRANK RICHARDS

I have always thought it would be better for critics to write about the things they did like rather than the things they did not. The worst that should happen to artists is that no one will write about them. No artist is confident; for an artist to fail is like a man being impotent and failing at making love. I don't think people realize the enormous cost of creation.

Also … most people cannot imagine that you would stay awake the night before teaching a class, knowing that the next day you have to cross the threshold into the studio and try to tie together the dancers, music, technique, the daily issues we live with, and the fact that these dancers are looking for some grounding in their existence. They are dealing with their sexuality, with society, with their imaginations; and there is potential for progress in all those areas within a single class. But will it provide that? There are no guarantees.

I think that critics have been shallow. Did they visit the studio? Did they want to know how our work was evolving? There has been no involvement … just judgement. The only credible role for a critic in the contemporary arts is to act as a liaison between the artist and their public. I would have to say that in my fifty years in the theatre, the biggest egos I have encountered belonged to the critics.

INTERVIEW: JULY 23, 2002

SWEET AND LOW DOWN

(1978)

Duration: 10 minutes
Composer: George Gershwin
Costume Designer: Carol Crawley
Lighting Designer: Ron Snippe
Premiere Date: September 1978.
Toronto Dance Theatre
Premiere Location: Casa Loma, Toronto
Cast: (1) Charles Flanders,
Wendy Chiles; (2) Charles Flanders,
Claudia Moore; (3) Charles Flanders,
Nancy Ferguson

SUMMARY NOTE

In each duet, the woman eventually
succumbs, in her own fashion, to
Charles Flanders' charms: Wendy
Chiles – sassy and compliant, Claudia
Moore – distant and seemingly
unattainable, Nancy Ferguson –
coquettish.

INTERVIEW: JUNE 2003

As a child I performed with Toronto
Children Players to the three Gershwin
preludes. The play was *Little Black
Sambo* by Helen Bannerman, which at
the time seemed innocent enough and
was very successful, although it's not a
very sensitive grasp of another culture.
I loved moving to that music and took
the opportunity to create *Sweet and Low
Down* to the preludes as a light-hearted,
up-tempo pièce d'occasion.

CLAUDIA MOORE AND CHARLES FLANDERS
IN *SWEET AND LOW DOWN*
PHOTO: FRANK RICHARDS

DAVID EARLE, DENNIS (RENÉ) HIGHWAY, SUSAN MACPHERSON IN *TIME IN A DARK ROOM*
PHOTO: FRANK RICHARDS

TIME IN A DARK ROOM

(1979)

Script by: Graham Jackson
Premiere Date: March 13, 1979
Premiere Location: Winchester Street
Theatre, Toronto
Cast: David Earle, Susan Macpherson,
Dennis (René) Highway, William
Douglas, Maya Toman

SUMMARY NOTE

Time in a Dark Room was a play for
dancers presented by Graham Jackson
and David Earle.

REJOICE IN THE LAMB

(1979)

Choreographers: David Earle,
Nancy Ferguson
Duration: 15 minutes
Composer: Benjamin Britten
Music Title: Rejoice in the Lamb
Text: Christopher Smart, "Jubilate Agno"
Conductor: John Barnum
Music performed by: Festival Singers
of Canada
Costume Designer: Carol Crawley. Masks
by Brefni Shuttleworth
Lighting Designer: Ron Snippe
Premiere Date: March 30, 1979.
Toronto Dance Theatre
Premiere Location: Convocation Hall,
University of Toronto
Cast: Claudia Moore, Charles Flanders,
Wendy Chiles, Suzette Sherman,
Karen Duplisea, Jeannie Teillet,
David Wood, Sherry Lanier,
David Hochoy, Steven Murillo

SUMMARY NOTE

Choreography was commissioned by
the Festival Singers of Canada, Giles
Bryant, Music Director; music arranged
by David Akal Jaggs. Performance of
this work was later forbidden by the
Britten estate.

PROGRAMME NOTE

When the Festival Singers
commissioned this choreography, it
was the visionary text as much as the
Britten score that prompted me to
pursue dance images. The text is taken
from a longer poem, "Jubilate Agno",
by Christopher Smart written in an
English asylum in the mid-eighteenth
century. Because of the unique quality
of the poetry I decided to approach the
work in a special way. I invited Nancy
Ferguson to choreograph the piece in
its entirety while I created a parallel
version. The challenge came in
combining these works, hoping to
create a unity, though also wanting to
suggest a two-ring sacred circus.

JEANNIE TEILLET AND GRACE MIYAGAWA IN *REJOICE IN THE LAMB*
PHOTO: FRANK RICHARDS

Unfortunately there is a sad story attached to this piece. TDT presented *Rejoice in the Lamb* and – as so often happened since our second European tour in 1974 – TDT received terrible reviews. I had recently bought a semi-detached house and when I met the adjoining neighbour I told him about TDT and our recent performance of *Rejoice in the Lamb* with the Festival Singers of Canada. It turned out that he worked for a music agency and asked if I had the music rights to choreograph the work. I told him that as a commissioned piece it would not have been the choreographer's responsibility and I presumed the Festival Singers had looked after it. He wrote to the Benjamin Britten Foundation informing them that I had used Britten's music without permission. He sent along the terrible review as proof. I received a letter from the Foundation forbidding me to choreograph to a note of Benjamin Britten's music ever again – under fear of being sued.

I was attempting to develop something where there was nothing before. I had been invited to create the piece, it gave the dancers work and we had a positive experience. Maybe it wasn't my best work but I put my heart and soul into it, the audience seemed to enjoy it, and I loved Benjamin Britten's music very much.

RAVEN

(1979)

Duration: 10 minutes
Composer: Michael J. Baker
Costume Designer: Carol Crawley
Set Designer: Aiko Suzuki
Premiere Date: 1979
Premiere Location: The opening of Aiko Suzuki's outdoor sculpture exhibition
Cast: Suzette Sherman, Charles Flanders

SUZETTE SHERMAN AND ERIC BOBROW IN *RAVEN*
PHOTO: FRANK RICHARDS

THE WEDDING DANCE

(1979)

Composer: J.S. Bach
Music Title: Air on a G String
Costume Designer: Carol Crawley
Premiere Date: December 8, 1979
Premiere Location: Bloor Street United Church, Toronto
Cast: Suzette Sherman, Charles Flanders

NOTE IN WEDDING BULLETIN

David Earle has choreographed this duet as a wedding gift in celebration of the marriage of Liz Macdonald and John McCloy. It is danced by Suzette Sherman and Charles Flanders to the *Air on a G String* by Bach.

INTERVIEW: JULY 23, 2002

In 1979, Liz Macdonald, a member of the Board of the School of TDT at the time, commissioned me to create an original work to be performed at her wedding ceremony. The bride's mother was uncomfortable with the idea of dance being presented in the church, but was relieved at the rehearsal when she saw Chuck Flanders and Suzette Sherman dressed very formally and graciously. Everything went well until the last climactic moment of the dance when Chuck swept Suzette onto his shoulder. He somehow managed to lift her entire dress up over her head so that much of her beautiful bottom was completely visible and revolving under the cross. The mother let out a panicked yelp and had to be helped from the church. We re-worked the piece, replaced the final lift and everything went very beautifully in the actual ceremony. But I'll never forget the wonderful moment when God's handiwork was visible in His very own home.

COURTYARD

(1980)

Duration: 27 minutes
Composer: Maurice Ravel
Music Title: String Quartet
Costume Designer: Marjory Fielding
Set Designer: Steve Gregg
Lighting Designer: Ron Snippe
Premiere Date: May 7, 1980.
Toronto Dance Theatre
Premiere Location: Winchester Street Theatre, Toronto
Cast: Bernardino de Prosperi – Charles Flanders; His wife – Claudia Moore; Their daughter – Sara Pettitt; The boy she is to marry – Robert Desrosiers; Nicolo d'Archangelo – Mitch Kirsch; His wife – Nancy Ferguson; Their son – Christopher House; The girl he loves – Karen Duplisea

PROGRAMME NOTE

In 1490 on the Strada degli Angeli, in Ferrara, the Roverella family built a splendid home. Since that date many families have occupied this noble building, but the courtyard, the heart of the palazzo, has changed little, if at all, since the fifteenth century. It has witnessed the passing of generations, the creation of new families and the demise of families who bore illustrious names. In 1530, it was the family of Bernardino de Prosperi, and in 1930, the family of Nicolo d'Archangelo.

REVIEW BY WILLIAM LITTLER

Courtyard turned out to be the evening's most ambitious work, a fascinatingly structured tale of two Italian families whose lives share a common courtyard, one in 1530, the other in 1930. The cleverness in the work resides in the way Earle has adapted a Graham-derived movement vocabulary to the portrayal of domestic relationships separated by four centuries. Without introducing historically authentic dance movements, he manages to give a period look to the 16th-century characters by making them move in a more formal, stylized manner. By the same token, the 20th-century characters move with a looser, more casual gait, which in turn leads to a different style of emotional communication.

– *Toronto Star*, May 8, 1980

INTERVIEW: JULY 23, 2002

Courtyard was a double quartet of dancers – two families living in the same palazzo four hundred years apart, but seen simultaneously by the audience. Both families had incestuous relationships that were expressed through their deportment and emotional responses according to the social behaviours of the period. The two groups never saw each other – though one of the young people sensed the presence of the others. Robert Desrosiers, who danced the role of the boy in the Bernardino de Prosperi family, was a physical phenomenon with an unbelievable persona of dark and light qualities.

I found it challenging to try to arrange the piece so the audience would see a vignette of each situation with each family. The greatest difficulty was to have the climax of both stories happening simultaneously in the last scene without complete chaos on stage.

Courtyard happened at a time when I felt I was beginning to lose control of what I was doing because of the economic and internal pressures at the studio. *Courtyard* had good material in it and could have been better if there had been more rehearsal time. Starting all over again with Dancetheatre David Earle (DtDE) has made it clear to me how much compromise had come into the second half of my life at TDT.

My independence has given me the time for process and the invaluable participation of people who are devoted to the realization of my vision.

Seth Walsh, Sara Pettitt, Grace Miyagawa, David Earle, Helen Jones, Christopher House, Karen Duplisea, Charles Flanders in *Courtyard*
Photo: Andrew Oxenham

AKHENATEN

(1980)

Duration: 38 minutes
Composer: David Akal Jaggs
Music performed by: Charleen Mignacco,
Ann Mortifee – voice; Tony
DesMarteaux – guitar; Paul Delons,
Gordon Philips – percussion;
Peter Telford – bass
Costume Designers: Carol Crawley,
Marjory Fielding
Set Designer: Edward Fielding
Premiere Date: May 15, 1980.
Toronto Dance Theatre
Premiere Location: Winchester Street
Theatre, Toronto
Cast: Aten – Charles Flanders;
Akhenaten (child) – Christopher House;
Akhenaten (older) – Charles Flanders;
Nefertiti – Susan Macpherson;
Smenkhkare – William Douglas;
Queen Tiye (Akhenaten's mother) –
Sherry Lanier; Pharaoh (Akhenaten's
father) – Mitch Kirsch; The God Horus
– Raul Trujillo; Priestesses – Suzette
Sherman, Sara Pettitt, Grace Miyagawa,
Karen Duplisea, Nancy Ferguson,
Claudia Moore, Billyann Balay;
Daughters – Grace Miyagawa, Claudia
Moore, Suzette Sherman; Attendants –
Michael Conway, Jimmy Saya.
Additional casting: Guards – Simon
Leigh, André Bédard, Jimmy Saya,
Michael Conway, David MacGellivray;
Female Attendants – Patricia Wynter,

Meredith Haupt, Jane Townsend, De
Tomkins, Diane Lacroix, Nenagh Leigh

*Note: William Douglas replaced Robert
Desrosiers in the role of Smenkhkare the
day before the performance.*

SUMMARY NOTE

Akhenaten is an adaptation of *Coronation
of the Boy King*, commissioned by the
Art Gallery of Ontario for the opening
of the Tutankhamen Exhibition in
November 1979. Akhenaten was the
pharaoh prior to Tutankhamen. The
piece is divided into the following
sections: (1) Prologue – A childhood
dream; (2) The death of his father King
Amenhotep III; (3) Coronation of
Akhenaten; (4) The banishing of the
gods; (5) Barges on the Nile – The
Temple of the Aten; (6) The Court of the
Sun; (7) Epilogue Eclipse – Apotheosis.

PROGRAMME NOTE

The sun is my first lover. The Pharaoh
Akhenaten, born around 1394 B.C.
appears to be perhaps the first
'individual' in human history. During
his reign he attempted to replace all the
traditional gods of Egypt with one god,
the Aten, or great disk of the sun. He
was a pacifist who based the universal
rule of god upon his fatherly love of
all men alike, irrespective of race or
nationality. In Akhenaten's teaching
there was also a constant emphasis
upon 'truth' which resulted in the
creation of a new movement in the
arts stressing realism rather than the
symbolic. Even his own misshapen
body was represented faithfully by his
artists. When he died (his fate is
obscure) almost every trace of his
existence was obliterated.

REVIEW BY WILLIAM LITTLER

… [This work] portrays the death of
(Akhenaten's) father, Amenhotep III,
the coronation of Akhenaten, the
banishing of the gods, a royal barge
ride down the holy river Nile and the
life of the court. Most of this is done in
a processional style involving slow,
dead-pan movements to a score by
David Akal Jaggs that is hypnotic in its
rhythmic repetitions and interweaving
of vocalizations.

– *Toronto Star*, May 19, 1980

WILLIAM DOUGLAS, RAOUL TRUJILLO, SHERRY LANIER, GRACE MIYAGAWA, SUSAN MACPHERSON, CHARLES FLANDERS IN *Akhenaten*
PHOTO: ANDREW OXENHAM

Chuck Flanders' costume as Aten, the Sun God, was covered with round, compact mirrors. The bright light projected on him from many angles made him almost impossible to look at. Inspiration for the set came from two L-shaped constructions displayed in the lobby of Sir George Williams University in Montreal. Similar multi-functional structures were created that became: a box-shaped seat to imitate a throne; royal barges when tipped the other way up; a room when laid sideways to enclose the space; and airborne chariots when carried overhead.

Because Akhenaten was possibly physically deformed, I created the idea that his parents were ashamed of him and locked him in a dark room. The room had a hole in the ceiling where, at noon, a shaft of the sun's light would shine down on him and warm him and he would think of it as his lover.

Akhenaten was performed only once and it is an ongoing tragedy for me that the promised videotape recordings by technical staff were never done, and the work is lost.

The desire to do an Egyptian dance stems from several inspirations. As a child with the Toronto Children Players I performed in a play about the Temple of Horus called *The Bird and the Princess*. It was a beautiful piece of theatre and triggered a fascination with Egypt. This interest continued during childhood visits to the Royal Ontario Museum where I was both frightened and intrigued by the mummies in the Egyptian rooms. The other inspiration is the starkness and angularity of the culture … stone and sand; relief sculptures in two-dimensional poses; many profiles; vast empty expanses; dark passageways; slices of light; religion and architecture as one.

As I think about it, I realize that I have always been in love with the sun. I have had fantasies of making love to the sun. I have lain naked in it and become soothed and serene. I have made love, sweating from the heat, confused and reckless from the intensity of the light. In the winters I put a chair in the front window and lie in the sun in the mornings, as in the arms of a parent. I remember in school turning often to Charles Lamb's essays of Elia and reading the section where he would creep into the orangery and lie ripening with the oranges.

I received the score for *Akhenaten* this summer from composer David Jaggs. It is of supernatural beauty! I used it last week for *Coronation of the Boy King*. It turned out to be one of my most beautiful creations. Four days before it was just a skeleton. The boy Peter Smith, who played the young king, has such beauty, such dignity, such self-possession that everyone loved him and more importantly believed in him. Susan Macpherson's Nefertiti was equally right. Now I have to return to my original plans for the score.

Tonight *Akhenaten* opens. It should have more music, should be longer. Much of it is beautiful. I think it could grow into successful narrative. Today was going well – then one of my dancers walked out. He's back – but I am demolished.

CHIAROSCURO

Chiaroscuro was an evening of dance-theatre by Graham Jackson and David Earle and includes *La Bilancia, Frost Watch* and *Emozioni*. *Chiaroscuro* is a term often used in the visual arts meaning the treatment of light and shade. *La Bilancia* and *Emozioni* were dance-theatre plays written by Graham Jackson; he gave them to David Earle to visualize into dance. *Frost Watch* was a choreography by David Earle for which he asked Graham Jackson to contribute text.

LA BILANCIA

(1980)

Duration: 20 minutes
Composer: David Passmore
Music performed by: David Passmore – piano
Text: Graham Jackson (a text for dance)
Costume Designer: Denis Joffre
Set Designer: David Earle
Lighting Designer: Ron Snippe
Premiere Date: September 19, 1980
Premiere Location: Winchester Street Theatre, Toronto
Cast: The Woman: dancer – Grace Miyagawa, speaker – Maya Toman; A Musician – Charles Flanders

PROGRAMME NOTE

"I saw your face everywhere /
Oh yes, the same face."

INTERVIEW: SEPTEMBER 26, 2002

The two women – the dancer and the speaker – represented one woman whose two halves were suffering constantly with each other while trying to find her lost lover. When Graham Jackson wrote *La Bilancia* he was writing about a very sophisticated, somewhat world-weary European woman and we asked Grace Miyagawa to play the part, despite the fact that she was very young. I first saw Grace in Ottawa when I went to assess a ballet school performance for the Canada Council. She must have been only fourteen or fifteen at the time and I remember thinking what an extraordinary, breathtaking dancer she was. A few years later I was teaching a class at TDT and in the door came Grace – I knew instantly who she was. Grace gave an unbelievable performance in *La Bilancia*. Her precise gift is difficult to describe – it's a kind of physical wisdom and consummate connection to instinct on a plane that you rarely see.

The arts, and modern dance in particular, have not had the funding and public recognition they so deserve … it will always be a source of anger for me that someone with Grace's gifts is not more widely seen and appreciated.

JOURNAL: 1980

I liked Graham Jackson's beautiful, enigmatic text very much when he presented the play in a TDT workshop. However, I imagined also using projected images – colour slides reinforcing the sense of setting and detail, and having appear in quotes – 'travel pictures' … though I understand that this imagery could not parallel the text any more than literal dance gesture can.

What is possible? Is the woman on the screen speaking – confronting the living woman? Is it sometimes one, sometimes the other? The text is a puzzle – a labyrinth – a wealth of evidence for an uncertain crime. It appears that during the course of the piece the two women will trade costumes – Grace will begin in the evening gown with white gloves and spike heels and a veil, Maya Toman will be in a kimono and slippers – and end in reverse. Both will have a black camisole underneath. I've brought Chuck into the piece as the trombone player – a beautiful ape of a man.

JOURNAL: TUESDAY,
SEPTEMBER 23, 1980

The brief three-night run is finished …
not an overflow audience, but very
enthusiastic. I realize that *La Bilancia*
was the piece that appealed least of the
three *Chiaroscuro* pieces I did with
Graham Jackson, but it is the one I feel
most fond of. The European aesthetic is
not popular with the North American
public. My psyche is really reinforced by
Graham Jackson's in this idiom. I wish
we could do the work in Europe.

GRACE MIYAGAWA IN *LA BILANCIA*
PHOTO: FRANK RICHARDS

FROST WATCH

(1980)

Poetry written and spoken by:
Graham Jackson
Costume Designer: Denis Joffre
Lighting Designer: Ron Snippe
Premiere Date: September 19, 1980
Premiere Location: Winchester Street
Theatre, Toronto
Cast: Dancers – Grace Miyagawa,
Charles Flanders; Poet – Graham
Jackson

GRACE MIYAGAWA IN *FROST WATCH*
PHOTO: FRANK RICHARDS

FROST WATCH

Like the red leaf in autumn
the human heart cannot bear
too much violence.
Outside my window
a wintry wind
tries in vain
to break this silence.
The midnight moon
bathes the floor
in ice.
I am already frozen with grief.
The irises you picked for me
just yesterday
on the banks of the Naniwa River
have also turned to marble.
Was your body as white
when it mounted the crest of the waves
like a lover?
Did you laugh then?
As I walked in
the pink garden
I heard cries falling through
the drifting petals.
I did not suspect they were yours.
Like the red leaf in autumn
the human heart cannot bear
too much violence.

                – Graham Jackson

JOURNAL: SATURDAY, SEPTEMBER 20, 1980

The debut of *Frost Watch* with text, costumes and lights was last evening. It must mark a moment of real achievement in my work. I can't believe how it unfolded – in so few days – with so little conscious preparation. Grace, in this work, becomes the most evolved artist in the company. Chuck's role doesn't allow the range that Grace's part does, but he is the solid core around which the piece revolves. They are devastating together.

    After the impact the piece had a week ago – performed in silence, work lights and practice clothes, I was worried about the addition of words. Yet, the text is splendid and makes even more of the piece. Graham spoke it last night. It was very moving.

    I was equally doubtful about the costumes, but they have turned out to be original and very beautiful. The colours are both sombre and rich overall – but flashes of brightness animate the still moments.

INTERVIEW: SEPTEMBER 26, 2002

In 1979 and 1980 TDT experienced financial instability, bad press and dancer layoffs. *Frost Watch* was presented at a time when the dancers were so divided in their focus and their values that they couldn't do my work the way it should be done. I was trying to overlook this because I admired them as dancers and loved them as people, but there wasn't enough belief and unification to support my vision. I realize now, looking back, how many of my works were presented inappropriately. Even *Cloud Garden* (1987), which was beautiful at Banff, suffered from the cynicism of the company dancers.

    My motivation to create *Frost Watch* was triggered by the loss of a number of people who I loved – my parents, and various lovers from the past – and I wondered how anyone could endure losing someone with whom they were passionately involved and devoted to. That kind of intimate loss would be very particular. What intrigues me about the structure of the piece is that I decided to do it in a Japanese style – very formal, archetypal and full of halts and empty spaces. The man enters, puncturing the space where a woman grieves over a body. What happens is very ambiguous. At the end the man has replaced the woman beside the body and sent her out of the space. Whether he has seduced her and banished her for her sake or for his own is unclear. Perhaps he had taken on her grief; perhaps the body was that of his lover; perhaps the man and woman were parents of a dead child. It could be read any way. All the characters could change as well – it could be three men, three women or any combination of three people. I liked the look of the piece – the forms and the progression of action. It's one quintessential statement of my individual vision of theatre and dance. I consider it a personal classic.

    Chuck Flanders was a great, muscular presence that was a wonderful foil for a woman and he was a stupendously conscious and conscientious partner. In *Frost Watch* Chuck was always there to work with Grace, to support her, to help her to be the vessel of the pure passion that she was. He was a very conspicuous presence in every work he performed – not just in my repertoire, but in Trish's and Peter's as well. Chuck died in 1987 in New York days before my Banff opening of *Cloud Garden*. His partner told me that in the days preceding Chuck's death he spoke of extraordinary visions and light, and at the moment of his death there was a change in the atmosphere and Chuck was gone. It was the first death in my experience where I felt some kind of inspiration – if anyone could give me this it would be Chuck.

EMOZIONI

(1980)

Composer: Mina – arranged by
Michael J. Baker
Script: Graham Jackson
Costume Designer: Denis Joffre
Lighting Designer: Ron Snippe
Premiere Date: September 19, 1980
Premiere Location: Winchester Street
Theatre, Toronto
Cast: Young Man – Charles Flanders;
Mom – Karen Borczak; Dad – John
Sweeney; Linda – Suzette (Pompei)
Sherman; Vince – Neil Clifford

CHARLES FLANDERS IN *EMOZIONI*
PHOTO: FRANK RICHARDS

JOURNAL: 1980

We've been working evenings on *Emozioni*. I thought this play was going to be insurmountably difficult – but it is developing. I had sat in on some rehearsals in July – mostly reading rehearsals in the lounge. One, with Nancy Ferguson, seemed like an incredibly valuable experience for all of us – Nancy and Chuck, Graham and me. I was amazed at how candid Nancy was able to be in the role of Linda. (She is now off to greener fields, and Suzette is doing very well with Linda.) The play shows the effects on a young man of the four people closest to him – parents, boyfriend and girlfriend – who cannot relate to the side of his nature that is addicted to Italian pop music, specifically Mina.

Peter [Randazzo] and I discovered Mina in Florence on a jukebox in the café and every day we tried new songs with our capuccinni. In Toronto I found LPs of Mina – and Peter used a song of hers for the Tango in his work, *L'Assassin Menacé*. (The tango was inspired by the couple we saw wearing formal gear and dancing in the rain in the Piazza San Marco, on the same trip.) *Emozioni* is a Mina song and on Monday evening composer Michael J. Baker decided with us to extend it into one long song – picking out the arpeggios from the beginning and using them as a rhythm to underlie the action.

When I first saw Chuck improvising movement, while the characters read, I realized that this would be the most challenging play yet to make 'dance'.

JOURNAL: SATURDAY, SEPTEMBER 20, 1980

Emozioni finally came to life on Wednesday evening. Chuck's dance to a Mina Spanish-sounding song gives it energy and a climax. It was really the most balanced programme you could wish for. With *Emozioni* the audience was ready for a sense of identification. It seemed, like the *Ray Charles Suite*, to hit most people with the potency of sudden remembrance. The violent deaths of the four characters were very shocking – and very cathartic – and their resurrection seemed inevitable. Suzette sprawled on the floor with her popcorn is a great hyperrealist image.

I really did not believe that we were going to meet the challenge of that script. At dress rehearsal, asking the actors to walk around when they'd previously been seated for the whole play, caused tears and anger, but it brought a dead scene to life.

MOONCHASE

(1981)

Composer: Claude Debussy
Music Title: Sonata for cello and piano, 2nd movement
Costume Designer: Audrey Vanderstoop
Premiere Date: March 26, 1981.
Toronto Dance Theatre
Premiere Location: Winchester Street Theatre, Toronto
Cast: Christopher House

SUMMARY NOTE

Moonchase premiered at a TDT Company Choreographic Workshop.

INTERVIEW: SEPTEMBER 26, 2002

The music was Debussy's *Pierrot Angry with the Moon*. The moon was represented by a follow spot, which I operated as part of the choreography. *Moonchase* was not a solo but a duet for the dancer and the moon. Christopher House was attempting to catch 'the moon' or jump into it and it was always moving away from him – out of his reach, too high or too low.

TORONTO DANCE THEATRE

Artistic Directors: Peter Randazzo
Patricia Beatty
David Earle

COMPANY CHOREOGRAPHIC WORKSHOPS

10 NEW WORKS

**PROGRAMME COVER FOR PREMIERE
OF *MOONCHASE***

EXIT, NIGHTFALL

(1981)

Composers: J.S. Bach, Iannis Xenakis, Gregorio Allegri, Kirk Elliott
Music Titles: Chorale Prelude (Bach), Akrata (Xenakis), Miserere (Allegri)
Costume Designer: Denis Joffre
Lighting Designer: John Mackenzie
Premiere Date: November 4, 1981. Toronto Dance Theatre
Premiere Location: Winchester Street Theatre, Toronto
Cast: Grace Miyagawa, Charles Flanders, Suzette Sherman, Christopher House, Sherry Lanier, Karen Duplisea, Michael Conway, Sara Pettitt, Michael Moore, Merle Holloman

SUMMARY NOTE

The title was taken from the poem "Goodbye My Fancy" by Walt Whitman. Full title *Exit, Nightfall – five dreams after death*. The Miserere section of *Exit, Nightfall* is frequently performed alone.

Exit, Nightfall portrayed five different aspects of death that were in my imagination. The first was a very slow ritual with the dancers constantly rising from the ground into ascension like a fast-motion film of trees growing. The second was a playful, flirtatious passage of angels as beautiful beings. The third part was a horrendous depiction of hell that ended in a procession of monsters. The fourth segment, later known by its musical title *Miserere*, became an entity unto itself. And the last section was very 'city' oriented, isolated and lonely with people walking their daily routine – the ritual path to work and home – with music that sounded like subway trains. The dancers held little penlights and walked patterns that inter-connected but never met. Eventually everyone left the stage except for one dancer who walked on alone – a tiny, solitary piece of light in the descending darkness. It was an unsentimental section where each person was extinguished, one by one.

People suggested that Miserere should have been the last section but I did not want to put in a vote for Christianity as the solution – although Miserere's ending does portray a beautiful dream of a circle of harmony and is set to one of the world's most beautiful pieces of music by Gregorio Allegri. The Miserere has had a larger life than the rest of the piece. We have performed it with fifteen dancers, twenty dancers and often with five or ten. I prefer it with one group of five because the character of each individual is more visible and this carries greater impact. Although people often say they see sculptures and paintings from the history of European art in my work, I had no plan or direction for what I was going to choreograph. We started with three groups of five people and the piece unfolded itself. The beauty of the Miserere is perhaps its lack of pretension and the sheer humanity of it. It is literally a sixteen-minute demonstration of trust and support.

KAREN DUPLISEA, CHRISTOPHER HOUSE, LUC TREMBLAY, PHYLLIS WHYTE, JULIAN LITTLEFORD, SARA PETTITT, MICHAEL MOORE, SUZETTE SHERMAN, CHARLES FLANDERS IN *EXIT, NIGHTFALL*
PHOTO: ANDREW OXENHAM

JOURNEY

(1981)

Composer: Marsha Coffey
Music Title: Percussion
Premiere Date: December 6, 1981
Premiere Location: Bloor Street United Church, Toronto
Cast: Grace Miyagawa, Lucie Boissinot, Michael Conway, Julian Littleford, Michael Moore, Luc Tremblay

SUMMARY NOTE

Journey was commissioned by Bloor Street United Church for Amnesty International.

INTERVIEW: JULY 2003

It's curious how often in my work everyone is running towards the audience. I have trouble getting people on and off stage and often when I go to see dance performances I am disturbed by the way people have left the stage or are coming back on. Where are they going? Why did they leave? *Journey* was intended to be an image of people running away – fleeing from something dangerous and falling down and helping each other up or carrying people on their backs. It was a portrayal of people suffering for political reasons and trying to provide support for each other. Amnesty International's mandate to protect individuals and communities whose human rights are under attack is an issue that I tried to illustrate in dance.

CHRISTMAS CONCERTO

(1981)

Composer: Arcangelo Corelli
Music Title: Christmas Concerto
Premiere Date: December 19, 1981.
The Company and School of Toronto
Dance Theatre
Premiere Location: Winchester Street
Theatre, Toronto
Cast: Lucie Boissinot, Michael Conway,
Monica George, Sherry Lanier,
Julian Littleford, Grace Miyagawa,
Michael Moore, Sara Pettitt,
Luc Tremblay, Phyllis Whyte

CHRISTOPHER HOUSE AND HELEN JONES IN
BAROQUE SUITE DUET, WHICH WAS ARRANGED FOR
TEN DANCERS TO CREATE *CHRISTMAS CONCERTO*
PHOTO: ANDREW OXENHAM

DAVID EARLE: A CHOREOGRAPHIC BIOGRAPHY

ALL THE BOOKS IN HEAVEN

(1981)

Composer: Gerald Finzi
Scenario: Graham Jackson
Costume Designer: David Earle
Set Designer: David Earle
Premiere Date: December 19, 1981.
The Company and School of Toronto Dance Theatre
Premiere Location: Winchester Street Theatre, Toronto
Cast: The Young Man – Michael Conway; The Woman – Suzette Sherman; The people on the street – Ian Betts★, Lucie Boissinot, Tanya Evidente★, Monica George, Julian Littleford, Grace Miyagawa, Michael Moore, Allen Norris★, Sara Pettitt, Pamela Tate★, Luc Tremblay, Hal Walton★, Phyllis Whyte

★ *Students of The School of Toronto Dance Theatre*

PROGRAMME NOTE

"They're opening up," said Vivaldo, "all those books in heaven." He closed his eyes.
– James Baldwin, *Another Country*

This work was dedicated to Graham Jackson's father.

INTERVIEW: SEPTEMBER 26, 2002

It was a poignant piece about a young man who was visited by an angel. The angel gives him a pen, indicating a future as a writer. Michael Conway, who has since been lost to us, beautifully played the part of the young man. Hopefully he is reading "all the books in heaven" now.

DAVID EARLE AND SUZETTE SHERMAN
IN *ALL THE BOOKS IN HEAVEN*
PHOTO: FRANK RICHARDS

ORMAI

(1982)

Composer: Mina collage with poet
Graham Jackson
Music Title: Ormai
Premiere Date: March 7, 1982.
Toronto Dance Theatre
Premiere Location: Toronto
Cast: Michael Moore, Suzette Sherman

SUMMARY NOTE

Ormai was created for *A Moveable Feast*,
launching Toronto Dance Theatre's
1982 fundraising campaign.

DIDO AND AENEAS

(1982)

Choreographers: David Earle,
James Kudelka, Christopher House,
Phyllis Whyte, Kenny Pearl
Composer: Henry Purcell
Music Title: Dido and Aeneas
Music performed by: Phoebus/
Aeneas/Sailor – Mark Pedrotti;
Goddess/Dido – Catherine Robbin;
Goddess/Belinda – Carolyn Tomlin;
Venus/Second Woman – Katherine
Terrel; Page/Mercury – Bevan Keating
Costume Designer: Denis Joffre. Masks
by Daniel Tremblay
Lighting Designer: Ron Snippe
Premiere Date: July 6, 1982
Premiere Location: Stratford
Cast: Dido – Merle Holloman;
Aeneas – Charles Flanders; Amor –
Christopher House; Second Woman –
Sherry Lanier; Belinda – Grace
Miyagawa; Courtiers – Karen Duplisea,
Michael Conway, Lucie Boissinot,
Monica George; Aeneas' Companions –
Luc Tremblay, Julian Littleford

MERLE HOLLOMAN AND CHARLES FLANDERS
IN *DIDO AND AENEAS*

Summary Note

Dido and Aeneas was commissioned by the Stratford Music Festival.

Synopsis

Aeneas, the Trojan hero, destined by the gods to found Rome, has been washed ashore at Carthage. He has fallen in love with the Queen, Dido, who shares his passion, but dares not confess it. She has vowed never to marry again after the murder of her husband. Her sister, Belinda, and her courtiers, persuade her to accept her visitor's love. The gods, anxious to see Aeneas enroute to fulfill his destiny, send Amor to bring the dalliance to a conclusion. Amor works in league with a mystical cabal at court, which is intent on the overthrow of the pleasure loving monarch. His principal conspirator at court is a woman placed close to the Queen. He steals the masks that Dido and Aeneas have worn in court theatrical diversions and the cult puts a hex on them. When Dido and Aeneas have truly become lovers, Amor, disguised as Mercury, commands Aeneas to set sail immediately for Italy. While telling Dido of this decree, Aeneas decides to 'offend the gods and Love obey' – but Dido refuses to allow him to stay because he had dared to think, for even one instant, of leaving her. She sends him away and, abandoned by everyone, takes poison, meeting death as she once dreamed she would.

Review by Paula Citron

[*Dido and Aeneas*] represented what we have come to expect from Earle: an astonishing amount of beauty, emotional impact and a careful rendering of a delicate story.

– *Canadian Dance News*, August 1982

Interview: September 26, 2002

For this Stratford Music Festival commission, I invited contributions from James Kudelka, Christopher House, Phyllis Whyte and Kenny Pearl. We choreographed every single note from the first note of the Henry Purcell overture to the last note of the piece so there was dance for the entire opera. The concept started as a chamber performance with a few moments of dance and developed into a huge production. It was performed only once and I regret that it was not recorded.

Journal: January 1, 1982

And so … it would seem that we have embarked on a production of *Dido*. I very much enjoyed my Stratford visit yesterday to see Peter Taussig who was to direct *Dido*, and his wife, pianist Kathryn Root. Because Peter had initially spoken about not using dancers, I'd developed several concepts to animate the production with singers – e.g. having them carried like statues of gods – but when he seemed disposed to consider dancers, my imagination filled with fresh ideas. It will be a challenge in that little space – but the hall has charm and nice Serlioesque wooden doorways. I suggested using four singers instead of eight – plus a boy soprano – doubling the roles to conserve space. I've already listened to the music several hundred times.

Journal: Sunday, May 23, 1982

I imagine opening the door to the long corridor – a gallery I hope, with windows – along which we will pass in the creation of this piece. I'm to work with the singers tomorrow. I have to find an idiom that will meaningfully bring together the ancient world, the seventeenth century, and 1982. Although we have no budget I am determined to enjoy this process and be creative. I was happy to be asked to do this – I want to do this – so I cannot be neurotic about it.

Because the action is so drawn out in the text, I feel tempted to use one of my favourite devices of seventeenth-century painting, that is to fill the foreground with sensual and attractive bodies and behaviour, and relegate the essential subject matter to a distant plane like Abraham Bloemaert's painting, the *Baptism of Christ*, in the National Gallery.

Journal: Friday, June 11, 1982

Middle of the night – up to make some notes – the home stretch. I have almost nothing left to do except go back over everything I've blocked and review the movement and steps to see if it is too repetitive – or if it is expressive enough. I heard that James Kudelka did a beautiful group dance today and I did Dido's death – taking poison from a ring – and Dido's Lament. I couldn't believe we'd done it! Merle Holloman will be extraordinary!

Journal: Saturday, July 3, 1982

When I began this commission someone said to me, 'Do a good job – but nothing exceptional, or you'll never be asked back'. The project turned out to be a sort of Renaissance fresco commission – I sketched in the broadest outlines and had help filling in the details. James' sections are a great delight to me – so well wrought.

Journal: Tuesday, July 6, 1982

And so – I left the dining room in Banff at 6:30 pm to come to my room and pray. It is 8:30 pm in Stratford, the performance of *Dido* is beginning. I have never missed an opening of a work of mine before and I regret missing this one. However I felt it necessary to honour my commitment to teach at the Banff summer school.

God bless my dancers, the singers, Ellyakim, and Bob who directs the choir. God bless Merle, and make this night worth many years of work, years of self-doubt, hours of sweating, nights in tears. Help this to change Merle – open her heart. God bless Purcell – who created such beautiful music in his lifetime … 1659-1695! God watch over our little galleon as it sets forth into the dangerous sea. Let it reinforce the possibility of love.

By the 1980s, TDT's status as one of Canada's foremost modern dance companies drew people into the organization. However, it became evident that many did not share the artistic vision of the three founders. I think it was immoral for designers, technical people and administrative people to work with TDT when they didn't like us or like what we were doing artistically. Dancers would stay and complain about the choreographers (Peter, Trish and me), pressuring us to bring in other choreographers and making us feel very 'old school'. I told them that TDT began as – and continued to be – a creative forum for Peter, Trish and me and if they didn't like what we were doing they should leave the company. Despite that, dancers would stay and stay and stay, taking our money, our time and our lives and we would find out, often years later, that they hated it – hated me. They weren't our hostages. They should have left.

INTERVIEW: SEPTEMBER 26, 2002

REALM

(1983)

Composer: Kirk Elliott and traditional music from Japan, Africa, Peru and Ireland

Costume Designer: Denis Joffre. Mask design by Edward Fielding; Jewellery design by Danielle Fleury

Lighting Designer: Ron Ward

Premiere Date: March 24, 1983. Toronto Dance Theatre

Premiere Location: St. Lawrence Centre (Town Hall), Toronto

Cast: Grace Miyagawa, Christopher House, Merle Holloman, Sara Pettitt, Sherry Lanier, Miguel Moore, Michael Conway, Suzette Sherman, Karen duPlessis, Lucie Boissinot, Luc Tremblay, Algeron Williams

SUMMARY NOTE

Realm was also performed at UQAM (Université du Québec à Montréal). The music for sections 2, 3 and 5 was commissioned from Canadian composer Kirk Elliott. *Realm* is divided into six sections: (1) Kingdom of the Sun; (2) Kingdom of the Moon; (3) Procession; (4) Light in the Village; (5) Ritual of Sacrifice; (6) Celebration. In 1984, David Earle was commissioned by Erik Bruhn to set *Realm* for the National Ballet and, after substantial re-working, the piece premiered in May of that year.

PROGRAMME NOTE

In many parts of the world there remain peoples for whom worship is allied to instinct. I offer a collection of imaginary images inspired by the variety and richness of such communities.

ARTISTS OF THE NATIONAL BALLET OF CANADA IN *REALM*
PHOTO: ANDREW OXENHAM, COURTESY THE NATIONAL BALLET OF CANADA ARCHIVES

COURT OF MIRACLES

(1983)

Choreographers: David Earle, Peter Randazzo, Christopher House, Carol Anderson, Kenny Pearl
Guest Choreographer: James Kudelka
Duration: 60 minutes
Composer: Michael J. Baker
Music Title: Medieval Collage
Costume Designers: Denis Joffre, Susan Rome
Set Designer: Ron Ward
Lighting Designers: Ron Snippe, Peter McKinnon
Stage Manager: Pierre Lavoie
Assistant Stage Manager: Penny Olorenshaw
Seamstress: Lenore Ison
Scenic Carpenter: Barry Eldridge
Carpenter: Jon Bankson
Props Assistants: Anne Barry, Brenda Davis, Rachel MacHenry
Premiere Date: December 14, 1983. Toronto Dance Theatre, School of Toronto Dance Theatre and Dancemakers
Premiere Location: Premiere Dance Theatre, Toronto
Cast: Toronto Dance Theatre: Lucie Boissinot, Michael Conway, Karen duPlessis, Merle Holloman, Christopher House, Helen Jones, Benoît Lachambre, Grace Miyagawa, Sara Pettitt, Suzette Sherman, Luc Tremblay
Dancemakers: Artistic Directors – Carol Anderson, Patricia Fraser. The Company – Conrad Alexandrowicz, Francisco Alvarez, Carol Anderson, Richard Bowen, Patricia Fraser, Ken Gould, Susan McKenzie, Zella Wolofsky
Guest Artists from Toronto Dance Theatre's past companies: Ricardo Abreut, Billyann Balay, Kathryn Brown, Norrey Drummond, Nancy Ferguson, Donald Himes
Other Guest Artists: Jonathon Burston, Murray Darroch, Pam Tate, Eric Tessier-Lavigne, David Victor, Phyllis Whyte
Students of the School of the Toronto Dance Theatre: Sylvie Bouchard, France Salmon, Gina Desjarlais, Karen Forsey, Ian Betts, Anne Barry, Fiona Drinnan, Ricardo de la Fuente, Michael Menegon, Brenda Davis, Remi Falquet, Gillian Ferrabee, Emily Hackett, Suzanne Miller, Lynn Snelling, Rachel MacHenry, Anne Marie Lalancette
Roles were danced by the following:
Priests – David Earle, Peter Randazzo; Beggars – Carol Anderson, Lucie Boissinot, Karen duPlessis, Ken Gould, Christopher House, Benoît Lachambre, Susan MacKenzie; Acrobats – Christine Adderson, Diane Bartlett, David Victor; Courtesans – Patricia Fraser, Merle Holloman, Helen Jones, Sara Pettitt; Bishop – Ricardo Abreut; Banner Dancers: Duke – Conrad Alexandrowicz; Men at Arms – Francisco Alvarez, Michael Conway, Luc Tremblay; Lepers – Billyann Balay, Jonathan Burston, Ricardo de la Fuente, Donald Himes, Anne Marie Lalancette, Pamela Tate, Phyllis Whyte; Penitents – Patricia Beatty, Michael Conway, Murray Darroch, Remi Falquet, Suzette Sherman; Gypsies – Francisco Alvarez, Monica Burr, Grace Miyagawa, Eric Tessier-Lavigne, Luc Tremblay, Zella Wolofsky; Three Kings – Richard Bowen, Murray Darroch, Donald Himes; Bride – Suzette Sherman; Groom – Michael Conway; Townspeople – Billyann Balay, Jonathan Burston, Donald Himes, Suzette Sherman, Pamela Tate, Phyllis Whyte, and students of the School of Toronto Dance Theatre: Sylvie Bouchard, France Salmon, Gina Desjarlais, Karen Forsey, Ian Betts, Anne Barry, Fiona Drinnan, Ricardo de la Fuente, Michael Menegon, Brenda Davis, Remi Falquet, Gillian Ferrabee, Emily Hackett, Suzanne Miller, Lynn Snelling, Rachel MacHenry, Anne Marie Lalancette; Inmates – Patricia Beatty, David Earle, Ricardo Abreut, Murray Darroch, Donald Himes, Peter Randazzo, Pam Tate, Phyllis Whyte; Miracle Play: Mary – Carol Anderson; Joseph – Benoît Lachambre; Angel – Christopher House; Ox – Karen duPlessis; Ass – Ken Gould; Shepherds – Lucie Boissinot, Susan MacKenzie

SUMMARY NOTE

Court of Miracles was conceived by David Earle and directed by David Earle and Kenny Pearl. *Court of Miracles* is divided into two acts. Act 1: Pageant of the City. A square in a city in Northern Europe in the Middle Ages during the Feast of St. Nicholas. Pageant of the City does not tell a story, but rather presents the panorama of life in Medieval times. The Feast of St. Nicholas was a holiday when lepers and penitents shared the streets with courtesans and royalty, when townspeople were crowned and became kings, where a wedding of royalty was shared with the common, and when everyone, rich and poor alike, was confronted with the everyday realities of Life and Death. Act 2: Feast of Light. A home for the socially discarded, on Christmas Eve. Each inmate re-enacts one of the seven deadly sins: anger, pride, sloth, greed, hunger, lust and envy. Finally, envy steals each person's sin, which was their only remaining possession. The beggars arrive with their gifts to perform the miracle of Christmas and are themselves witness to an unexpected miracle.

PROGRAMME NOTE

The Court of Miracles was an area in Paris dating back to the Middle Ages, in which the inhabitants gained their livelihoods through their imaginations.

**MEMBERS OF TORONTO DANCE THEATRE AND GUEST ARTISTS IN *COURT OF MIRACLES*
PHOTO: ANDREW OXENHAM**

During the ten years that *Court of Miracles* was performed sections were re-staged and re-choreographed using many different companies and soloists. For example, in 1985 guest artists were Jackie Burroughs, James Kudelka, Veronica Tennant, Lawrence Adams, Brigitte Bourbeau, Donald Himes and members of the Canadian Children's Dance Theatre. Other guest artists through the years included Celia Franca, Lois Smith, Lilian Jarvis, Danny Grossman, Erik Bruhn, David Wood, Angela Leigh, Russell Kilde, Jeffrey Mayne, Susan Macpherson, Ken Irving, Cameron MacMaster, Michael Querin, Michael Trent, Julia Sasso, Gerry Trentham, Carolyn Woods, David Rose, Dion MacArthur, Gérald Michaud, Naoko Murakoshi, Kathleen Pritchard, Darryl Hoskins, Sasha Ivanochko, Janet Kearsey, Learie McNicolls. *Court of Miracles* was performed in Toronto, Windsor, Barrie, Waterloo, St. Catharines, cross Canada tour (1990) and Philadelphia (1991). Dancetheatre David Earle remounted *Court of Miracles* at the River Run Centre, Guelph, Ontario, in December 2003.

DAVID EARLE: A CHOREOGRAPHIC BIOGRAPHY

There was an area of Paris in the middle ages where the street people lived; people with every kind of physical disability. They would go into the city to beg and when they returned, legs, arms, hearing, sight were all miraculously restored. The people of Paris lovingly referred to this area as the Court of Miracles. It's all about street theatre. This area is still referred to in the *Michelin Green Guide to Paris*.

It broke my heart when I first saw the needy people during our stay in Lisbon, but when I remained after the tour I observed them donning their supposed infirmity and began to see behind the façade. A pitiful beggar woman (to whom I had previously given money) received an American twenty-dollar bill, marched into a store and bought a Fudgsicle. When a potential 'donor' came by she hid the Fudgsicle under her arm and resumed her grotesque, pitiful shape. Another beggar, huddled in front of a monastery, hailed a taxi and drove off when the people who had given her money had moved on. Begging in supposed need is undoubtedly a timeless occupation. So it seemed very timely, when so many people are depending on others for their well-being, to create my *Court of Miracles*.

I approached all the modern dance companies in Toronto hoping that, together, we could create a Christmas show to rival *The Nutcracker*, but the only interest came from Dancemakers. I chose the music, although James Kudelka later changed some sections. His contributions were epic – the Banner Dance, the Wedding, The Gypsy Dance and the Finale. Each year sections changed, were dropped, re-choreographed or added, depending on the cast and the guest artists involved.

The opening image of the acrobat crossing on a tightrope while carrying two candles came from an engraving I fell in love with in a Paris gallery. The image struck me as the perfect metaphor for the artist. You have been given a light and you have to carry it safely across the void, blindfolded.

I envisioned three large ladder-type structures for the set, but our set designer Ron Ward created phenomenal multi-purpose structures. For example, a large plank that the acrobat used as his tightrope to walk across the stage later became the table inside a set piece for the inmates' feast.

The curious thing about *Court of Miracles* is that, although it had a cast of sixty, ten good dancers could handle all the technically difficult roles. It became a kind of community on stage – from the very young members of Canadian Children's Dance Theatre to the seasoned guest artists.

In Act 1, I wanted to show the unchanging nature of society and the potential for play when people gather together for celebration. Act 2 opened in an asylum-like 'home for the socially discarded' with only grey costumes and grey hangings – a dramatic opposite to the colour, action and brightness of Act 1. Each inmate represented one of the seven deadly sins until 'Envy' stole everyone else's sin, leaving them with nothing. The beggars arrived and offered the inmates the things they had begged or stolen from people in Act 1. The first gift, an orange, stems from my childhood memories during the war when an orange in December in Toronto was an exceptional treat – almost miraculous in itself. The beggars enacted a Miracle Play that concluded with the set pieces revolving to display a Nativity scene. The inmates then gave up their gifts to the Christ Child. So it really was about the poor giving to the even poorer, giving to God. In that moment a miracle transformed the asylum into a great castle hall where the inmates were entertained and dined on gold platters. Just when the people thought they had given everything possible to transform the inmate's existence, the inmates took the tablecloth – which was actually seven rainbow robes lined with gold – and to the astonishment of the assembled company ascended the ladder as seven saints.

One of my unforgettable memories of *Court of Miracles* was in the first year when Benoît Lachambre played a beggar in Act 1 and Joseph in Act 2. He had injured his leg so we choreographed everything for him with a crutch or a staff. He did a phenomenal job and was utterly unforgettable.

ORPHEUS AND EURIDICE

(1984)

Composer: Opera by Christoph Willibald Gluck, Libretto by Ranieri da Calzabigi, Translation by Andrew Porter
Conductor: Nicholas Goldschmidt
Assistant Conductor and Rehearsal Pianist: José Hernandez
Music performed by: Hamilton Philharmonic Orchestra – Boris Brott, Musical Director; Guelph Chamber Choir – Kathryn Laurin, Director
Costume Designer: Rita Brown. Masks created by Ted Ross
Set Designer: Thierry Bosquet. Set painting by Jack King
Lighting Designer: Lynne Hyde
Stage Director: Bill Glassco
Stage Manager: Bernie Fox
Assistant Stage Manager: Suzanne Maynard
Premiere Date: April 27, 1984
Premiere Location: Ross Hall, University of Guelph
Cast: Orpheus – Janet Stubbs; Euridice – Heather Thomson; Amor – Jane MacKenzie; members of The Toronto Dance Theatre; The Guelph Chamber Choir; The Hamilton Philharmonic Orchestra

SUMMARY NOTE

This production of *Orpheus and Euridice* was recorded by CBC Radio for broadcast on the CBC stereo network on June 9, 1984 on the programme *Saturday Afternoon at the Opera.*

PROGRAMME NOTE

Amor, god of love, touched by the grief of Orpheus at the grave of his young wife Euridice, offers him the opportunity to go down to the underworld to rescue her. He is armed only with the sweetness of his song and limited by a condition: he must not look at Euridice until he has brought her back. So much in love he yields to her pleading, he turns to embrace her, thus losing her to death once more until his ravishingly beautiful song of love again melts the hearts of the gods.

PERFORMANCE HISTORY
PROGRAMME NOTE

Christoph Willibald Gluck (1714-1787) and his librettist Ranieri da Calzabigi reformed opera by increasing the human interest and dramatic intensity and by striking a balance between the vocal and instrumental portions. More than two hundred years after the first performance, which was in Vienna in October 1762, this opera is the earliest work still in the repertory of the modern opera house. Gluck composed the opera first for Vienna in 1762 and then for Paris in 1774. Berlioz presented a revision of the opera in Paris in 1859, in a run of a hundred and fifty performances. It was Berlioz who said of the opera: "It is a complete masterpiece and one of the most astonishing productions of the human mind."

INTERVIEW: DECEMBER 3, 2002

CBC Radio recorded *Orpheus and Euridice* at Ross Hall in Guelph for a later broadcast on the programme *Saturday Afternoon at the Opera.* We were undoubtedly radio's foremost dance company! I remember that the music was played so painfully slow that even the singers jokingly said they couldn't stand up at that tempo. A turn in two counts became four counts and it didn't contribute positively to the choreography to be performed at that speed. But still, it was visually very beautiful and the singers – as happens so often – were very supportive and appreciative of our work.

JANET STUBBS AS ORPHEUS WITH MEMBERS OF TORONTO DANCE THEATRE IN *ORPHEUS AND EURIDICE*
PHOTO: NIR BAREKET

CAPE ETERNITY

(1984)

Composer: Milton Barnes
Costume Designer: Denis Joffre
Premiere Date: June 1, 1984.
Toronto Dance Theatre
Premiere Location: The Forum at
Ontario Place, Toronto

SUMMARY NOTE

Cape Eternity was commissioned for the opening of the Toronto International Festival celebrating Toronto's sesquicentennial year and Ontario's bicentennial.

SOUVENIR PROGRAMME COVER FOR THE
TORONTO INTERNATIONAL FESTIVAL
DESIGN: HEATHER COOPER

SACRA CONVERSAZIONE

(1984)

Duration: 28 minutes, 30 seconds
Composer: W.A. Mozart
Music Title: Requiem Mass K 626
(Introit, Kyrie, Dies Irae, Tuba Mirum,
Recordare, Offertorium, Lacrimosa)
Costume Coordinator: Julia Tribe
Lighting Designer: Peter McKinnon
Premiere Date: July 26, 1984.
Banff Centre for the Arts
Premiere Location: Eric Harvie Theatre,
Banff Centre for the Arts
Cast: Original cast, Banff: Allan Barry,
Francine Liboiron, Jocelyn Paradis, Karin
Wakefield, Lorna McConnell, Nancy
Shainberg, Learie McNicolls, Jay Gower
Taylor, Clark Blakley, Anita Bostok,
Kenneth Cooper, Marilyn Gabriel, John-
Eric Kent, Marie Josée Lecours, Laurence
Lemieux, Jessica Manzo, Elaine Pollock,
Dawn Pyke, Robyn Richards, Chip
Seibert, Thomas Walker. Cast for Toronto
Dance Theatre's premiere, March 18, 1986:
Almond Small, Dennis (René) Highway,
Monica Burr, Merle Holloman, Grace
Miyagawa, Learie McNicolls, Karen
duPlessis, Christopher House, Sylvie
Bouchard, Michael Kraus, Suzette
Sherman, with members of the School
of Toronto Dance Theatre: Laurence
Lemieux, Suzanne Landerman,
Christiane Larouche, Ron Ladd

SUMMARY NOTE

Sacra Conversazione was commissioned
by the Banff Festival of the Arts, Banff
School of Fine Arts and was performed
by the Banff Centre Dance Performance
Class with the Alberta Ballet Company.
In 2002 *Dance Collection Danse Magazine*
gathered a panel (Michael Crabb, Jeanne
Renaud, Cathy Levy and Max Wyman)
to consider and select the ten top
Canadian choreographic masterworks
of the 20th century; works that
'advance the art itself' and trigger the
audience's emotion, intellect and
imagination. *Sacra Conversazione* was
chosen as one of the ten.

PROGRAMME NOTE

The first performance of this work is
dedicated to Douglas Earle, my
brother, who taught me the meaning
of compassion. Many years ago, during
a visit to France, I went to the Abbey of
St. Denis, north of Paris, to see the
tombs of the French Kings. As I stood
amidst the fabulous white marble
monuments, the great centre doors of
the church opened on a scene of
unforgettable poignance. A family
dressed with all the dignity evident
poverty would allow, stumbling wild-
eyed with grief, under the precious
weight of a wooden coffin, entered
the pantheon of French royalty from a
violent, wind-blown, rain-lashed world.
And on a wreath … 'à Jean 18 ans'. This
vision is perhaps the seed of this work.
Mozart died at 35 – of poverty – of
neglect – and left his Requiem Mass
unfinished.

Programme Note from Toronto Dance Theatre Premiere, March 18, 1986

A people encountering violent death pass through feelings of grief and anger: they struggle to retain their unity and come to terms with their own mortality. Surely it is against the dark background of Death that our small flame of existence appears the most brilliant.

Review by Janet Martineau

Writing about the piece is difficult since it is an emotional experience rather than an intellectual one. There is no denying the powerful spiritual sense of Mozart's aching work, his last project before he himself dies, and what Earle has miraculously managed to do is choreograph it as one with the music. When a female soloist sings, a female soloist dances. As a male voice is added and the work becomes a duet, a male dancer joins the female soloist. Gradually it becomes a quartet, and then a full chorus, as dancers rise from the floor. As the music implores of the heavens, so do the bodies. As grief sounds through the notes, the bodies move as if pained beyond endurance. And as the music swells, the dancers sway to and fro … that magical uplifting, overpowering moment when dance and music become one and the soul quenches its insatiable thirst.

– *The Saginaw News* (Michigan), 1990

Interview: December 3, 2002

There is a particular photograph in a book called *The Family of Man* that shows a community of Jews walking down the centre of the street – probably on their way to a death camp – scornfully watched by onlookers. If there was one central image in my creation of *Sacra* it was this targeted destruction. The *Sacra* programme note relates an experience that moved me deeply at the Abbey of St. Denis in France, and the contrast between the white marble magnificence of the memorials and a grieving family's simple wooden casket. What I was trying to evoke in *Sacra* was the comparison between that scene and Mozart's great vaulting *Requiem*, which portrayed working class people. At the heart of my vision was humanity at its humblest and most sincere.

When *Sacra* was performed in Mexico and Venezuela, men from the audience came backstage in tears. The piece was all about community and going through tragedies and coming out the other side, a concept that they deeply understood. We were the first North American dance company to perform in Poland after the Berlin wall came down. We did fourteen curtain calls each night. As soon as we perform outside of southern Ontario we seem to do well. Works will find their audience if you just have the courage to keep presenting them.

Interview with dancer Suzette Sherman, December 3, 2002

Sacra made a great impression on the dancers as well as the audiences. Dancing it you felt that sense of journey and community. Many dancers were very devoted to *Sacra* allowing themselves to experience each performance as though for the first time. On tour *Sacra* was at the end of long, difficult programmes and we often wondered where we would find the energy to sustain another thirty minutes of dancing. But the opening moments of *Sacra* drew us in and we would travel to the other end realizing that we had used our strength as a 'community'. The piece was incredibly powerful both emotionally and physically; from performing it most dancers learned a great deal about themselves, their dancing and the world.

MEMBERS OF TORONTO DANCE THEATRE
IN *Sacra Conversazione*
PHOTO: JOHN LAUENER

Journal: Sunday, May 13, 1984

First choreographic images: Playing the Mozart *Requiem* – Angels coming forward on orchestral introduction – a staggered line progressing downstage, in random canon … perhaps from knees. An illusion of distance – with words – falls backwards, sits in contraction, rolling upstage, some backfalls and backbends caught by kneeling figures. Perhaps the figures of the Passion noticed one by one by the crowd – turning – whispering and recognizing – leaving them isolated.

Journal: Saturday, July 7, 1984

I realized today that the walking forward at the beginning is Life – the 'execution' they encounter is their own – it is Death they see. The entire work is the gamut of reaction. Mozart's death illustrates the tragedy of the artist refused – but his work speaks of immortality. In this music I find many images – beseeching a reprieve, rage at the end of the familiar, passionate love, and hope, reaching to an understanding God – Peace in a sense of struggle ended.

Journal: Friday, July 20, 1984

I am in a state of shock. There is a great beauty to be had in this work. In its unfinished state I can see that I could work the material into a very moving piece. The dancers look so magnificent in Peter McKinnon's light. Learie McNicolls was the piece – he was shining – he spent himself without reserve. The dancers applauded me afterwards – and I told them that I feel I have achieved what I had hoped for. I have made them no less beautiful than they really are – and, perhaps, more than they knew. But it is the music … we don't detract from its splendour. It is the chance to hear that feast of sound with some imagery drawn from it that is so moving. It is even more incredible than I knew when I came here to Banff. I have listened for so many years now. Only after taking it apart and drawing images from every bar am I really able to hear it. Now it is part of me. Though the lighting was just being improvised tonight there were many extraordinary moments. I liked it best when I couldn't see the whole stage – when the dancers moved in and out of the light – it is very supportive of this style of movement … of my random canons and freedom of interpretation. The light makes the stage glitter with differences.

Note to Cast at Banff Premiere

I believe that a fear named, is a fear diminished. It is my hope that through this work which we created here together, we can, by dancing half an hour of our Lives, give each person who watches some release from the undefined fear of Death. By enacting for them a ritual of our own Death, we can make conscious and beautiful the inevitable end, and inspire the passion to Live!

Article by Carol Anderson

David Earle: I remember I decided in Banff that I didn't want the dancers to wear any make-up … A ballerina from the Alberta Ballet … danced, for the first time in her life, with no make-up. She moved herself beyond recovery. She had unleashed something so gigantic in herself by being herself. She had never been seen as herself. I suddenly realized that it wasn't about fantasy, it was about reality. Everything off the stage is a fantasy that we all contribute to, that we've all agreed to. I call it the Great Lie. We've all bought into it because everyone we ever knew did. There didn't seem to be any choice. Then I thought, we have this chance to show these fragments of reality to people … I realized when I was onstage performing that I felt my unique existence as a being more intensely than I did in any other context. Very shocking. That's why it takes time to come back. It's not coming back to reality, it's coming back to the lie …

– Extract from "Beatty – Earle – Randazzo", *Dance Collection Danse Magazine*, No. 47, 1999

ADAGIO FROM 'THE THEATRE OF MEMORY'

(1985)

Composer: David Akal Jaggs
Music Title: The Theatre of Memory
Premiere Date: May 30, 1985
Premiere Location: Winchester Street
Theatre, Toronto
Cast: Suzette Sherman, Luc Tremblay

SUMMARY NOTE

Adagio from 'The Theatre of Memory' was
performed for On The Threshold, three
evenings of new choreography.

PROGRAMME NOTE

On The Threshold is a collaborative
dance-theatre production utilizing the
multi-faceted talents of independent
choreographic dance artists, Susan
McNaughton and Claire Piggot, along
with two of the well known co-
founders/resident choreographers
of Toronto Dance Theatre, Peter
Randazzo and David Earle. This is an
innovative project for us. We are two
generations of Dance. We meet ON
THE THRESHOLD.

LUC TREMBLAY AND SUZETTE SHERMAN
IN *ADAGIO FROM 'THE THEATRE OF MEMORY'*
PHOTO: FRANK RICHARDS

EMOTIONAL GEOGRAPHY

(1985)

Composer: J.S. Bach
Music Title: Chorale
Music performed by: Paul Jacobs, piano
Costume Designer: Denis Joffre
Premiere Date: June 1, 1985.
Toronto Dance Theatre
Premiere Location: Dalhousie Arts
Centre, Halifax
Cast: Christopher House,
Learie McNicolls

SUMMARY NOTE

Also called *Emotional Geography: Four Studies.* Choreographed for Dance in Canada Gala, 1985. The first study is a eurhythmic duet; the second is two blind figures journeying together who recover their sight at the end; the third is a solo of life and death tension; the fourth is a zany allegro. The second and third sections of this piece are often performed independently.

INTERVIEW: MARCH 26, 2003 AND JULY 2003

Donald Himes' teaching of Dalcroze Eurhythmics while I was a student at the National Ballet School has inspired much of my work. In *Emotional Geography* I chose to have one dancer follow one line of melody and another dancer simultaneously follow the other – making the music visible. The Paul Jacobs recordings of these Bach Chorales are wonderful pieces of music; I felt the kind of gestures I had the dancers doing to that music was very Dalcrozian. I particularly liked the solo section. It was built on the diagonal line and had a sense of resignation about it – life and death – the tension between the two corners of the stage.

LEARIE MCNICOLLS AND CHRISTOPHER HOUSE IN *EMOTIONAL GEOGRAPHY*
PHOTO: ANDREW OXENHAM

SACRED GARDEN

(1986)

Duration: 7 minutes
Composer: Giovanni Battista Pergolesi
Music Title: Stabat Mater, first movement
Premiere Date: February 1, 1986. Toronto Dance Theatre
Premiere Location: Solar Stage – Lunchtime Theatre, Toronto
Cast: Suzette Sherman with Learie McNicolls or David Earle

SUMMARY NOTE

Sacred Garden was performed at Solar Stage as a duet for a man and a woman and as a duet for two women. In future performances it was always a duet for two women. *Sacred Garden* became part of *Palace of Pleasure* and was later performed with *Zefiro Torna* (choreographed by Christopher House) as part of *Two Renaissance Songs.*

PROGRAMME NOTE, 1990

At the cross her station keeping, /
Stood the mournful Mother weeping, /
Close to Jesus to the last.

— *Stabat Mater*

SUZETTE SHERMAN AND LEARIE MCNICOLLS IN *SACRED GARDEN*
PHOTO: FRANK RICHARDS

SUNRISE

(1987)

Duration: 19 minutes
Composer: Johannes Brahms
Music Title: Symphony No. 1, in
C minor, Op. 68 – first movement
(Un poco sostenuto – Allegro)
Costume Designer: Denis Joffre
Lighting Designer: Ron Snippe
Premiere Date: January 1987.
Toronto Dance Theatre
Premiere Location: Toronto
Cast: Grace Miyagawa, Karen duPlessis,
Merle Holloman, Suzette Sherman,
Learie McNicolls, Almond Small,
Monica Burr, Sylvie Bouchard,
Ron Ladd, Laurence Lemieux,
William Elias, Michael Sean Marye

MICHAEL SEAN MARYE AND LAURENCE LEMIEUX IN *SUNRISE*
PHOTO: MICHAEL COOPER

DAVID EARLE: A CHOREOGRAPHIC BIOGRAPHY

Summary Note

In 1987 David Earle received the Dora Mavor Moore Award for best new choreography for *Sunrise*.

Programme Note

One day it occurred to me that the 19th century had just that moment died, and having fought with its images and values all my life its sudden absence, like the loss of a parent, created an instant nostalgia in me for the romance, heroism and pursuit of freedom that this period embodied. I turned to the German composers, and the painters Delacroix, Gericault and Turner. Their storms and shipwrecks spoke to me of passion and adventure and breaking free from hollow forms that, no matter how beautiful, must be abandoned like shells on a seashore.

Interview: November 4, 2002

Sunrise began for me in a coffee shop near the Winchester Street studio. The Brahms music came on the radio, the first movement opening with a gripping, powerful pounding that I immediately felt I must use. I saw an opening image of the past coming toward us – resurfacing in a way – with heroic forms from the Romantic period. Since my early twenties I had found the early nineteenth-century orchestral music to be very bombastic and on a scale that I couldn't relate to. However, the Brahms symphony took me to a place where I felt that the courage, idealism and romantic passion of the nineteenth century had just died. I wanted to create forms from the ballet idiom without actually being in the idiom, a new kind of ballet that would strike people as having a similar elegance and grandeur.

The piece began in a very fragmented way, seemingly arbitrary sections of movement that gradually turned into a narrative of war; the climax pattern shaped in a 'V' for victory. There was a passage of pure beauty of lifts and love duets, trios and solos in an idyllic mode, and a section of running and panic, and a coming together in a wall-like formation that revolved … people peeling off into death, leaving one woman alive to hear the signs of the future. The sun rises at the end of the piece and the new age is born. It signified, for me, the dawn of feminism and the positive aspects of the twentieth century. After everyone gathers to watch, they leave to go off as individuals, each in their own direction, as though it were the moment of the end of Romanticism, when people felt empowered to choose their own, unique path.

CANTATA

(1987)

Composer: J.S. Bach
Music Title: Cantate Christ Lag in
Todesbanden – Sinfonia, Versus I,
Versus II
Costume Design and Construction:
Sigrid Kay
Lighting Designer: Donald Scarrow
Premiere Date: May 23, 1987.
Goh Ballet Company
Premiere Location: Queen Elizabeth
Theatre, Vancouver
Cast: Wang Caijun, Andrea Allen,
Yaming Li, Chan Hon Goh,
Steven Bremner, Camilla Fishwick,
Alice E. Gerbrecht, Sheena-Alexandra
Dickson, Corinne S. Hertel,
Dong Sheng Wei, Naoko Murakoshi,
Kee Juan Han, Ella H. Newton-Mason,
Marianne Hallal Rostand. Second
Cast: April Chow, Che Chun, Bai Lan,
Luke H. Newton-Mason

SUMMARY NOTE

Cantata was commissioned by the Goh
Ballet Company of Vancouver and
performed in over thirty-two cities
throughout the People's Republic of
China. In 1988, the work was renamed
The Triumph of Love.

PROGRAMME NOTE

Someone once told me that during a
lecture Martha Graham picked up a
piece of white paper and, tearing it in
half, said "this is the only tragedy".
Division – what was one becomes two.
The loss of a love tears us apart.
Loyalty sometimes wins a reprieve.
We are reunited. Sing the wholeness
of the heart.

INTERVIEW: NOVEMBER 4, 2002

I began the piece with a woman
embracing a man on the stage. The
man breaks her embrace and walks
away, which in my mind is a kind of
death, as is separation in love. The
community eventually joins her in her
grief and with their help the couple re-
unite, brought together in a sculptural
pyramid with the lovers at the apex.

MEMBERS OF TORONTO DANCE THEATRE IN *CANTATA/THE TRIUMPH OF LOVE*
PHOTO: ANDREW OXENHAM

CLOUD GARDEN

(1987)

Music: Traditional Japanese
Costume Designer: Denis Joffre
Set Designer: Denis Joffre
Lighting Designer: Ron Snippe after Jane Reisman
Premiere Date: July 15, 1987
Premiere Location: Eric Harvie Theatre, Banff Festival of the Arts
Cast: Cast for Banff Centre premiere performance (double cast): Old Poet – David Earle, Christopher Jean-Richard; Death – Learie McNicolls, Bernard Sauvé; First Story: Woman – Barbara Moore, Ainslie Cyopik; Man – Mario Marcil, Marc Leclerc; Spirit – Yseult Lendvai. Second Story: Woman – Lorna McConnell, Marie-Joseé Dubois; Man – Gérald Morin, John Kellner. Third Story: Dead Samurai – John Ottmann, Christopher Jean-Richard; Comrade – Martin Vallée, Jay Gower Taylor; Cloud Gallants and Moon Lords – Joel Boudreault, Paul Reich, John Kellner, Christopher Jean-Richard, Martin Vallée; Ladies of the Shadow of the Willow – Eva Cairns, Eleanor Sande, Fiona Macdonald, Marthe Leonard, Alison Skinner
Cast list for Toronto Dance Theatre premiere, November 25, 1987. Old Poet – Ron Ladd; Death – Learie McNicolls. First Story: Woman – Karen duPlessis; Man – Christopher House; Spirit –

Suzette Sherman. Second Story: Woman – Merle Holloman; Man – Michael Sean Marye. Third Story: Dead Samurai – William Elias; Comrade – Almond Small; Moon Lords – Christopher House, Benoît Lachambre, Almond Small, William Elias, Michael Sean Marye, Crispin Redhead*, Graham McKelvie*; Ladies of the Shadow of the Willow – Karen duPlessis, Monica Burr, Sylvie Bouchard, Laurence Lemieux, Rosemary James, Miriane Braaf, Sharon Moore*, Coralee McLaren*

Students of the School of Toronto Dance Theatre

LEARIE MCNICOLLS IN *CLOUD GARDEN*
PHOTO: MONTE GREENSHIELDS
COURTESY OF THE BANFF CENTRE

SUMMARY NOTE

This work is dedicated to Chuck Flanders, who inspired me in life, as in creation, and who gave of himself generously to dance in this country.

– D.E.

PROGRAMME NOTE, BANFF PREMIERE

David Earle is the 1987 recipient of the Clifford E. Lee Choreography Award. This award was established in 1978 by the Edmonton based Clifford E. Lee Foundation and The Banff Centre School of Fine Arts to encourage the development of Canadian choreography. Award recipients, selected on an annual juried invitational basis, receive a cash award and use Banff Centre resources to showcase original works premiered as part of the annual Festival Dance presentation.

CHOREGRAPHER'S NOTE

The old poet hides from Death, but Death is everywhere. He is caught but escapes to see another year. Three stories are told to pass the time in the journey from Spring Blossoms to bare-branched Winter. The spirit of a young bride returns from the exile of death to find her husband happy with a new love. A woman whose lover is much younger sees that she is losing her beauty. She leaves her sleeping lover in the night. A young samurai is taken from Life in the full flower of his youth. His comrade mourns his loss. As the year passes, the poet has an opportunity to choose the moment of his death, and makes it a gift.

JOURNAL: FRIDAY, MAY 8, 1987 (NEW YORK)

A major breakthrough at last – everything has been building to it, and in the new room of Japanese Art at the Metropolitan Museum today I resolved to do a piece in Japanese style. Through the iris screens, the view of the Noguchi Fountain, and a wondrously made young man in grey pants, reinforced the realization. I will create this work in Banff and have always envisioned Banff as a Japanese creation – the setting cries for that sensibility. I am thinking of the four seasons. This week I even bought myself *The Pillow Book* by eleventh-century lady-in-waiting Sei Shonagon – "In spring it is the dawn…". Maybe I will have my head shaved and dance in the piece. I made a list of elements while I was in the museum: masks, figures pressing through fabric, oranges, irises, rocks, pine boughs, a branch of cherry blossoms, white sheets for snow. A 'travelling garden' – carrying on the rocks upstage left, and gradually shifting them off downstage right. Men with fabric binding women's legs – lowering women with fabric. Sacred undressing (silhouette), lanterns. Various screens.

I have a truly gorgeous display of images and forms before me. The wind brought down many little branches so I have sprays of green leaves in a glass on my table. I have my favourite postcards from Japan laid out – buildings, interiors, scenes of nature – and the little knife I bought with its red tassel, calligraphy on its sheath. Beyond, in the bookcase four little screens (printed as cards, all folded in three) with gold backgrounds; two wooden balls I bought in New York; two green apples; an orange; a green pear; pine cones; the stones I bought in China; candles; cards with Japanese paintings; some special pictures of friends; and one of the Noguchi Water-stone. And beyond that – from my window – the pine covered mountain, pure white clouds and a sky of the gentlest blue.

ARTICLE BY ENA E. SPALDING

David Earle: The dancers at Banff were advanced enough that the possibility of being imperfect did not threaten them. They were particularly responsive to my ideas about what part of the self is really being asked for; how developing the artist in themselves transcends the idiom. They were hungry for imagery and for the philosophy of performance and I always enjoy the opportunity to make my beliefs concrete and perceptible for them. The advantage of working with living instruments is that they have insight of their own and, knowing my nature, they felt encouraged to make suggestions. I think I helped them to find confidence in their own abilities and opened a window to some of the possibilities of how and why to dance.

I was overwhelmed when *Cloud Garden* came to me. I'd had so many separate ideas, then during one night I kept waking up with new pieces for the puzzle. All three stories are sad but not depressing and the structure of the dance is seasonal with a tale of love and death for each story. The Monk, the central figure, is old enough to be able to play and move gracefully with the elements of life and death. At the opening there is a procession across the stage carrying cherry blossoms and the Monk is hiding among rocks. But Death, disguised as a rock, almost catches him. The piece ends with a procession of bare branches – a young girl falls behind the others and, when Death closes in on her, the Monk saves the child and he is taken in her place. The cherry blossoms appear again as Death pulls the Monk offstage and the Monk reaches back to the new year he won't have. He feels nostalgia for what he's leaving but knows it's only a matter of time – choosing the moment himself is a kind of victory. For artists ... life is life and death ... in every moment.

– Revised extracts from "New Work by
David Earle", The Banff Centre
Centre Letter, July 9–16, 1987

PALACE OF PLEASURE (OR DEATH BY LOVE)

(1988)

POSTER FOR *PALACE OF PLEASURE*
PHOTO: JOHN LAUENER
DESIGN: R.K. STUDIOS LTD.

Music: Collage of Baroque composers
Costume Designer: Denis Joffre
Set Concept: David Earle and
Patrick Matheson. Set Realization:
Patrick Matheson
Lighting Designer: Ron Snippe
Sound editing: Penny Olorenshaw
Set Construction: Ed Curtis,
Howard Munroe
Set Painter: Denise Lisson
Wardrobe Assistant: Alison Conway
Premiere Date: April 5, 1988.
Toronto Dance Theatre
Premiere Location: Premiere Dance
Theatre, Toronto
Cast: Feste, the jester – Benoît
Lachambre; The Old Master – Donald
Himes; His Apprentice Orsino, as a
child – Coralee McLaren; A goddess –
Suzette Sherman; Viola/Cesario –
Karen duPlessis; Sebastian – Ron Ladd;
Orsino, as a man – Benoît Lachambre;
His models, lovers, creations – Miriane
Braaf, Sharon Moore, Peter Nishimura,
Cameron MacMaster, Coralee McLaren,
Crispin Redhead; Olivia – Merle
Holloman; Her lady – Suzette Sherman;
The men of her Court – Kate Alton,

William Elias, Michael Sean Marye,
Graham McKelvie, Crispin Redhead;
The ladies of her Court – Sylvie
Bouchard, Monica Burr, Marie-Joseé
Dubois, Rosemary James, Ron Ladd,
Laurence Lemieux, Kathy Martin; The
Cardinal – Donald Himes; The Gods of
Olympus – Members of the Company

SUMMARY NOTE

Palace of Pleasure was a full-evening
work in three acts. "Palace of Pleasure
was inspired by William Shakespeare's
Twelfth Night but only the principal
characters and a few of their
entanglements remain. My principal
concern has been the creation of two
courts, two worlds co-existing,
connected only by a young girl, equally
a stranger in both."   – D.E.

Prologue – The Artist's Garden. The old master, having used up all his vision, wanders with his apprentice, the young Orsino, amidst the memories of loves and the beloved creations they inspired. The child is chosen by the gods and led to Olympus to witness their revels. Scene (1) The Banquet of the gods. The deities pursue their endless pleasures. The child, envious of their splendour, steals the crown that holds the power of the gods; Scene (2) A street. The gods pursue him to Earth and quickly taste the realities of mortal existence. The boy had been away only moments, but an hour in Olympus is twenty years on Earth. While carousing in the streets he rescues one of the gods, whom we will call Viola, and, mistaking her for a boy, offers shelter in his studio. Viola's twin brother Sebastian, mistaken for a girl, is abducted by a gentleman from Olivia's court; Scene (3) Orsino's studio. Viola watches the artist use the powers he has stolen from the gods; Scene (4) The Chapel in Olivia's Palace. The Court is harbouring an unspeakable plague to which Olivia's brother has succumbed. Hiding at the funeral, Orsino points out to Viola the woman who is his ideal and his inspiration. Olivia has sworn to remain in mourning, receiving no one for seven years; Scene (5) Cesario (Viola) pays the first five calls on Olivia, eventually meeting with a curious response. Olivia has fallen in love with the messenger;

Scene (6) Olivia's Court perform their daily ballet mass. Viola is now a regular guest. Viola – discovering Sebastian amongst Olivia's ladies – decides to give her role over to him as she is breaking Olivia's heart. Olivia and Sebastian know brief happiness, but after all this is not really the lover who started the flame in Olivia's heart. Meanwhile her Court is succumbing to the plague and she is gradually becoming a lonely wanderer in her marble halls; Scene (7) The lovers are finally united.

I feel that it was in the 17th century that we recognized the full extent of our aloneness. With the advances in science and the corruption of the Church, we were banished from the centre of the universe. We became outcasts, wandering aimlessly on a star in endless space with no longer an absolute belief in eternal life. At its best it was the dawning of the great adventure we carry on today. At its worst it was a feeling of utter displacement and desperate clinging to every moment of pleasure and pain as a confirmation of existence. *Palace of Pleasure* was a book of Renaissance stories published in 1566 by William Painter, that contains the tale of Apolonias and Silla on which Shakespeare based *Twelfth Night*. In England at this time, sexual ecstasy was referred to as the little death, and the words of many songs told of lovers longing to 'die'. In my father's favourite book, the autobiography of Benvenuto Cellini, I read, "At the time while I was a young man of about twenty-three, there raged a plague of such violence that many thousands died of it every day in Rome. There arrived in Rome a surgeon of the highest renown who was called Maestro Giaconi de Carspi. This able man in the course of his other practices undertook the most desperate cases of the so called French disease. In Rome this kind of illness is very partial to the priests and especially the richest of them." In notes, written by Edward Tatnall Canby, with some Bach Cantatas I found: "The 'love-death' motive after all, is much older than Richard Wagner. It is a theme rich in scientific Freudianism today but it has been the inspiration for many a poetic tale, both sacred and profane, since the beginnings of the human race. In Bach's sacred imagery, love and death are very nearly synonymous and they are described in extraordinarily vivid, sensuous terms. Those of us who have been brought up in the prim religious attitudes of today are apt to find these portrayals somewhat bewildering, as if a frank expression of human passion were not quite proper in a sacred text. It is our fault if we think so. The Hebrew and Christian writings are full of love-death imagery of the sort, most notably in the poetic Psalms but in many another place as well."

Journal: Sunday, February 28, 1988

My Brother's Birthday. I was just thinking that I have no letter, book or present for Douglas. I imagined myself saying "I'm buried in my Palace of Pleasure" – but I have always been. I escaped to it in my first years. Is it that I am ready to leave it? Is my interest in the East and nature making me want to sum up my lifetime of 'theatre'? Certainly everything has gotten swept into it – Fontainebleau, Anet, Diane de Poitiers, Ferrera, the Este, Mantua, the Gongagas, Michaelangelo, the Medici, Pomona, Mannerism, the Toronto Children Players, Bach, Decoration, Death & Sexuality – all my themes.

Journal: Sunday, March 27, 1988

The last week of rehearsal. I still have about five scenes to do ... well, there will be a worth – but I can't yet see it in its entirety. An artist is a person with the confidence to live with their imagination – to tap it, to channel and nourish it – it is an act of faith. The imagination includes the best and worst, the most glorious and the most appalling images that we contain.

Journal: April 6, 1988 (the morning after opening night)

I realized in the night that the *Palace of Pleasure* was my belief in love – romantic love, I guess. The passion that, in its full power, defies death.

Interview: November 4, 2002

Benoît Lachambre, who played the part of Feste, the jester, is one of those dancers who is all instinct and, without ever studying Graham technique, he is the product of what I believe Graham is about – moving from your gut with every fibre of your being connected to that.

One of the successful sections in *Palace of Pleasure* was the Sculptor making sculptural forms with three couples; shaping and molding the men and placing the women into their form, the way Rodin placed the crouching figure into the man's arms – both already made and then fitted together. I wanted to make a statement about AIDS as well, so I decided to invent a plague based on love – love being the dangerous element – with Olivia mourning her brother's death from this plague. The premise being that she was in love with her brother. Unfortunately, the piece was too confined on the small stage at Premiere Dance Theatre and the work was only about two-thirds realized when it was presented. The best part about *Palace* was the poster, which was a photograph taken from a ladder. I organized everybody on the floor in their unitards in sculptural forms and shot down – as if from a ceiling. The poster encouraged a lot of people to come to the theatre, and, in some regards, I'm sorry about that!

LA VALSE

(1988)

Composer: Maurice Ravel
Conductor: Charles Dutoit
Music performed by: Montreal Symphony
Orchestra, Alicia de Larrocha, Victoria
de los Angeles, Jean-Phillipe Collard,
Agustin Dumay
Premiere Location: Filmed in
St. Lawrence Hall, Toronto
Film's copyright date: 1988
Cast: Suzette Sherman, Karen duPlessis,
Merle Holloman, Monica Burr,
Sylvie Bouchard, Laurence Lemieux,
Rosemary James, Miriane Braaf,
Sharon Moore, Michael Sean Marye,
Learie McNicolls, Almond Small,
Ron Ladd, Michael Conway,
Benoît Lachambre, William Elias,
Graham McKelvie, Crispin Redhead

SUMMARY NOTE

La Valse was part of the Rhombus
Media film *Ravel*, a portrait of the
composer Maurice Ravel's life, directed
by Larry Weinstein. The film received
the Crystal Apple, National Educational
Film & Video Festival award; Golden
Gate Award, San Francisco
International Film Festival; Best
Performing Arts, Gemini Awards; Best
Canadian Television Program, Banff.

REVIEW

An outstanding example of what an
entertaining musical biography should
be … The performances are astonishing
… brilliant rhythmic editing … weds
the video's images to the music. It is a
genuine work of art in itself … There is
a large audience for *Ravel* ranging from
high school and college students to
adults who enjoy voice, opera, dance,
and music. It is highly recommended for
anyone who loves the finer things in life.

– Video Rating Guide for Libraries

MEMBERS OF TORONTO DANCE THEATRE IN *LA VALSE*
PHOTO: DAVID EARLE

CHICHESTER PSALMS

(1988)

Composer: Leonard Bernstein
Musical Director: Ned Hanson
Music performed by: The Toronto Boys Choir, The Hanson Singers and instrumentalists Ian Sadler, Sarah Davidson, Michael Côté, Richard Armin, Paul Shilton, Michael J. Baker, Kirk Elliott, Stuart Elliott
Costume Designer: Diana Smith
Lighting Designer: David Morrison
Premiere Date: December 20, 1988. Canadian Children's Dance Theatre
Premiere Location: Premiere Dance Theatre, Toronto
Cast: Rebecca Armstrong, Shanyn Bishop, Arwyn Carpenter, Eliza Gibson, Anna Jaeger, Asha Joseph, Jennifer Laidlaw, Tara Lee, Andrea Lill, Rachael Lutes, Keat Maddison, Alorani Martin, Robin McPhail, Lara Munro, Amanda Porter, Patricia Quevedo, Cindy Rose, Matthias Sperling, Barbara Stekly, Rachel Tucker. Special guest dancers: Michael Conway and the students of the School of Toronto Dance Theatre – Darryl Hoskins, David Pressault, Dan Wild

ROBIN McPHAIL AND AMANDA PORTER IN *CHICHESTER PSALMS*
PHOTO: CYLLA VON TIEDEMANN

Summary Note

Chichester Psalms was commissioned by the Canadian Children's Dance Theatre and was dedicated "to all that unites". Assistant to the choreographer was Suzette Sherman.

Interview with Michael deConinck Smith and Deborah Lundmark, Directors of Canadian Children's Dance Theatre, April 12, 2003

Michael: I think what David did most for Canadian Children's Dance Theatre (CCDT) is what he did for so many artists in Canada and elsewhere, and that was to invest his confidence in what we were doing, put his name behind it, put his talent behind it and say "have a look at these people". It was his authority that had people taking a look at us in 1988 when he did *Chichester Psalms* because that was really what we consider a breakout year for CCDT. It was the first year that we staged WinterSong and there was a lot riding on that production. Along with numbers choreographed by Deborah Lundmark, Holly Small and Carol Anderson, David Earle made that show work.

Chichester Psalms was unique because David used dancers from Toronto Dance Theatre and professional freelance dancers along with the young dancers of CCDT. It was a hallmark David Earle piece in that it projected the sense of a complete community, which David is known for in *Court of Miracles*. David has always had the vision that dance starts when you leave the womb and ends when you re-enter the ground – and maybe not even then. So it was a real transformative experience to work with him and to have him look at our dancers in ways that choreographers had not looked at them before.

I think *Chichester Psalms* had one of the most dramatic openings and closings of any dance I've seen in thirty years. Even on our pitiful amateur video it still packs the power that only David can assemble consistently.

Deborah: David influenced many of those young dancers and made them feel that they were part of the modern dance community. That was incredibly important because it is difficult for us to nurture young modern dancers if the community is not willing to accept them.

ANCIENT VOICES OF CHILDREN

(1989)

Composer: George Crumb
Poetry by: Federico Garcia Lorca
Conductor: Robin Engelman
Premiere Date: April 11, 1989
Premiere Location: Slee Concert Hall,
Amherst Campus, University at
Buffalo, SUNY
Cast: Benoît Lachambre,
Amanda Porter

**BENOÎT LACHAMBRE AND AMANDA PORTER
IN *ANCIENT VOICES OF CHILDREN*
PHOTO: DAVID EARLE**

SUMMARY NOTE

Ancient Voices of Children is divided into
five sections. (1) The little boy was
looking for his voice. Dance of the
Ancient Earth; (2) I have lost myself in
the sea many times; (3) From where do
you come my love, my child?; (4) Each
afternoon in Granada, a child dies each
afternoon. Ghost Dance; (5) My heart
of silk is filled with lights.

The Toronto Dance Theatre
premiere, with Bill Coleman and
Amanda Porter, premiered on April 14,
1991 at the Chamber Concerts Canada
presentation of An Evening of Love,
Magic and Mysticism, Sunday Stage,
Lawrence Cherney, Artistic Director.

TRANSLATION OF "ANCIENT VOICES OF CHILDREN"

1. The little boy was looking for his
voice. / (The king of the crickets had
it.) / In a drop of water / the little boy
was looking for his voice. / I do not
want it for speaking with; / I will make
a ring of it / so that he may wear my
silence / on his little finger. /

2. I have lost myself in the sea
many times / with my ear full of
freshly cut flowers, / with my tongue
full of love and agony. / I have lost
myself in the sea many times / as I
lose myself in the heart of certain
children. /

3. From where do you come, my
love, my child? / From the ridge of
hard frost. / What do you need, my
love, my child? / The warm cloth of
your dress. / Let the branches ruffle
in the sun / and the fountains leap all
around! / In the courtyard a dog
barks, / in the trees the wind sings. /
The oxen low to the ox-herd / and the
moon curls my hair. / What do you
ask for, my child, from so far away? /
The white mountains of your breast. /
Let the branches ruffle in the sun /
and the fountains leap all around! / I'll
tell you, my child, yes, / I am torn and
broken for you. / How painful is this
waist / where you will have your first
cradle! / When, my child, will you
come? / When your flesh smells of
jasmine-flowers. / Let the branches
ruffle in the sun / and the fountains
leap all around! /

4. Each afternoon in Granada, /
a child dies each afternoon. /

5. My heart of silk / is filled with
lights, / with lost bells, / with lilies,
and with bees, / and I will go very
far, / farther than those hills, / farther
than the seas, / close to the stars, /
to ask Christ the Lord / to give me
back / my ancient soul of a child.

– Federico Garcia Lorca

PROGRAMME NOTE

George Crumb suggests in the score that several parts in this work might be danced. When I was invited to contribute to the Chamber Concerts Canada performances at the University of Buffalo, I wanted to integrate dancers into the musical performance rather than create a piece of choreography – so that the dancers, like the singers and musicians, could be a constant element. Benoît Lachambre, the original male dancer in the work, contributed largely through improvisation to its creation.

JOURNAL: SATURDAY, MARCH 25, 1989

The first rehearsal with Benoît Lachambre and Amanda Porter. We blocked through the second dance – Dance of the Sacred Life Cycle – Benoît a parent figure and Amanda a playful spirit. They were, as I imagined, utterly magical together, truly two of a kind.

JOURNAL: TUESDAY, APRIL 11, 1989

The day has come. The instruments are set up on stage. We set some lights this morning – all white – isolating the stage as much as possible, trying not to have it uniform. I've learned to like the piece rehearsed to the tape recording, with all the emptiness and stillness, though the dance is created to be integrated with the chamber concert performance. George Crumb, the composer, will be there. I hope that I haven't transgressed his wishes. Having the dancers onstage for the entire piece will offer more continuity than the composer's comment that "the three dance sections may be danced by a solo dancer" as he noted in the score. I hope he will find something of himself in the little narrative we have created.

After the onstage dress rehearsal we went to hear George Crumb interviewed – a great experience – a wise, modest man. I was in a sweat hearing him talk about *Ancient Voices* – and the two "danced intermezzi!" What will he feel when he sees the dance element present from the beginning? He talked so much about his work being organic – surely my addition is inspired by and respectful of that. He mentioned that sometimes he liked to listen to music in the dark – but that in the concert hall even the most traditional performances have action and therefore distraction. So why not organize the action somewhat? Still, it will be a very tense experience.

JOURNAL: WEDNESDAY, APRIL 12, 1989

A time of darkness, death and sudden light. Last night was one of my greatest experiences. It was an extraordinary stretch of time – the piece was literally hanging in silence. The dancers made not one sound – the audience sat forward in their chairs – not a breath – the musicians gave an inspired performance. Benoît was a lion, Christ and the sea. Amanda stepped onstage with awesome purpose – never faltered – wove and deepened a spell made of all that is delicate on the earth. The composer said, "a performance like that of one of your works makes you want to go on creating". He saw great things in the dance.

DAVID EARLE: A CHOREOGRAPHIC BIOGRAPHY

EL AMOR BRUJO (WEDDED TO WITCHCRAFT)

(1989)

Composer: Manuel de Falla
Conductor: Robin Engelman
Music performed by: Sharon Festival Ensemble; Odette Beaupre – mezzo-soprano; Raymond Spasovski – piano; Colin Tilney – harpsichord
Costume Designer: Denis Joffre
Premiere Date: July 8, 1989
Premiere Location: Sharon Temple, Sharon
Cast: The Bride – Suzette Sherman; The Groom – Graham McKelvie; The Ghost of Her First Husband – Michael Sean Marye; The Woman He Loved – Laurence Lemieux; Friends of the Bride – Rosemary James, Miriane Braaf, Kate Alton; Friends of the Groom – Crispin Redhead, Darryl Hoskins, David Pressault, Dan Wild

MICHAEL SEAN MARYE, SUZETTE SHERMAN,
GRAHAM MCKELVIE, LAURENCE LEMIEUX
IN *EL AMOR BRUJO (WEDDED TO WITCHCRAFT)*
PHOTO: CYLLA VON TIEDEMANN

Summary Note

This piece was commissioned by the Music at Sharon summer festival, Lawrence Cherney, Artistic Director.

Synopsis

At her wedding the bride is visited by the spectre of her first husband. A gypsy girl who also loved him, senses his presence and conjures up his spirit to declare his still violent passion. The bride, discovering that her husband was unfaithful, banishes him and gives herself utterly to her new love. The gypsy girl renounces life for her dead lover.

Interview: November 4, 2002

The Sharon Temple, in Sharon, Ontario, is a round building where we performed in the centre of the space and the piece worked very well there.

There is a horrible rehearsal story of Suzette Sherman as the Bride. She was supposed to fling herself, distraught, near a chair but managed to somehow actually hit her head on the chair. It made a terrible crack that everyone in the room could hear. Suzette insisted that she was fine and refused to stop dancing despite the fact that she was reeling uncontrollably around the stage. It became a rather famous story of heroism and dedication.

ANDREW GIDAY IN *SCHÉHÉRAZADE*
PHOTO: MICHAEL SLOBODIAN

SCHÉHÉRAZADE

(1989)

Choreographers: David Earle, James Kudelka
Composer: Nikolai Rimsky-Korsakov
Music Title: Symphonic Suite, 1st, 2nd and 4th Movements
Set and Costume Designer: Peter Horne
Lighting Designer: Nicholas Cernovitch
Assistant Costume Designer: Sylvain Labelle
Violin Solo: Denise Lupien
Premiere Date: October 27, 1989. Les Grands Ballets Canadiens
Premiere Location: Place des Arts, Montreal
Cast: (all casts) King's Wives – Gioconda Barbuto, BetsyAnn Baron, Anik Bissonnette, Andrea Boardman, Katia Breton, Donna Croce, Yvonne Cutaran, Judith Johnson, Seung-Hae Joo, Josée Ledoux; The Ladies of the Court – Nathalie Buisson, Suzanne Gagnon, Emmanuelle Gill-Houpert, Katrenna Marenych, Audrey Papegaey, Dale Peacocke, Renée Robert, Nadya Chiacig; The Queen – Min Tang, Rosemary Neville, Leslie Jonas; The Golden Slave – Rey Dizon, Andrew Giday; The Slaves – Joel Boudreault, Nicolo Fonte, Aaron Hartnell, Dennis Lepsi, Michael Reed, Johnny Rougeolle, Douglas Vlaskamp; The King – Min Hua Zhao, Kevin Irving; The Warrior Princes – Pedro Barrios, Philippe Delorme, Benjamin Hatcher, Kenneth Larson, Jocelyn Paradis, Kevin Thomas

Summary Note

Danny Jackson and Linda Stearns, the co-artistic directors of Les Grands Ballets Canadiens (LGBC), commissioned David Earle to collaborate with James Kudelka, resident choreographer of LGBC at the time. James Kudelka choreographed the chorus work and David Earle choreographed the duets. This was one of many successful collaborations between Kudelka and Earle.

Choreographers' Note

Rather than reconstructing the original creation by Fokine and Bakst for Diaghilev in 1910, we have chosen to allow ourselves to be inspired by their characters and the passion for the exotic that caused the production to have a great impact on Paris in the early part of this century.

Interview: November 4, 2002

For this work created for Les Grands Ballets Canadiens, James Kudelka gave me the pas de deux sections and he took the chorus sections to choreograph, which was the reverse of the way we usually worked together. His opening scene of women bathing surrounded by elaborate draping fabric was reminiscent of my style and, because the programme did not list which parts each of us had choreographed, everyone assumed it was mine. At intermission people said to me, "Oh, I really love it, *especially* the opening scene", and I was happy to respond, "It was all James."

I've known James since he was a little boy. He's a very complicated man and it's always a privilege to work with him. I lived with him in his Montreal apartment while we were working on *Schéhérazade*, and I used to tease him a great deal. In fact, he would go off to the studio first, before I was due to be there, and the office would phone and thank me for making James laugh before he arrived.

In rehearsals we would run the whole piece, both sitting in front of the company. After the work's devastating and moving conclusion I would start to say, "that was very beautiful …" and beside me James would be saying the opposite. It was almost comical and the dancers were very confused by our differing opinions.

Journal: July 1989

As we pulled into the Dorval Airport the sky looked like a negative of itself – black and grey and white – ominous and magnificent. The heat has been so weakening that I feel reckless, wanting to escape into that darkness. The rain has come.

Lying on the parched grass in the park – feeling welcome cool air announcing this storm, I imagined writing a programme note: "The slave – at first a favourite, a toy – has become almost a son – too well loved by the King. Whether the queen plotted the young god's destruction, or truly felt the tragic passion she used to encompass it, we shall never know". All three casts were excellent today. When the piece is done it will be rewarding to coach in detail.

Journal: Thursday, August 10, 1989

The last day of this period of creation. Very emotional. I spoke after the second run, but it was all I could do to keep from breaking down. The end is so passionate. The music after the destruction of the court – as the King goes toward the Queen, lying beside the dead slave – is unspeakably beautiful. I felt empty and lost afterwards.

Journal: Sunday, October 29, 1989 (following the first two performances)

This is the kind of ballet that enchants – makes children want to enter that world of illusion – makes adults remember their first attraction to theatre. All of the production elements worked perfectly – the gauze traveler opening and closing as if people were moving it … the opening vision was applauded. And now the post-birth letdown can underline loneliness.

QUODLIBET

SUMMARY NOTE

Quodlibet is composed of *Scherzo*, (by Christopher House), *Debate* (by Christopher House), *Capriccio* (by David Earle) and either *Autumn Leaves* (David Earle) or *Romance* (David Earle). *Quodlibet* was later titled *Quodlibet – (as you will) A humorously incongruous musical medley.*

CAPRICCIO

(1990)

Composer: J.S. Bach
Music Title: Overture #5 in G Minor
Costume Designer: Denis Joffre
Lighting Designer: Ron Snippe
Premiere Date: March 6, 1990.
Toronto Dance Theatre
Premiere Location: Premiere Dance Theatre, Toronto
Cast: Karen duPlessis, Christopher House, Suzette Sherman, Laurence Lemieux, Michael Sean Marye, Kate Alton, Miriane Braaf, Monica Burr, Bill Coleman, Pascal Desrosiers, Rosemary James, Graham McKelvie, Coralee (McLaren) Moen, Crispin Redhead

SUMMARY NOTE

Capriccio later became a section of *Visible Distance.*

ROMANCE

(1990)

Composer: Henry Purcell, arranged by J.S. Bach
Costume Designer: Denis Joffre
Lighting Designers: Ron Snippe, Howard Munroe
Premiere Date: March 6, 1990.
Toronto Dance Theatre
Premiere Location: Premiere Dance Theatre, Toronto
Cast: Kate Alton, Miriane Braaf, Monica Burr, Pascal Desrosiers, Christopher House, Rosemary James, Laurence Lemieux, Michael Sean Marye, Graham McKelvie, Coralee (McLaren) Moen, Crispin Redhead, Suzette Sherman, Michael Trent

SUMMARY NOTE

Romance later became a section of *Visible Distance.*

AUTUMN LEAVES

(1990)

Composers: Joseph Kosma, melody; Jacques Prevert, lyrics
Music Title: Autumn Leaves
Costume Designer: Denis Joffre
Lighting Designer: Ron Snippe
Premiere Date: March 6, 1990.
Toronto Dance Theatre
Premiere Location: Premiere Dance Theatre, Toronto
Cast: Miriane Braaf, Monica Burr, Graham McKelvie

MONICA BURR, MIRIANE BRAAF,
GRAHAM MCKELVIE IN *AUTUMN LEAVES*
PHOTO: CYLLA VON TIEDEMANN

DREAMSEND – A MELODRAMA IN 12 MOVING PARTS

(1990)

Composer: Anton von Webern
Music Title: Five Movements for String Orchestra, Op. 5; Six Pieces for Large Orchestra, Op. 6; Two Songs, Op. 8
Costume Designer: Denis Joffre
Lighting Designer: Ron Snippe
Premiere Date: March 13, 1990.
Toronto Dance Theatre
Premiere Location: Premiere Dance Theatre, Toronto
Cast: The boy – Christopher House; His sister – Karen duPlessis; A boy who loves him – Graham McKelvie; A girl who loves him – Suzette Sherman; The school hero – Michael Sean Marye; An angel – Bill Coleman; Girls – Kate Alton, Miriane Braaf, Monica Burr, Rosemary James, Coralee (McLaren) Moen, Laurence Lemieux; Boys – Bill Coleman, Pascal Desrosiers, Crispin Redhead

PROGRAMME NOTE

Have adults forgotten how corrupted – that is, incited and aroused – by the sex impulse they themselves were as children? Have they forgotten how the frightful passion burned and tortured them while they were all children? I have not forgotten for I suffered terribly under it.
– Egon Schiele, *Prison Diary*, 1912

The actual tragedies of life bear no relation to one's preconceived ideas. In the event, one is always bewildered by their simplicity, their grandeur of design, and by that element of the bizarre which seems inherent in them.
– Jean Cocteau, *Les Enfants Terribles*, 1929

A Melodrama in 12 Moving Parts:
(1) Brother, sister, angel; (2) School hero; (3) Girls dance; (4) A scene in a schoolyard; (5) Three children witness love as an ideal; (6) Night scene; (7) Games; (8) Three mirrors; (9) The wall – labyrinth; (10) Dance hall; (11) Midnight; (12) The path of flowers.

INTERVIEW: NOVEMBER 4, 2002

Dreamsend was my effort to pay homage to *Les Enfants Terribles*, a book that gave me permission to be myself when I was sixteen. After reading the book I turned in a new direction and have stayed on that course for the rest of my life.

I've always had sympathy for the concept of incestuous relationships because my mother was very cold and unsensual. I felt isolated and somewhat starved for affection, craving an intimacy with my family. So I thought that if anyone ever found that closeness in a family it would be kind of beautiful – even with a sexual element – which struck me as, probably, not that unnatural.

The tragic deaths of Julien and Marguerite de Ravalet, brother and sister executed for their love in the sixteenth century inspired me to create a story about a brother and sister who were in love and have a guardian angel with whom they play. At school the boy has an infatuation with a school hero and, bullied for his puny size, he experiences violence because of his sensitivity. The brother and sister go to the city where the tragic and discarded city people find the siblings' love ridiculous and destroy them – stripping and killing them. It ends in a mock funeral. Shrouded in black veils, the people who refused to accept them in life offer the brother and sister flowers as they pass with their angel, but they are oblivious to anything except the path they are on. I started at least three new pieces and got lost before I started *Dreamsend*. It was a nightmare time when Toronto Dance Theatre was divided in two and I had to prove my worth moment by moment as all the people I loved and had brought into the company vacillated from side to side, depending where the power was. I was artistic director then, but close at my heels were the hounds of fate. So it took an awful lot of nerve to create under those circumstances but I did press the piece through.

Michael Sean Marye, who played the school hero, is probably the best male dancer I have ever seen anywhere in the world on any stage with any company and yet he is still unrecognized. How does the artist get through the net to find the public, I wonder? Christopher House is also one of the great dancers of this country. Lar Lubovitch was the initial inspiration for Christopher's choreography and the fact that Christopher brought that element – with its wonderful freedom and ease of movement – into the studio affected me and my choreography – as does everything around me. When Christopher and I lived together we exchanged thoughts and ideas and unconsciously played a part in each others' creations.

JOURNAL: SUNDAY, JANUARY 21, 1990

I choreographed 3½ of the Berg Songs this week – that is I put movement to them: the drunken waltz, the ugly shapes solo, the canon that looks like Cocteau's drawings while on opium, and another duet passage. Friday we videotaped all my material. It is like so many random bolts of fabric. What are the elements that appeal to me in *Les Enfants Terribles*? The love between the brother and sister; hiding from the world; the mother that is not in the same universe; the shared love of young men – the anarchist in them; the fatality of obsession; the inability to compromise.

JOURNAL: SUNDAY, FEBRUARY 11, 1990

Friday evening I thought – it will be movement – it will be what it becomes. I've consumed images and the score to the point of delirium. I'm sweating the work out in the night. I will go into the studio with my excellent dancers and the piece will evolve. I can't solve it mentally. Today at the Art Gallery of Ontario bookstore I saw a new book on Egon Schiele and his contemporaries. He has been a continuing theme from *10 Moving Pictures* on through *Dreamsend* – sexuality and angst – that must be the theme.

JOURNAL: THURSDAY, FEBRUARY 15, 1990

Rough ride – I don't think I can do it – not to the Berg *Lulu Suite*. Today we videotaped everything I've done. It seems to be a film – very little 'dance'. Poor me – poor everybody. I went to the A&A music store – $200 more in CDs – one of them has promise.

JOURNAL: SATURDAY, FEBRUARY 24, 1990

Tough, tough, tough – I'm feeling completely shitty – very painful cough. I was very disheartened seeing it yesterday – not the physical content, though it doesn't seem very inspired to me – but the music – too big, too rich. I have two weeks …

JOURNAL: THURSDAY, MARCH 1, 1990

Running scared – still very sick, and new music!!! Anton von Webern. God, I hope I'm learning whatever this is supposed to teach me. I'm counting the days till I am delivered. I started with Webern late Tuesday evening: *Five Movements for String Orchestra*, *Six Pieces for Large Orchestra*, *Two Songs* with Rilke text. I've woven them together into twelve sections. I have two hours today to try to accomplish it.

BILL COLEMAN, CHRISTOPHER HOUSE, KAREN duPLESSIS IN *DREAMSEND – A MELODRAMA IN 12 MOVING PARTS*
PHOTO: CYLLA VON TIEDEMANN

DAVID EARLE: A CHOREOGRAPHIC BIOGRAPHY

OPENINGS AND INVENTIONS

(1990)

Composer: J.S. Bach
Music Title: Partitas
Costume Designer: Evelyn Bastien
Lighting Designer: Penny Olorenshaw
Premiere Date: May 16, 1990.
School of Toronto Dance Theatre
Premiere Location: Winchester Street
Theatre
Cast: Courante – Sasha Ivanochko,
Dan Wild; Gigue – Barbara Grant,
Gérald Michaud; Allemande – Jane
Fothergill; Burlesca – Jacqueline Casey,
Natalie Plante; Allemande – Wendee
Rogerson, Ilana Rubinsztein;
Sarabande – Hope Terry, Darryl
Hoskins; Fantasia – Cari Campbell,
Kris Evans, Charmaine Headley;
Allemande – Kathleen Pritchard,
Gérald Michaud; Capriccio – Darryl
Hoskins, David Pressault

Openings and Inventions was performed
by the third-year students of the School
of the Toronto Dance Theatre as part
of their year-end presentation and was
later performed by the company at
Toronto Dance Theatre's Rhapsody in
the Late Afternoon, a fundraiser
organized by the volunteer committee
of Toronto Dance Theatre.

SCHOOL OF TORONTO DANCE THEATRE
STUDENTS IN *OPENINGS AND INVENTIONS*

ROMEOS & JULIETS

(1991)

Composer: Sergei Prokofiev
Conductor: Charles Dutoit
Music performed by: Montreal
Symphony Orchestra
Costume Designer: Michael Harris
Premiere Date: February 14, 1991
Premiere Location: Adrienne Clarkson
Presents (Canadian Broadcasting
Corporation Production)
Cast: The Family Section,
choreographed by Marshall Pynkoski
and Jeannette Zingg: Juliet – Coralee
(McLaren) Moen; The Nurse – Joan
Karasevich; Paris – Paul Haddad; Lord
Capulet – David Earle; Lady Capulet –
Linda Goranson. The Bedroom Scene,
choreographed by James Kudelka:
Juliet – Peggy Baker; Romeo – Sylvain
Lafortune. The Balcony Scene,
choreographed by David Earle: Juliet –
Andrea Boardman; Romeo – Benoît
Lachambre. Minuet, choreographed
by David Earle: Juliet – Suzette
Sherman; Romeo – Graham McKelvie;
The Nurse – Susan Macpherson; with
dancers from the Toronto Dance
Theatre. Juliet the Young Girl,
choreographed by David Earle: Juliet –
Amanda Porter; Mercutio – Christopher
House; Lord Capulet – Bill Coleman;

Paris – Eric Gauthier. The Montagues
& Capulets, choreographed by David
Earle: Juliet – Miriane Braaf; Romeo –
Michael Sean Marye; with dancers from
the Toronto Dance Theatre. Dancers:
Kate Alton, Miriane Braaf, Bill Coleman,
Pascal Desrosiers, Karen duPlessis,
Christopher House, Rosemary James,
Laurence Lemieux, Graham McKelvie,
Michael Sean Marye, Gérald Michaud,
Coralee (McLaren) Moen, David
Pressault, Kathleen Pritchard, Suzette
Sherman, Michael Trent

Romeos & Juliets was a film produced
by Rhombus Media and directed by
Barbara Willis Sweete. The film
received the Press Award from France's
Grand Prix International de Vidéo-
Danse de Sète, as well as a Gemini
Award. It consisted of six dances – each
a different interpretation of the classic
story, each danced by a different Romeo
and Juliet.

Romeos & Juliets was a film produced by Rhombus Media which I co-choreographed with Marshall Pynkoski and Jeannette Zingg of Opera Atelier, and James Kudelka. James choreographed The Bedroom Scene duet and then dropped out of the project. It was a little awkward in that I had not been the person developing the context or choosing the sets and costumes, so I was left with a production that was fully realized except for most of the choreography and some dancers that I might not have chosen to work with on this theme. However, despite working with dancers from both the ballet and the modern idiom, despite running out of time at the end of the day, despite exhaustion, it looked very beautiful.

I love film and was eager to create for film. In The Balcony Scene duet I wanted it to appear as if they were running forever. I think that is what young love feels like – it is like getting out on the highway and stepping on the gas. It's a kind of boundless elation and sudden freedom from the minimizing aspect of consciousness.

The Montagues and Capulets 'tribal' section at the end was meant to seem barbaric in the way that the Renaissance was barbaric – its extreme violence hidden behind a veil of culture. Those two families are an expression of that kind of ruthless war for power and wealth that the Renaissance was about, socially. So I wanted to make the scene as primitive as it was, then take away all the trappings and show the lovers sacrificed in a ritualistic way.

BENOÎT LACHAMBRE IN *ROMEOS & JULIETS*
PHOTO: CYLLA VON TIEDEMANN

DAVID EARLE: A CHOREOGRAPHIC BIOGRAPHY

THE VOICE OF THE ANCIENT BARD

(1991)

Composer: Kirk Elliott
Music performed by: Kirk Elliott
Costume Designer: Katharine Mallinson
Premiere Date: December 1991.
Canadian Children's Dance Theatre
Premiere Location: Premiere Dance Theatre, Toronto
Cast: Rebecca Armstrong, Anneke Garnett, Emma Howes, Anna Jaeger, Tara Lee, Claire Marshall, Lara Munro, Amanda Porter, Patricia Quevedo, Matthias Sperling, Jennifer Stockfish, Rachel Tucker

SUMMARY NOTE

The Voice of the Ancient Bard was choreographed for the Canadian Children's Dance Theatre as part of an hour-long collage by nine choreographers called *Songs of Innocence and of Experience*, conceived by Michael deConinck Smith and directed by Michael deConinck Smith and Deborah Lundmark. *The Voice of the Ancient Bard* was also performed at the fifth annual Dancers for Life performance to benefit the AIDS Committee of Toronto.

PROGRAMME NOTE

Songs of Innocence and of Experience springs from a cycle of forty-five poems published in London by William Blake between 1789 and 1794. The author of the *Songs* was also a painter and engraver who interwove his verse with intricate pictures, and so "illuminated" the text.

With the *Songs'* appearance two hundred years ago, an astonishing new voice enters the language. The voice of the child, of individual children, here begins to rise above the self-serving adult ventriloquisms familiar to every age. The stories they tell – of trust and betrayal, of poverty amid wealth, of jealous tyranny and youthful desires, of simply joy – are timeless.

Songs of Innocence and of Experience is dedicated to the memory of Northrop Frye.

INTERVIEW WITH MICHAEL deCONINCK SMITH, APRIL 12, 2003

We asked David to choreograph the last section of *Songs of Innocence and of Experience* because he is so good with endings. Although all the choreographers we selected had an affinity for Blake, David was a natural because Blake was a visionary, a whole artist conscious of visuals as well as the sound of words and music and that is the way David approaches art too. It is very holistic.

Another indication of his generosity was gifting us *Angelic Visitation #1* and *#2* for our tenth anniversary celebration at Premiere Dance Theatre. It was a proud moment because it allowed us to show range in our company and to show a classic work at the same time.

PROGRAMME COVER FOR PREMIERE OF *THE VOICE OF THE ANCIENT BARD*

ARCHITECTURE FOR THE POOR

(1992)

Composer: Marjan Mozetich
Music Title: Fantasia, Procession
Music performed by: Amadeus Ensemble
Costume Designer: Joanne Lamberton
Set Designer: Ken Alexander
Lighting Designer: Ken Alexander
Premiere Date: February 8, 1992.
Ballet British Columbia
Premiere Location: National Arts Centre,
Ottawa
Cast: Allan Barry, Leigh-Ann Cohen,
Ainslie Cyopik, Anne Dryburgh,
John Laurence Grady, Kirk Hansen,
Patti Hines, Marc LeClerc, Martin
Laemmerhirt, Allegra Mia Lillard,
Fiona Macdonald, Gwyneth Obrecht,
John Ottmann, Crystal Pite, Sylvain
Senez, Miroslaw Zydowicz

CHOREOGRAPHER'S NOTE

Architecture for the Poor is the title of a book I saw on a remainders table in a bookshop in Victoria. I believe it is about public housing in North Africa. It shocked me to see the poor as an accepted static segment of human society. Perhaps that is what I found affecting in the title. Since then, in creating this work, I have come to think of the "architecture" as social structures and "the poor" as those who, despite the lack of material wealth, have allowed their spirits to be held captive by the values of the age. I believe that you are never completely a prisoner if you have imagination. I have used the composer's titles for the two parts of this work.

INTERVIEW: NOVEMBER 4, 2002

I find the concept of 'architecture for the poor' shocking … the fact the poor would have such permanence that one would conceive of architecture for them instead of eliminating the reason for their poverty.

It was a pure-movement piece – the first section ritualistic with a lot of floor work and the second much more moving through space.

JOURNAL: NOVEMBER 1991

I've been thinking of a Martha Graham quote in connection with a programme note for this piece. When charged with obscenity by an American congressman, Miss Graham responded, "I can think of two things offhand that are obscene – one is war and the other is poverty."

I don't want 'dancers' on stage … I want people. No unitards. No unisex. My mind is going over and over the theme – Poverty. "The poverty of the spirit that allows the vulgarity of wealth", I thought today. Architecture – "social architecture that holds the spirit prisoner". It seems clear that the 'poor' are those who live in this time, in this culture, and have forsaken the real treasures of existence.

JOURNAL: THURSDAY, FEBRUARY 6, 1992

The run-through was not perfect … mistakes in the opening section, a month later, people not into it. The difference in training shows. I can tell that they can't feel the movement – it is in their heads. I know this is the result of my nature, of not driving people to accomplishment, but considering the recent death of Ballet BC's artistic director Barry Ingham, I can't help but be supportive. But I was disappointed today.

JOURNAL: SATURDAY, FEBRUARY 8, 1992, NATIONAL ARTS CENTRE, OTTAWA

And so, the day arrives. It should be thrilling to be in this space realizing a very unique process – an extraordinary situation. Jacob Siskind from the *Ottawa Citizen* wrote an inflammatory advance, quoting me very liberally – using my phrases "red-neck rich" and "dumb money" – so my life is on the line again. No – I can't even think of that. I need to remember the Tao Te Ching. I need to reject all notion of success or failure. This has been a good piece of my life. I will learn what I can and go on.

MEMBERS OF BALLET BRITISH COLUMBIA IN *ARCHITECTURE FOR THE POOR*
PHOTO: COURTESY OF THE VANCOUVER BALLET SOCIETY

UNTITLED MONUMENT

(1992)

Composer: Toru Takemitsu
Music: Collage of film scores
Costume Designer: Denis Joffre
Set Designer: Ken Shaw
Lighting Designer: David Othen
Premiere Date: February 25, 1992.
Toronto Dance Theatre
Premiere Location: Premiere Dance
Theatre, Toronto
Cast: Miriane Braaf, Monica Burr,
Bill Coleman, Pascal Desrosiers,
Susanna Hood, Christopher House,
Rosemary James, Laurence Lemieux,
Michael Sean Marye, Graham McKelvie,
Coralee McLaren, David Pressault,
Suzette Sherman, Michael Trent,
Crispin Redhead. Apprentices: Sasha
Ivanochko, Naoko Murakoshi,
Kathleen Pritchard

PROGRAMME NOTE

If the hero join combat with night and
conquer it, may shreds of it remain
upon him!
— Jean Genet, *The Thief's Journal*

INTERVIEW: NOVEMBER 4, 2002

There was a large pedestal at the back
of the stage and the first monument
revealed a bride's dress on a headless,
armless dummy skirted with a row of
red votive candles. The second
monument was Crispin Redhead, a
gorgeous, muscular dancer. The
costume he wore consisted only of a
phallic extension that surrounded him
about three times and with which he
wrestled – the metaphor was Hercules
wrestling the Hydra. The third vision
depicted men and women attempting
to step on each other's faces to see
which gender would successfully reach
the top of the heap. It concluded with
a vision of three women who let their
hair down and then stripped three men
naked, washing them with three crystal
clear bowls of water. It was a strong,
dark piece and one that I would like to
do again.

JOURNAL: SUNDAY, JANUARY 12, 1992

I started the piece on Thursday and
worked on Friday again – although only
about forty-five minutes at the end of
the day. The general thrust seems
interesting. I think I have to go on
trusting that I have something to say
through movement and human
presence even if I have no precise idea
to illustrate as yet.

JOURNAL: SUNDAY, FEBRUARY 2, 1992

The title *Untitled Monument* seems
perfect. It occurred to me while
looking through a *Galeries Magazine* I
bought at a second-hand bookstore.
Making a monument – the Longo
frieze – and behind it two people
bathing each other's chests – people
falling from the top of the frieze –
caught by straps.

JOURNAL: MONDAY, FEBRUARY 10, 1992

I was awake much of the night. Was it
indigestion? Starting a new piece with
so little time? Starting to teach again?
The cold air from the door? Lust?
Recovering from my premiere
Saturday? Jet lag? Time change? Any,
and I presume all, could be the reason.
I envisioned a great deal of this piece in
very extreme ways. I pictured (as
always) many objects appearing onstage
– brass musical instruments, fruit.
What else? A body builder – weight
lifter – on a pedestal. There is a picture
that started me in that direction – a
photograph taken in Rome with
colossal body parts, scraps of epic
proportions of giant sculptures – statues,
monuments, columns. Rome – fascism
– this seems relevant. I pictured the men
having bestial games – ape-like
'masculinity'. I did one section today with
them on their knees and on their knuckles,
and another of an acrobatic girls' game.

JOURNAL: THURSDAY, FEBRUARY 13, 1992

Monument is moving well. So far the
sequence seems powerful … I have a
clear image of the closing. Now I need
music, so I'm listening yet again to all
my Takemitsu film scores. I started the
choreography for Part 2 on Tuesday
with the dancers forming a line in
single file from which couples slide out.
It turned ominous – cruel, rather –
today. Yesterday we did a very free and
vital lift section, the dancers
contributing constantly. I'm not sure
about the men's costumes – maybe
start all silver, switch to red shirts or
finish in the full metallic look …?

JOURNAL: SATURDAY, FEBRUARY 15, 1992

Of course, now I realize that the piece
is about what I call the new fascism.
It is also about violence between the
sexes, which seems to be a principal
theme in this time. I'm concerned that
it not seem *too* violent to women,
although some of it is very much part
of my attack on the current social
structure. Soon I will have to write the
programme note. Should I mention the
redneck rich? Should I say "how long
will people tolerate the obscenity of
the redneck rich – their preposterous
limousines that would even be absurd
in the water?"

Journal: Saturday, February 23, 1992

Today we lit the piece in the theatre. It was arduous and, as in Ottawa, I was left feeling that I'd lost what I liked about the work. I came home with the video and my notes – trying to remember what worked and what didn't work for me. Tomorrow I have two hours at the studio. I need time in the theatre to change cues. The nudity at the end needs work – I think I'll just have the men naked. The pedestal wasn't lit well – so, though quite beautifully painted, it didn't show. Crispin will be added on Tuesday.

Journal: Wednesday, February 25, 1992

It happened. It was a very extraordinary evening. *Monument* went well – it was horrifying but received a great response. Crispin was a powerful icon – Hercules and the Hydra. Someone made reference to it at the reception; and the reception felt like the real thing – people staying and staying, despite the length of the programme, to chew on the content of the evening.

ROMAN SCULPTURE *THE LAOCOÖN GROUP*;
INSPIRATION FOR *UNTITLED MONUMENT*

VISIBLE DISTANCE: A BACH SUITE

(1992)

Duration: 17 minutes
Composer: J.S. Bach
Music Title: Sonata in E minor for Violin and Continuo
Costume Designer: Denis Joffre
Lighting Designer: David Othen
Premiere Date: July 3, 1992.
Toronto Dance Theatre
Premiere Location: Ottawa
Cast: Kate Alton, Miriane Braaf, Monica Burr, Bill Coleman, Pascal Desrosiers, Susanna Hood, Christopher House, Rosemary James, Laurence Lemieux, Michael Sean Marye, Graham McKelvie, Coralee McLaren, Naoko Murakoshi, David Pressault, Suzette Sherman, Michael Trent

Summary Note

Visible Distance consists of five sections: Capriccio; a suite of three newly choreographed pieces; and Romance. *Visible Distance* received its world premiere in Ottawa as part of the Northern Telecom 1992 Canada Dance Festival. In September 1997 the quartet from *Visible Distance* was performed as part of the gala opening of the River Run Centre in Guelph.

Miriane Braaf, Laurence Lemieux, Michael Sean Marye, Kate Alton, Pascal Desrosiers, Naoko Murakoshi, Bill Coleman
in *Visible Distance: A Bach Suite*
Photo: Cylla von Tiedemann

ANGELS AND VICTORIES

(1992)

Composer: Valerie Ross
Costume Designer: Wladyslaw Wigura
Premiere Date: 1992.
Polish Dance Theatre
Premiere Location: Warsaw
Cast: Ewa Wycichowska, Aleksander
Rulkiewicz, Beata Wrzosek, Robert
Szymanski, Magdalena Gaworzewska,
Przemyslaw Grzadziela, Marzena
Kilinska, Adam Klafczynski, Honorata
Mickiewicz, Pawel Kromolicki,
Aleksandra Musialowska, Witalij
Litwinienko, jr, Iwona Pasinska,
Pawel Mikolajczyk, Patrycja Przybl,
Miroslaw Ogorek, Inessa Sawczuk,
Andrzej Platek, Ewa Sobiak, Krysztof
Raczkowski, Iwona Wojtkowiak

Summary Note

Angels and Victories was choreographed
for the Polish Dance Theatre for the
World Music Days Festival in Warsaw.
This work was also presented at the
1992 Edinburgh Festival.

Interview: November 4, 2002

There were wonderful people in the
Polish Dance Theatre, however, there
were also the usual dancers who could
make 'pictures' very fast, but producing
the continuity between the shapes was
quite alien to them. The men, in
particular, were determined to ignore
the choreographic process and just
practice their *tours-en-l'air*. During the
last studio dress rehearsal I realized that
they were never going to learn their
steps. The soloists were great and the
women, as always, were great, but the
men lacked commitment. So using a
combination of mime, drawings, single
words and my pen, I asked the
production assistants if they could find
some penlights. An hour later they
returned and I told them to give two
penlights to each male dancer at the
back of the group.

At the theatre I asked the lighting
crew to dim all the back lights on the
stage so that only the beams from the
penlights were visible in each of the
dancer's hands. The performers in the
front who knew their steps were
beautifully lit and behind them was an
incredible firefly effect. When push
comes to shove and performance time
has arrived, you've got to do what
you've got to do to make the piece
work.

EWA WYCICHOWSKA AND ALEKSANDER RULKIEWICZ IN *ANGELS AND VICTORIES*
PHOTO: ANDREJ GRABOWSKI

UNDETERMINED LANDSCAPE

(1992)

Composer: Arvo Pärt
Music Title: Stabat Mater (excerpt)
Premiere Date: August 21, 1992.
Victoria Arts Collaborative
Premiere Location: Victoria
Cast: Darryl Hoskins, David Pressault, Laurence Hartz, Kathleen Pritchard, Alisoun Payne, Danielle Baskerville, Rachel Anderson, Jenny Wilkey, Jennifer Dahl, Sandra Botnen, Peter Czerner, Evadne Fulton, Susan Holtz, David Ferguson

SUMMARY NOTE

Nature fashions and dissolves us as she wills. Do we require a miracle greater than birth? Are we too proud to lend our nourishment to the earth? And in the heart of life how lovely the strands of desire that bind us all together.   – D.E.

Choreographed for six couples for the Victoria Arts Collaborative, *Undetermined Landscape* was premiered in Victoria on August 21, 1992.

Undetermined Landscape was then re-worked and a shorter version, half the length of the original work, became a duet performed by David Earle and Suzette Sherman, which premiered September 26, 1992 in Toronto at The Dance Goes On! benefit performance.

DAVID EARLE AND SUZETTE SHERMAN IN *UNDETERMINED LANDSCAPE*
PHOTO: CYLLA VON TIEDEMANN

THE CLAY FOREST

(1992)

Composer: Arvo Pärt
Music Title: Stabat Mater (excerpt)
Lighting Designer: Ron Snippe
Premiere Date: 1992. Ballet Creole.
Premiere Location: Vancouver
Cast: Ballet Creole company members

SUMMARY NOTE

The original, longer version of *Undetermined Landscape* was re-worked and evolved into a group piece for Ballet Creole.

DIVING FOR THE MOON

(1992)

Duration: 10 minutes, 30 seconds
Composer: Rodney Sharman
Music Title: Dark Glasses
Costume Designer: Denis Joffre
Lighting Designer: David Othen
Premiere Date: November 10, 1992. Toronto Dance Theatre
Premiere Location: Premiere Dance Theatre, Toronto
Cast: Kate Alton, Bill Coleman, Pascal Desrosiers, Susanna Hood, Christopher House, Graham McKelvie, Naoko Murakoshi, David Pressault

SUMMARY NOTE

This piece was intended to be 'Autumn' in a series of nature studies inspired by contemporary Japanese sculpture although this project has yet to be realized.

PROGRAMME NOTE

To me, autumn suggests separation. Hakuin, Japan, 18th century: "The monkey is reaching for the moon in the water, / Until death overtakes him he will never give up. / If he would only let go the branch and disappear into the deep pool, / The whole world would shine with dazzling clearness."

KATE ALTON,
BILL COLEMAN,
DAVID PRESSAULT,
PASCAL DESROSIERS IN
DIVING FOR THE MOON
PHOTO: CYLLA
VON TIEDEMANN

Diving For The Moon was an AIDS piece symbolic of the kind of grieving that was around us during that painful period in the 1990s. The work was largely inspired by Eric Hawkins' natural, abstract movement that is humane but more interested with sculptural form than programmatic concerns – just arranging people in space, making complimentary shapes.

It was one of my many attempts to use the inspiration of the Japanese gardens I had visited in Kyoto. The costumes were genderless red silk shirts and pants. It ends with a single figure sitting on another dancer as on a stone in a garden – remembering and thinking.

The Chinese poet, Ly Po, is said to have been out on his boat, drunk (a poetic ideal of the time). He was so in love with the moon that, seeing its reflection in the water, he reached over to embrace it and, falling in, he drowned. Diving for the moon is something we all do. To choreograph a piece is 'diving for the moon'; it is dangerous and yet you're after something illusive that may in fact be merely the reflection of something else, but it's all you can see. I always say no artist is confident. It doesn't matter if you have every award, in fact, it makes it worse, because then you have to meet and maintain an expectation – that's the irony. It's true that you learn as you grow but no artist says, "Now I will paint a masterpiece". As soon as you have more confidence than humility you are getting to a very dangerous place because we all know that we do our best work in spite of ourselves.

My brother did not appreciate this piece or the choice of music and told me as much. It's interesting how people automatically think the fault is with the work or the artist and not a lacking in themselves. Maybe – if they truly believe the person is an artist – they should see it twice to appreciate it. When I listen to new music and don't like it the first time I hear it, I'm not surprised – maybe I'll like it the fifth time. I once had the great good fortune to see Leonard Bernstein conduct a new work by a contemporary composer at Lincoln Center. At the conclusion he received a very slight response and he said to the audience, "From your response to this work I feel that you've failed to grasp its real significance – so I'm going to play it again. If you want to start your intermission early you can leave now." He waited – no one dared to move. He conducted it again – needless to say – to very enthusiastic applause. Leonard Bernstein – one of my heroes!

PILLOW OF GRASS

(1993)

Composer: Rodney Sharman
Music Title: Towards White
Costume Designer: Judy Bishop
Premiere Date: March 19, 1993.
Suddenly Dance Theatre
Premiere Location: Kaleidoscope
Playhouse, Victoria
Cast: David Pressault, D.A. Hoskins,
Lynda Raino, David Ferguson,
Danielle Baskerville, Michael Conway,
Sasha Ivanochko, André Gingras,
Kathleen Pritchard, Laurence Heartz,
Lori Hamar, Elen Gueorguiev

SUMMARY NOTE

Pillow of Grass was presented at a show called Between the Shadows and Light, produced by Suddenly Dance Theatre Society – artistic directors David Ferguson, Lori Hamar and Miles Lowry. *Pillow of Grass* was an abstract, sculptural piece with an Asian influence.

PROGRAMME STATEMENT

Between the Shadows and Light could describe a Night – a time of seasonal change – a Life. Shadows might be a metaphor for unknowing. Light can be wisdom or understanding. In the contemporary arts the spectator is invited to collaborate by bringing their feelings and thoughts to complete the experience. Interpretation is individual and open-ended. Between the Shadows and Light is a realm of dreams. No one can say that their dreams were not realized if they did not carry them to every encounter.

ANDRÉ GINGRAS AND SASHA IVANOCHKO IN REHEARSAL
FOR *PILLOW OF GRASS*

ERRATA

(1993)

Choreographers: David Earle,
D.A. Hoskins
Composer: David Darling
Costume Designer: Hua Fang Zhang's
dress by Judy Bishop
Premiere Date: March 19, 1993.
Suddenly Dance Theatre
Premiere Location: Kaleidoscope
Playhouse, Victoria
Cast: (1) Sasha Ivanochko, Elen
Gueorguiev, Kathleen Pritchard,
Danielle Baskerville; (2) Hua Fang
Zhang; (3) Ricardo Abreut,
D.A. Hoskins, David Earle

SUMMARY NOTE

Errata was part of Suddenly Dance
Theatre's presentation Between the
Shadows and Light.

The years of David's sole artistic
directorship of TDT, from 1987-1994,
had taken their toll artistically, physically
and mentally and he required time to
rejuvenate. The first part of a Canada
Council project grant enabled him to
take five dancers, plus accompanist
Ricardo Abreut, to create two new
works – *Pillow of Grass* and *Errata* – to
perform in Victoria. The second part
of the grant allowed him to explore
Europe.

David visited Paris, Arles, Cahors,
Toulouse, Provence and London. He
haunted art galleries, museums,
chateaux, reconditioned Renaissance
hotels, churches, gardens and exhibitions
for inspiration. He purchased CDs of
many formerly unfamiliar composers,
including Alfred Schnittke, a composer
he would use extensively in the coming
years. He photographed brick walls,
gardens, and a favourite image – a
gigantic archway filled with glass.
Through filling notebooks with images,
collages, dreams and concepts for new
dances, David recorded experiences that
would become catalysts for future
works.

INTERVIEW: JULY 2003

The second phase of my project was
one of new stimulation and input – my
work has always had a Eurocentric bias
through my attraction to historical art,
and Renaissance art in particular. I have
a new fascination for European avant-
garde art and an interest in combining
classical architectural values with
contemporary developments. As I
travelled in Europe, I documented my
interests on still film as well as attended
live performances in theatre, music,
dance and performance art.

INTERVIEW: JULY 2003

"When thinking stops wisdom enters"
occurred to me one day.

Near the Museum of Modern Art in
Paris I noticed an automated 'golden'
man in a window. He is seated, then sits
up … stands up … screams several
times … and sits again. I watched it
over and over … me! I took pictures of
him, I always carry one with me now, a
talisman – me learning to scream.

In Fajac I stayed with John Sime –
founder of the Three Schools of Art in
Toronto and owner of Longhouse
Books – in his wonderful rented cottage
surrounded by 400 acres of fields and
forests. We made a videotape in which I
was the principal actor … *The Man Who
Wears Hats*. But mostly I rested, my
very deep fatigue had time to surface.
So much life to digest and so much
experience from this voyage. It was
very creative time – soul time – healing
time. I started by allowing myself to
get ill.

DAVID EARLE, 1992
PHOTO: MICHAEL ENGLISH

I think the story of TDT is too big to be told – it would have to be broken down into the separate lives that it consumed, reflected and illuminated – so many lives, and love affairs – all of mine have been woven through this river called a dance company. I have been through the white water personally and professionally often in outright terror, and I have known ecstasy and peace in their turn. And so many wasteful deaths – Chuck Flanders and René Highway – both whom I loved as men as well as collaborating artists.

The dancers are the reason I go to the studio – their complicated beauty, their animal power, the challenge they offer me in every instant – and most of all their unrivalled generosity in performance. When we have been in parts of the world where this [their artistry] is recognized, they have received the overwhelming response that they constantly deserve. We all live in the memory of those moments in which a great wave of love held us aloft for an instant and all of the hardships and slights of the past fall away like grains of sand. In those moments we have the confidence to recognize that everything teaches humility.

PROGRAMME NOTES BY DAVID EARLE, TDT SILVER ANNIVERSARY SEASON (1993/94)

THE PAINTER'S DREAM

(1993)

Composer: Peter Landey
Music performed by: Douglas Perry,
Marc Sabat, Ann Armstrong,
Paul Widner
Costume Designer: Denis Joffre
Lighting Designer: Ron Snippe
Premiere Date: December 10, 1993.
Toronto Dance Theatre
Premiere Location: St. Catharines
Cast: Solos – Suzette Sherman,
Coralee McLaren, Graham McKelvie,
David Pressault. The Company –
Kate Alton, Miriane Braaf, Bill
Coleman, Pascal Desrosiers, Susana
Hood, Laurence Lemieux, Michael
Sean Marye, Naoko Murakoshi,
Michael Trent

DAVID PRESSAULT AND CORALEE MCLAREN
(CENTRE) IN *THE PAINTER'S DREAM*
PHOTO: ALAN SHISKO

Summary Note

The Painter's Dream was commissioned by the Centre for the Arts, Brock University, to celebrate its twenty-fifth anniversary. Peter Landey created an original score for this work. *The Painter's Dream* was divided into five sections: (1) In the Forest; (2) Descent to the Underworld; (3) A Clearing; (4) The Kingdom of Hades; (5) Return to Earth.

Interview: December 3, 2002

Composer Peter Landey wrote the music specifically for this commission from the Centre for the Arts at Brock University. It was very much my kind of material – the perils of Eros and mythology woven into the lives of innocent village people in a somewhat historical setting.

Journal: Tuesday, October 12, 1993

Yesterday Peter brought me the completed score. Very, very powerful – epic – sounds like a string orchestra, not a quartet. Peter had said he wanted to expand on it and he definitely has. Now I will have to listen to it a thousand times.

Journal: Tuesday, October 20, 1993

I bought a book on Edvard Munch at the Art Gallery of Ontario yesterday and found a wonderful painting on a postcard – *Girls on the Beach*. A band of long-haired girls in white are standing together in a tight circle and a girl in red is emerging from the group – or passing them – at the edge of the sea.

Journal: Sunday, November 7, 1993

I played Peter's score in the theatre last night to hear how it will sound. It was overwhelming and suggested Armageddon. It certainly is atonal – dissonant – excruciating in parts. Now I have to find life in it. I said to the soundman, "It is telling a very big story, I just have no idea what it is." I have two days to find out.

Journal: Monday, November 8, 1993

Images upon listening – women as girls in white, men in sombre colours. I see the men standing like a forest, sweaters pulled over their heads; the women on a summer night playing hide and seek – ecstatic in the moonlight – running amongst them, being lifted by them. Men begin to turn. Two girls walking hand in hand, or mother and daughter. Suzette Sherman as Munch's *Woman of Sorrow*.

Journal: Monday, November 15, 1993

I reworked the opening – much more control and simplicity – taking the audience through conscious imagery. I also did a passage for David Pressault and Coralee McLaren – Hades and Persephone where David is tender, yet forceful. I worked on a scene with Bill Coleman, Michael Sean Marye, Pascal Desrosiers and Michael Trent as the 'Mouth of Hell', the gateway to Hades – writhing muscled bodies – with Suzette being sucked into the centre of it. I've been trying to decide whether to give the last entrance to Cora or Suzette – Demeter or Persephone. But I think it's the Mother's triumph – it was her battle, her journey – her lesson. I talked with the company about the programme and decided against naming the characters. I had originally written "The girl, Her mother, The young man who loves her, The king of Hades", but, considering the title, the content should be more open-ended.

Journal: Wednesday, November 17, 1993

I did the ending today and found it very moving. I have imagined it almost from the beginning. Suzette, carrying flowers or leaves, leads on the couples. In the last moment, after connecting Cora and Graham she passes under their arms, kneels and offers the gift of renewal to the audience – to the world.

Journal: Friday, December 10, 1993 (premiere)

The day dawns. The lighting is beautiful: the branch 'gobos' evocative, the red light on the gate of Hades effective. David carrying Cora to the spirit kingdom with the little lights like fireflies is truly enchanting. How I love my little fable.

Journal: Saturday, December 11, 1993

Was it good? People reacted well. A gracious woman and her husband spoke to me at some length at the reception. She told me that she had been an overprotective mother and now her daughter was having a very extreme experience as a reaction to it. So … it was understood!

*transparent white cloth
and a woman in white*

[David Earle:] My favourite things in Japanese culture are those beautiful silver and gold abstract paintings with calligraphy. I asked Yoichi (Peter Nishimura) to translate the words on a gorgeous poster and he said it says, "Life and death, that is the only matter." It was an amazing moment for me. When I was teaching yesterday I told the dancers, "You're wasting time in this class because you're not allowing yourself to feel suspended between life and death. You're dancing generalizations and there's no time for that. You're putting off connecting yourself to the essential principles of life, but there isn't enough time." I wanted to say, "Don't you see, 'life and death is the only matter,'" you have to be dancing exactly in the space between those two things. Nothing else is worth it.

I always tell dancers, "Don't come here if you don't have to. If you can live [without dance] then you must … and the rest of us will join you when we can." I think it's the same in a personal relationship. A personal relationship with another human being should be pursued with the idea of eventual separation and if pursued with that idea it could last a lifetime. But if you set out to create a relationship through compromise, the imposition of control or a notion of possession or any other false parameters, then I think its days are numbered. When both are aligned with an inner necessity to be constantly working toward the realization of the self, then it becomes a true and creative partnership.

EXTRACT FROM "DAVID EARLE: THE TORONTO DANCE THEATRE IN JAPAN AND CHINA"
BY DAWN SUZUKI, *THE NEW CANADIAN*, MARCH 16, 1995

THREE BACH ARIAS

(1994)

Composer: J.S. Bach
Premiere Date: Summer 1994
Premiere Location: Winchester Street
Theatre, Toronto
Cast: Leica Hardy

SUMMARY NOTE

Three Bach Arias was commissioned by
Leica Hardy of Halifax, Nova Scotia.

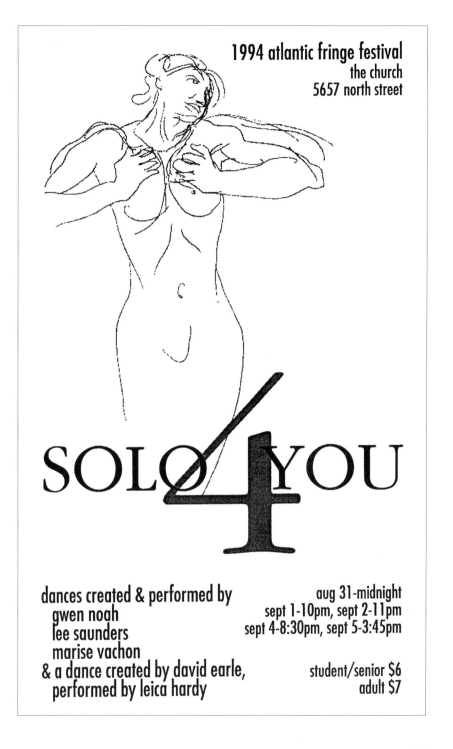

POSTER FOR *THREE BACH ARIAS*

FURNITURE

(1995)

Duration: 29 minutes, 10 seconds
Dance Titles/Composers/Music Titles:
The Long Farewell/Michael
Longton/Miniature; Manhattan
Cowboy/John Beckwith/Scene;
The Undertaker's Lunch/Owen
Underhill/Swizzle Stick; The Sailor's
Revenge/Stephen Parkinson/Desires
are Already Memories; The Uninvited
Guest/Christos Hatzis/Hurraymusic;
Sleeping Beauty/Rodney Sharman/
Sleeping Beauty; Evening Out/Michael
J. Baker/Red Brick; The Interrupted
Dream/Linda C. Smith/Passacaglia
Music performed by: Arraymusic
Ensemble
Costume Designer: Denis Joffre
Lighting Designer: Roelof [Ron] Peter
Snippe
Premiere Date: March 7, 1995.
Toronto Dance Theatre
Premiere Location: Premiere Dance
Theatre, Toronto
Cast: The Long Farewell – Kate Alton,
Stephan Beckon, Pascal Desrosiers,
Susanna Hood, Ron Stewart; Manhattan
Cowboy – Andrew Giday, Coralee
McLaren; The Undertaker's Lunch –
Stephan Beckon, Pascal Desrosiers,
Megan Hayes, Susanna Hood, Naoko
Murakoshi, Suzette Sherman, Michael
Trent; The Sailor's Revenge – Andrew
Giday, Sasha Ivanochko, Ron Stewart;

The Uninvited Guest – Kate Alton,
Graham McKelvie; Sleeping Beauty –
Stephan Beckon, Susanna Hood;
Evening Out – Kate Alton, Pascal
Desrosiers, Andrew Giday, Sasha
Ivanochko, Graham McKelvie,
Coralee McLaren, Naoko Murakoshi,
Ron Stewart; The Interrupted Dream –
David Earle, Suzette Sherman,
Michael Trent

SUMMARY NOTE

Full title is *Furniture: 8 Modern Ghost
Stories in Red and White (and Black and
Blue).*

INTERVIEW: DECEMBER 3, 2002
Furniture was a great, nutty, theatrical
piece performed to the live music of
the Arraymusic Ensemble and I loved
doing it. Christopher House had just
taken over as TDT artistic director and,
in retrospect, it was very gutsy for me
to attempt comedy during that
unsettled time.

The 'gimmick' was that the stage
was full of junk-shop furniture that we
re-arranged to suit each section. Some
of the stories were: Manhattan Cowboy
– a woman is not amused when her
New York urban lover is more
interested in playing cowboys than he is
in her; The Sailor's Revenge – a young
lady dressed as a sailor lures a man
home and locks him in a trunk;
Sleeping Beauty – two naked people
rob Sleeping Beauty of her jewellery by
flashlight; Evening Out – a murder is
committed when two women arrive at
a nightclub wearing identical dresses;
The Interrupted Dream – a deceased
King lies on a bier being mourned by
the Queen and a Jester. Eventually the
Queen and Jester begin to make love.
Partners change and the piece ends
with the Queen dead and the Jester
and the King as lovers.

STARDUST

(1995)

Composers: H. Carmichael and
M. Parish
Premiere Date: 1995
Cast: Veronica Tennant, Michael
Sean Marye

SUMMARY NOTE

This duet was commissioned by
Veronica Tennant and was included in
Timothy Findley's touring show *The
Piano Man's Daughter.*

MICHAEL SEAN MARYE AND VERONICA TENNANT
IN *Stardust*
PHOTO: CYLLA VON TIEDEMANN

The essential purpose of the Graham Technique is to reconnect oneself with instincts that were surrendered after childhood. The purpose is not to be a great Graham dancer but to be a whole and unique individual. Martha used dancers in her school to demonstrate her technique in class but wouldn't invite them into the company. Then some lunatic would come in off the street and Martha would want him or her in her next work because she never confused the technique with the purpose of the technique. If someone was already in touch with their instincts and had total presence then she knew they didn't need to study the Graham Technique to access it. The purpose of the technique is to burn away those blockages so that the body can once again become the clear, pure and open channel that it was born to be.

The recovery of instinct is not a simple situation. We're talking about the recovery of honest terror and a sense of epic darkness. It's not just a simple holistic solution that allows you to be benign and happy for the rest of your life. It's getting in touch with life and death and having the courage to confront your own fears. One has to step out of middle-class values, step out of institutional thinking and look at what's happening and say, "Are we delivering the flower?". Zeami, the Noh player wrote a beautiful book, "The Transmission of the Flower and Style". I think of that constantly: Is it an artificial flower? Is it still in the box? Has anyone looked? Does anyone know if they have a gift left to give? It requires daily assessment of yourself, of your motivations, of your ability to communicate.

EXCERPT FROM "DAVID EARLE: THE TORONTO DANCE THEATRE IN JAPAN AND CHINA"
BY DAWN SUZUKI, THE NEW CANADIAN, MARCH 16, 1995

ELSEWHERE

(1996)

Composers: Gyorgy Kurtag, Arvo Pärt
Premiere Date: February 6, 1996
Premiere Location: Kiss Festival,
Vancouver
Cast: Danielle Baskerville, David Earle

SUMMARY NOTE

Elsewhere was commissioned by
Judith Marcuse for the Kiss Festival in
Vancouver. It became the opening duet
in *Maelstrom*.

INTERVIEW: DECEMBER 3, 2002

I remember it was a freezing January
day in Victoria and the rehearsal studio
was so cold that the director, Lori
Hamar from Suddenly Dance Theatre,
brought in a pile of clothes – sweaters
and coats – including a huge army coat.
I chose to wear the army coat.

Because I can't read music I often
draw a chart, with a visible melodic
line through it, using marks for the
beats. I had one for *Elsewhere* and,
holding the chart I began walking on
the beats. It suddenly occurred to me
that I was creating an interesting visual
image. What could the paper be? A
letter perhaps, a map – certainly very
ambiguous. The piece developed from
there and, I decided to carry Danielle
Baskerville on my back.

The title, *Elsewhere*, is taken from
Henri Coulette's poem "Night
Thoughts" in which 'elsewhere' means
death – and that is how I used it in my
piece, "The word *elsewhere* was always
on your lips, / A password to some
secret, inner place … / Now you are
elsewhere, *elsewhere* comes to this /
The thoughtless body, like a windblown
rose, / Is gathered up and ushered
toward repose…. / The Horn of
Nothing, the classical abyss, / The only
cry a cry of recognition. / "

The pieces in the Kiss Festival,
curated by Judith Marcuse in
Vancouver, were to be five minutes
long and include a kiss. At the end of
Elsewhere, Danielle kissed me and
smothered me with my coat – the kiss
of death. I thought it would be a
wonderful piece to use as the beginning
of a longer work and that is how
Maelstrom developed.

JOURNAL: WEDNESDAY, FEBRUARY 7, 1996

Many people spoke of the character
Danielle was portraying. I told them
that it was open. She could be a girl I'd
raped, shot, or a beautiful corpse I'd
stumbled over – or a girl I'd loved thirty
years ago whose memory I'd carried
like a burden all my life. Or, if I am
simply a choreographer carrying my
music notation she could be the dancer
I'm wishing to create with / for. Or she
might be my muse – the very thing I'm
seeking, concealed from my view. She
could by my innocence. In the second
section her role changes from
guide / protector to the angel of death.

David Earle and Grace Miyagawa in *Elsewhere*
Photo: Cylla von Tiedemann

MAELSTROM

(1996)

Duration: 33 minutes, 20 seconds
Composers: Gyorgy Kurtag, Arvo Pärt,
Michael Thomas, Gavin Bryars,
Dmitri Yanov-Yanovsky
Music: various selections
Costume Designer: Lori McLean
Lighting Designer: Aisling Sampson
Premiere Date: May 2, 1996
Premiere Location: Betty Oliphant
Theatre, Toronto
Cast: Kate Alton, Danielle Baskerville,
Bill Coleman, Todd Durling, Laurence
Heartz, D.A. Hoskins, Sasha Ivanochko,
Gérald Michaud, Grace Miyagawa,
Naoko Murakoshi, David Pressault,
Kathleen Pritchard, Suzette Sherman,
Jason Troan, Dean Vollick

SUMMARY NOTE

Maelstrom, a Life Cycle in Dreams, is the
development of the duet *Elsewhere*.
Maelstrom was commissioned by
Nenagh Leigh for Spring Rites '96.
The work is divided into five parts:
Elsewhere, Youth, Love Part 1, War
Part 1, Love Part 2. The Toronto Dance
Theatre premiere was on December 10,
1996.

PROGRAMME NOTE

Why present a piece about war – the
word should be banned, like "bomb" in
an airport. It should demand prosecution.
It is too late for war, we are already
on the path of self destruction
environmentally. There is now a whole
generation who imagine they are
untouched by the horrors of the 20th
century – but the decline in the values
of humanity, so vividly present in our
society, have their roots in the appalling
history of humanity's unspeakable
crimes against itself. *Maelstrom* offers a
depiction of what is lost when our
cruelty is allowed free reign. As the
Western world seeks a confirmation of
destruction we need to be reminded
of the price that must be paid.

– Dancetheatre David Earle,
September 19, 2002,
River Run Centre, Guelph

INTERVIEW: DECEMBER 3, 2002

The love duet in *Maelstrom* to Gavin
Bryars' music, with Danielle Baskerville
and Darryl Hoskins, is so much in their
blood that they can walk in after three
or four months and perform it exactly
as you would wish it done. I was very
affected by that duet – any duet in
which Darryl is involved as a performer
receives the gift of his choreographic
genius because it's impossible for him
not to add something of his own. He
and Danielle are as close to family as I
will ever have, and shaping that duet
with them was very meaningful.

Grace Miyagawa went to buy the white dress I saw on Yonge Street – it is beautiful on her. We'll get one for each of the women. My long-time friend Bill Glassco donated $500. I will have to put $1000 of my own into it (on top of the $259 I already spent on costumes in Victoria). Today in my *Beaux Arts Magazine* on Symbolism I found the word "maelstrom" describing the whirling lines that surround the figures on paintings by Munch.

In the Youth sectionthe men should wear light coloured slacks and shirts – then change for the war into the army greens I bought in Victoria. Should some be in blue or black to distinguish them as two armies? It hardly matters which side anyone is on, or even if there are two clear sides in men's appetite for cruelty and violence. In the last scene all the dancers will be arranged as if at an army dance. Bill and I will wear berets. When I lift Suzette on my back it reminds me of my premonition of carrying death. I take my pants off – like Marlon Brando in *Last Tango in Paris* – and my shirt – don my army coat – helped by another soldier – while Suzette, my wife, is being supported, or restrained, by others. I find the paper in my pocket. I'll probably take the beret off first – drop it – Suzette could pick it up. Grace is walking in a curve from the back to meet me. Everyone else will leave.

We lost a dress – $35! It shrank to half its size when Todd Durling dyed it. Danielle went to get another. We still need three more pairs of green pants and two large sweaters from the army surplus on Yonge Street.

The last day ... what an epic experience. I don't remember such a response to a work of mine in this city. It was like a European audience. I was astonished – so many people in tears afterwards. I feel so rewarded. Clearly being away from TDT is a fresh start on my work in Toronto – though it's not where I want to be. The Anglo establishment and their mainstream media translate everything exceptional, everything miraculous, into the ordinary. When I began this work I didn't imagine that I could realize my larger vision. It was late Wednesday evening last week – pressed to have the structure and composers' names for the programme when I suddenly decided to end with *Waltzing Mathilda* which led to tying up the implied narrative by returning to the opening image of the piece – *Elsewhere*. I have completed this work ... it astonishes me.

Such sadness. I am "dirt poor" as they say. I put my last cent into the piece. I hear it was very appreciated in the press – I won't read it. Saturday was the greatest response, but both Thursday and Friday were greater than any Toronto reaction I can remember.

DANIELLE BASKERVILLE AND D.A. HOSKINS IN *MAELSTROM*

ARK OF THE COVENANT

(1996)

Duration: 20 minutes
Composer: Milton Barnes
Set Designer: Décor by Artists Choice
Lighting Designer: Aisling Sampson
Premiere Date: June 25, 1996
Premiere Location: Ford Centre, Toronto
Cast: King David – Michael Sean Marye; Saul – Kenny Pearl; Prophet – David Pressault; Michal – Grace Miyagawa; Young David – Jason Troan; Jonathon – Michael Mackid; with Danielle Baskerville, Bill Coleman, Pascal Desrosiers, Todd Durling, D.A. Hoskins, Gérald Michaud, Kathleen Pritchard

SUMMARY NOTE

Choreographic assistant to David Earle was D.A. Hoskins.

PROGRAMME NOTE

Ark of the Covenant is an original work commissioned by Lawrence Cherney and Erica Goodman to celebrate the 3000th Anniversary of the City of Jerusalem (the City of David) in the coming year of 1996. The substance of the musically illustrated Biblical text composed in a Mid-Eastern Mediterranean style is drawn from Samuel II Chapter I and following a recounting of the time in the life of David when King Saul and Jonathon are slain in battle and David proceeds to lead his people to the capture of Jerusalem bearing the Ark of the Covenant. *Ark of the Covenant* is scored for Bass Oboe, English Horn, Oboe, Oboe D'Amore and Shofar (played by one player), Harp and Percussion (one player) with a performance time of approximately twenty minutes. The work is divided into four main sections bearing the subtitles: (1) Invocation is characterized by alternating motifs of prophetic, religious and warlike nature; (2) Recollections describes David recounting his memory of war played by Shofar and Percussion, his playing the Harp for King Saul (harp solo) and his Elegiac Lament over the death of Saul and Jonathon, and English Horn solo; (3) Rituals and Cortege symbolizes the celebration and event of the march from Kiriat Jirim bearing the Ark to Jerusalem; (4) Bacchanal represents the formal climax of the work where David joyously enters the City of Jerusalem to a series of four fiery dances interrupted by the admonitions of Michal chastising David for his crude public behaviour. The first dance is utilized as a Ritonello and a Coda recalling previously heard motifs and themes bringing the work to an 'upbeat' close.　　　　– Milton Barnes

SANG

(1996)

Duration: 47 minutes
Composer: J.S. Bach
Music Title: excerpts from the
St. Matthew Passion, St. John Passion,
Masses and Cantatas
Costume Designer: Lori McLean. Costume
Builder: Katharine Rose
Lighting Designer: Roelof [Ron] Peter
Snippe
Premiere Date: December 10, 1996.
Toronto Dance Theatre
Premiere Location: Premiere Dance
Theatre, Toronto
Cast: (1) Bill Coleman and The
Company; (2) The Company; (3) Sasha
Ivanochko, Michael Sean Marye;
(4) Darren Bonin, Graham McKelvie,
James Robertson, Ron Stewart,
Michael Trent; (5) Bill Coleman,
Grace Miyagawa; (6) Kirsten Andersen,
Marie-Joseé Dubois, Sasha Ivanochko,
Coralee McLaren, Robin McPhail,
Naoko Murakoshi, Suzette Sherman,
Laura West; (7) Michael Sean Marye,
James Robertson, Suzette Sherman;
(8) Darren Bonin, Marie-Joseé Dubois,
Ron Stewart; (9) The Company;
(10) The Company

SUMMARY NOTE

Consider, His bloodstained back in
every way, is like unto Heaven.
– *St. John Passion*

Sang premiered at the special
programme in David's honour to mark
his final season with Toronto Dance
Theatre.

Sang is a suite of dances to arias
from Bach's sacred works – the St.
Matthew Passion, the St. John Passion,
the B Minor Mass and several cantatas.
An intensely physical work on a large
scale, *Sang* reveals not only the depths
of this great music but also the
incredible gift of light it offers us 200
years later. *Sang* (French for "blood")
suggests not only the passions of
humanity but the passion of Christ –
two polarities that David has tried to
connect throughout his lifetime. In
June 1997, four sections of *Sang* were
re-set under the title *Passions* for Robyn
Allan's Dance and Desire show at the
Vogue Theatre in Vancouver.

PROGRAMME NOTE

This work was created to honour the
life of Michael Conway, friend and
lover, who died on July 16 of this year.
It is dedicated to all lovers living and
dead, and to the sacred nature of
desire. I would like to express my
gratitude to Bill Glassco for his
generous donation to the making of
Sang, in memory of Michael Conway,
for whom he was a constant support.

INTERVIEW: DECEMBER 3, 2002

Sang opened with Bill Coleman as the
Christ figure, walking along a lit
pathway, trailing long red ribbons from
his hands. It is a vision I have often
imagined – Christ wandering through
a crowd of people who fail to identify
him. There was a scene of Christ
praying in the garden and being led
away with his wrists bound; a scene of
angels; a scene of the death of a loved
one. The final scene was a long,
flowing procession of figures en route
to paradise – a summation of
individuals transcending human
concerns. We borrowed a red floor
from Robert Desrosiers and used
vintage red and black velvet dresses.
Despite this being my final work with
TDT, the dancers were enthusiastic
with the collaboration. I also invited
Grace Miyagawa and Suzette Sherman,
two of my muses and most extraordinary
artists, to be in the piece and I was
surrounded by some of the best
modern dancers in the world.

Journal: Friday, September 27, 1996

It seems that I will do a new work for my final season with TDT. I thought of doing all of Bach's St. John Passion, which I heard at the Elora Festival in a vast barn only a few days after the death of my beautiful Michael. I wanted to do it in his memory, but it is too daunting – the recitative would be perilous. I love arias from it and began to find other Bach arias. I've thought of a collection of songs for some time now.

Journal: Sunday, October 6, 1996

I was about to throw away a magazine picture of an El Greco portrait when I decided that I liked it and, very spontaneously, with two scraps of paper put a white X across his mouth. Underneath in large letters is written SANG – blood. It strikes me that *Sang* would be a good title for a collection of songs and this image a good poster for my season. It's nicely perverse, the past tense of sing – and blood.

Journal: Friday, October 18, 1996

Today I started a new section – a tango to a soprano aria from the St. John Passion. I spoke to the dancers about the realization that the names we are given in our childhood pervade every moment of our existence. Also, the notion of life going on around a tragedy – people out participating in rituals oblivious to the dramas being re-enacted within the people around them.

Journal: Friday, October 25, 1996

Michael Sean and I are working very closely on the creation of this work. He has so many perceptions that are clear and powerful. What began as a series of very full dance pieces to sacred music now has a theme emerging. It is a "sacred marathon" I thought yesterday – "a walk with Love and Death". It is the consummate statement of my principal theme – Death and Sensuality. It is also how the suffering inherited from a Christian conditioning finds its way into love relationships … of course it is perilous tying all this together. But sharing the task is much easier.

Journal: Thursday, October 31, 1996

A breakthrough in the men's section based on Michael Sean's suggestion that Graham McKelvie sit down during the duets. It gave me a sudden image of one of my themes – The Night in the Garden. I felt, on the entrance, that he was a Christ figure – everyone touching him to take strength from him. And when he lifts each body as if to waken it, each falls back into slumber … perhaps I've set it up unconsciously. All I added was a kiss in the last moments and Graham being led away with his hands bound behind his back. I should use a red ribbon.

Journal: Monday, November 11, 1996

I realized what the theme of this piece actually is: "The war between Christianity and Nature has brought us to this dead end". When I decided to call it *Sang* it took off on this course. The flyers came out Friday; the original design trendy and frigid – but I made changes – the colours especially. I think it is very striking although more horrifying than I would have wanted. The poster is to have more humanity. I particularly like the red for *Sang*.

Journal: Wednesday, December 11, 1996

The day after. Epic response … overwhelming … humbling … inspiring. Standing ovation after *Maelstrom*, but many many cheering calls after *Sang*. Veronica Tennant came onstage in floods of tears and said it was the most beautiful performance she'd ever seen. She used the word humanity several times. So many friends at the reception – like drowning pleasantly.

POSTER FOR *SANG* AND *MAELSTROM*
DESIGN: IN ORBIT/GARY STÜBER

The Dance Theatre of David Earle is dedicated in loving memory to Michael Conway. Michael Conway, former dancer with TDT, passed away July 16, 1996.

In this time of unreasonable loss we are called upon to release from our lives young and gifted friends; a task I cannot accomplish in losing my loving friend Michael Conway. My past year and a half spent in great intimacy with his noble struggle has brought me closer to myself than any other experience. It is impossible to express the detailed nature or the scale of our loss. This was a young man of incandescent spirit and passionate humanity whose gifts as a dancer were just coming to the fullness of maturity.

I met Michael in the early 1970s with his lover of that time, the poet Graham Jackson, and both of them had a profound influence on my life and work. I watched Michael's transition from classical dance to modern, training in our studio, and the development of his beautiful clear instrument and the expression of innate wisdom in all his movement.

We created many roles together but my strongest memory of Michael's warmth and luminous clarity is in the brilliant Wedding from *Court of Miracles* created by James Kudelka for Michael and Suzette Sherman, as well as Michael's boyish angel in act two of the Miracle Play. Everyone will remember Michael in different roles from his years with TDT, with Dancemakers, and as an independent artist. Michael's presence in my life contributed to the forming and growth of my character. I am a stranger to myself without him.

DAVID EARLE, TORONTO DANCE THEATRE HOUSE PROGRAMME, DECEMBER 10–14, 1996

WALKING IN VENICE

(1997)

Composer: Alfred Schnittke
Music Title: Hymn #4
Premiere Date: February 1997
Premiere Location: Granville Island,
Vancouver
Cast: Kathleen Pritchard, Mike Moore,
Danielle Baskerville, Edmond Kilpatrick

Summary Note

Walking in Venice was commissioned by
Judith Marcuse for the Kiss Festival.
Originally a highly kinetic physical
marathon for two men and two
women, the idea expanded into *Walking
in Venice II*.

DANCETHEATRE DAVID EARLE
IN *WALKING IN VENICE*

DANNY BOY

(1997)

Choreographers: David Earle,
Michael Sean Marye
Music Title: Danny Boy
Premiere Date: March 1997
Premiere Location: Leyanders Café, Elora
Cast: Michael Sean Marye, David Earle

SUMMARY NOTE

Danny Boy was first performed at
Leyanders Café, Elora, where Iain
Hutchinson arranged an evening of
dance. This is one of the few pieces
that David Earle continues to perform.

INTERVIEW: DECEMBER 3, 2002

When I was performing *Undetermined
Landscape* at Dancers for Life in Victoria
with dance artist Lynda Raino, one of
the dancers in another piece was unable
to be there at the last moment so I told
Rex Harrington, who was there
performing with Evelyn Hart, that I
had a short duet we could do called
Danny Boy. He asked how many steps
were in it and I told him "six". So he
said OK and learned it during the day
and we performed it that night.

DAVID EARLE IN *DANNY BOY*
PHOTO: VINCENT WONG

WALKING IN VENICE II

(1997)

Duration: 25 minutes
Composers: Alfred Schnittke, Gavin Bryars, Damian le Gassic
Premiere Date: June 19, 1997
Premiere Location: Betty Oliphant Theatre, Toronto
Cast: Kate Alton, Danielle Baskerville, Bill Coleman, D.A. Hoskins, Laurence Lemieux, Michael Sean Marye, Graham McKelvie, Alex Michael, Mike Moore, Kathleen Pritchard, Suzette Sherman, Sonya Stefan, Jason Troan, Dean Vollick

SUMMARY NOTE

Walking in Venice II premiered at Spring Rites '97. Based on Earle's highly kinetic quartet, the idea was expanded into a twenty-five minute piece in three sections – the original quartet and two group sections.

PROGRAMME COVER FOR PREMIERE OF *WALKING IN VENICE II*

LAST, HOUR OF LIGHT

(1997)

Composer: Aleksander Lasson
Music Title: String Quartet #2
Music performed by: Penderecki String Quartet
Premiere Date: July 19, 1997. Dancetheatre David Earle
Premiere Location: Gambrel Barn, Elora Festival
Cast: Kate Alton, D.A. Hoskins, Michael Sean Marye, Suzette Sherman, Laura West, Bill Coleman, Laurence Lemieux, Grace Miyagawa, Dean Vollick

SUMMARY NOTE

From a book David Earle was reading at the time: "The fin de siècle is upon us, illuminated as Théophile Gautier said of the last one by slanting suns, in whose half light we might mistake beauty for hope." This piece marked the debut of Dancetheatre David Earle and was "... about the transitory nature of love".

GRACE MIYAGAWA, D.A. HOSKINS, BILL COLEMAN, MICHAEL SEAN MARYE, LAURENCE LEMIEUX IN *LAST, HOUR OF LIGHT*
PHOTO: COURTESY OF THE ELORA FESTIVAL

UNE CANTATE DE NÖEL

(1997)

Composer: Arthur Honegger
Music Title: Christmas Cantata
Costume Designer: Katharine Mallinson
Lighting Designer: David Morrison
Premiere Date: December 6, 1997.
Canadian Children's Dance Theatre
Premiere Location: Humanities Theatre,
University of Waterloo
Cast: Miranda Abbott, Tawny
Andersen, Alix Bemrose, Jordana
Deveau, Clare Ellis, Kristen Foote,
Davidson Jaconello, Kristin Konnyu,
Brian Lawson, Samantha Lazzaro,
Claire Marshall, Laura Morrison,
Nina Shach, Gillian Tinsley. Appearing
courtesy of Dancetheatre David
Earle and the Danny Grossman Dance
Company: Danielle Baskerville,
D.A. Hoskins, Eddie Kastrau,
Gérald Michaud, Mike Moore,
Suzette Sherman, Dean Vollick

SUMMARY NOTE

This piece was commissioned by the
Canadian Children's Dance Theatre
while David was Artist-in-Residence.

PROGRAMME NOTE

I first heard Honegger's *Christmas
Cantata* in 1960, seven years after its
premiere, and I have listened to it
faithfully every Christmas since. I have
always wished to realize some
theatrical imagery to make visual this
great tapestry of sound. It was
originally conceived as part of a passion
play – the entire life of Christ, so the
end is in the beginning. Work on the
score began in 1941 during the German
occupation of Paris. After the
Liberation, the project was abandoned
and was only completed two years
before Honegger's death. In every child
born there lies the hope for one who
can bring peace and humanity into a
profoundly troubled world. The world
was not created in seven days – in fact
it's far from finished, and until the
creative gift in every individual is
encouraged we will never know the
potential this world holds for
affirmative life. Though the origins of
the piece are in darkness, the
luminosity of the score triumphs over
all fear and the climax of the work is
transcending – profoundly moving.

INTERVIEW: DECEMBER 3, 2002

In this piece I was trying to point out –
as in *Court of Miracles* – that the idea of
Christmas is not about receiving, it is
about giving. Today's commercial
Christmas is really the opposite of
everything I believe it should be. I have
the feeling that the end of the piece –
being rather sad – didn't appeal to
everybody, but I heard this sadness in
the Honegger music and thought it
might serve as a reminder to people
who have forgotten the true meaning
of Christmas.

INTERVIEW WITH MICHAEL deCONINCK SMITH, APRIL 12, 2003

In 1997 when we learned that David
was going to be leaving TDT we
immediately made our studios available
to him in the hope that we could repay
a little of what he had given us. And
out of it, of course, David did all the
paying by creating two more fantastic
pieces for us. *Une Cantate de Nöel* was a
beautiful, powerful experience for our
dancers. The only trouble with it was
that, like *Chichester Psalms*, it was really
difficult for us to tour because it
required bringing in another whole
company.

DESIGN: JERRARD SMITH
PHOTO: COURTESY OF CANADIAN CHILDREN'S DANCE THEATRE

VERTICAL THOUGHTS 3

(1998)

Composer: Morton Feldman
Music Title: Vertical Thoughts
Lighting Designer: Aisling Sampson
Premiere Date: April 16, 1998.
Dancetheatre David Earle
Premiere Location: Betty Oliphant
Theatre, Toronto
Cast: Suzette Sherman, D.A. Hoskins,
Danielle Baskerville, Mike Moore,
Michael English

SUMMARY NOTE

Vertical Thoughts 3 premiered at Spring
Rites '98.

PROGRAMME NOTE

In New York I choreographed Morton
Feldman's *Vertical Thoughts 5* as a duet
for Artis Smith and Germaine Salsberg.
It is my aim to put together a collection
of Feldman pieces including this
quintet based on World War I images.

INTERVIEW: DECEMBER 3, 2002

This was an interesting, abstract piece
with dramatic elements and no actual
narrative thread intended, and was
inspired, once again, by the work of
Eric Hawkins.

DANCETHEATRE DAVID EARLE
IN *VERTICAL THOUGHTS 3*

SERIOUS GAMES PART 1

(1998)

Composer: Erkki-Sven Tüür
Music Title: 1st movement string quartet
Costume Designer: Katharine Mallinson
Lighting Designer: Aisling Sampson
Premiere Date: April 16, 1998.
Canadian Children's Dance Theatre
Premiere Location: Betty Oliphant
Theatre, Toronto
Cast: Alix Bemrose, Kristin Konnyu,
Belinda McGuire

SUMMARY NOTE

Serious Games Part 1 was commissioned
by the Canadian Children's Dance
Theatre as part of David Earle's Artist-
in-Residence year and premiered at
Spring Rites '98.

DAVID EARLE: A CHOREOGRAPHIC BIOGRAPHY

SERIOUS GAMES PART 2

(1998)

Composer: Erkki-Sven Tüür
Music Title: 1st movement string quartet
Costume Designer: Katharine Mallinson
Lighting Designer: Penny Olorenshaw
Premiere Date: May 23, 1998.
Canadian Children's Dance Theatre
Premiere Location: Winchester Street
Theatre, Toronto
Cast: Tawny Andersen, Alix Bemrose,
Clare Ellis, Kristin Konnyu,
Claire Marshall, Belinda McGuire

SUMMARY NOTE

Serious Games Part 2 was commissioned
by Canadian Children's Dance Theatre
and marked the end of David Earle's
year as Artist-in-Residence.

INTERVIEW: DECEMBER 3, 2002

Serious Games Part 1 begins with the
girls crossing the stage in various light,
allegro hopscotch patterns. An
ominous presence ends their play and
the movement becomes dark and
quieter. Toward the end they repeat the
hopscotch diagonally, leaving the stage
one by one. On the final, strange chord,
the last girl looks back over her
shoulder in a chilling moment – the
dawn of the age when she is old
enough to know and acknowledge fear.

In *Part 2* three older girls dance a
much more passionate and sensual
piece with the trio from *Part 1* entering
and exiting occasionally. It concludes
with the older girl embracing and
comforting the one who was afraid –
her first motherly instinct.

INTERVIEW WITH MICHAEL deCONINCK SMITH, APRIL 12, 2003

In *Serious Games* David created a very
challenging, very dramatic work using
only Canadian Children's Dance
Theatre dancers. It was difficult for him
not to use his own dancers who he had
come to depend on as his instruments.
But once he started he created an
amazing work. *Serious Games* is one of
those classic threshold dances, the little
tipping point between childhood and
adulthood – innocence and experience.
That interplay is so brilliantly handled.
David always knows how far to push it
and when to round it off.

**CANADIAN CHILDREN'S DANCE THEATRE
IN *SERIOUS GAMES, PARTS 1 AND 2***

THREE DUETS FOR TWO FRIENDS

(1998)

Composers: Peteris Vasks, Morton Feldman, Arnold Schoenberg
Premiere Date: November 13, 1998
Premiere Location: Cunningham Studios, New York
Cast: Artis Smith, Germaine Salsberg

Summary Note

This trilogy of duets was commissioned by Artis Smith and Germaine Salsberg, two founding members of Toronto Dance Theatre. The last section, called Prisoners in the Garden, is often performed independently.

Interview: March 26, 2003

Artis (Barry) Smith and Germaine (Merle) Salsberg were two of the original Toronto Dance Theatre company members. It was wonderful to create this trilogy and to work with them again. They are extraordinary people and have evolved unique dance styles over the years. In the first piece they were continually separating, there were many lifts and the motif was cruciform. In the second piece they remained in continual physical contact and in the third they stayed apart. The concept of repeatedly coming together, never separating and never touching being the basic choreographic premise.

Artis Smith and Germaine Salsberg in *Three Duets for Two Friends*

IN MEMORIAM

(1998)

Composer: Alfred Schnittke
Lighting Designer: Alex Kordics
Premiere Date: November 13, 1998.
Dancetheatre David Earle
Premiere Location: Waterloo Community
Arts Centre
Cast: (1) Requiem Aeternam – full
company; (2) Lacrimosa – full company;
(3) Sanctus – Todd Durling, Evadne
Fulton. Company – David Earle, D.A.
Hoskins, Suzette Sherman, Kate Alton,
Danielle Baskerville, Todd Durling,
Michael English, Stephen Filipowicz,
Evadne Fulton, Janet Johnson,
Mike Moore, Dean Vollick

SUMMARY NOTE

In Memoriam was presented as part of
Passchendaele, a Waterloo Dance
Frontier presentation with
Dancetheatre David Earle and D.A.
Hoskins Dance. Waterloo Dance
Frontier is a collective division of
Dance Foundation David Earle (DFDE)
established to organize and develop the
growing number of dance projects in
this region of Ontario. Largely
managed by Mike Moore, this collective
of DFDE artists brings professional
training and performance opportunities
to the community at a grass-roots level.
Our goals are to: expand the audience
for modern dance; offer training of the
highest calibre; encourage creativity in
all people; provide a vision that inspires
and affirms the positive nature of
existence. *In Memoriam* was the
foundation for David Earle's *Three
Winter Prayers*.

PROGRAMME NOTE

Known as the third battle of Ypres, the
Canadian contribution to the battle
began on Friday, October 26, 1917 and
continued until the Canadians took
Passchendaele on Friday, November 6,
1917. The cost was 15,654 lives. The war
memorial beside the city hall in
Waterloo, Ontario, lists sixteen young
men who died in World War I. In 1994
this inscription was added to recall
those days eighty years ago when these
sixteen young men "Felt dawn, saw
sunset glow / Loved and were loved."

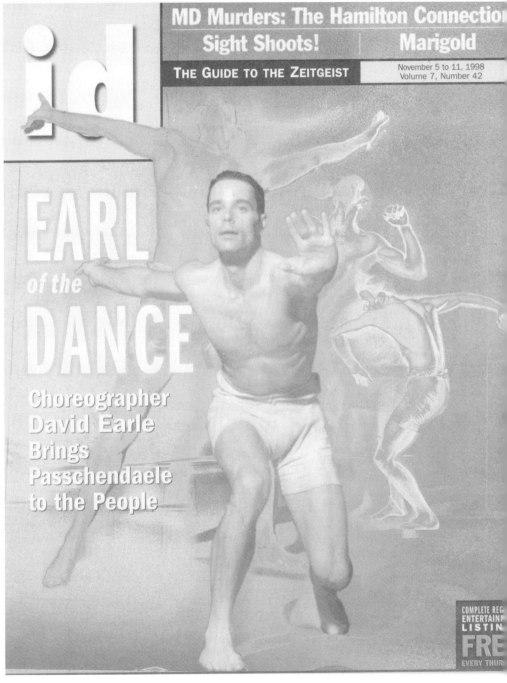

DEAN VOLLICK ON THE COVER OF *ID* **PRIOR TO PREMIERES OF** *IN MEMORIAM* **AND** *KYRIE*

KYRIE

(1998)

Composer: J.S. Bach
Lighting Designer: Alex Kordics
Premiere Date: November 13, 1998.
Dancetheatre David Earle
Premiere Location: Waterloo Community
Arts Centre
Cast: Danielle Baskerville, Todd
Durling, Michael English, Evadne
Fulton, Stephen Filipowicz, D.A.
Hoskins, Janet Johnson, Mike Moore,
Suzette Sherman, Dean Vollick

PROGRAMME NOTE

Our approach to dance is based in
expression as well as concern for
sculptural form. In our experience
people are moved by powerful music
and highly evolved physical theatre. We
are consciously attempting to engage
the deepest feelings in our audience.

REMARKS

Kyrie was presented as part of
Passchendaele 1998, a Waterloo Dance
Frontier presentation with Dancetheatre
David Earle and D.A. Hoskins Dance.

ARTICLE BY KATHE GRAY

David Earle: I used to be indignant that
there was a section in bookstores called
"War". I felt that documenting it –
writing books about it, making films
about it – glorified the idea of men

killing one another. Now, however, I
have a reluctant fascination with how
humans react to war and are changed
by their exposure to it. Two thousand
years ago when Homer wrote the *Iliad*
its description of war should have
brought war to an end – but it hasn't.
We read this book; we recognize
ourselves and wonder why we haven't
learned from the past. War itself has
changed so much and, despite this, lives
go on even though battles might be
raging all around.

I don't think we ever healed from
the loss of honour we experienced in
World War II. Technology and industry
had as much impact on the battlefield
as did ideology and patriotism.
Humanity became inhumane because
of the weapons.

Although the Canadian Passchendaele
experience is symbolically important,
the performance is not about this
specific battle. We can't pan over the
field of action like a film might. We
show close-ups instead: a soldier and his
girlfriend trying to say good-bye, an old
soldier going mad knowing the pain
he's inflicted. This is where dance has
its place. It isn't like seeing reality. It has
a dream-like quality. It doesn't require
words to communicate. It can be a raw
and emotional experience that
audiences respond to instinctively.

– Extract from "In Remembrance of Dance",
id magazine, November 5-11, 1998

Passchendaele was conceived and produced by Mike Moore and was a Waterloo Dance Frontier presentation. *In Memoriam* opened the Passchendaele programme and *Kyrie* closed it. I choreographed a fairly abstract piece to three adage sections and used the same movement in both pieces. They turned out very differently, in fact, because the Schnittke music for *In Memoriam* is mysterious and evocative and not particularly rhythmic and the Bach *Kyrie* is more ecstatic. Passchendaele is a very dark programme and I wanted to frame it with prayers, starting with *In Memoriam* as a way to bring people's consciousness to a quiet place and then closing with *Kyrie's* healing flow of music and movement.

Artist's statement: 1998

Here chivalry disappeared for always. Like all noble and personal feeling it had to give way to the new tempo of battle and to the rule of the machine. Here the new Europe revealed itself for the first time in combat.   – Ernst Junger

I was born in September 1939 at the very start of World War II, and my first memory as a child was being taken to the playing field behind Runnymede Collegiate in Toronto to watch Mussolini burned in effigy. How old could I have been? The war ended in 1945 … I remember the VE Day parade on Yonge Street.

In past works I have used war images: In *Field of Dreams* I brought a war monument to life, a dead soldier with three women in robes – the three Marys at the crucifixion? Or three Fates? In *Maelstrom* in 1996 I played an old soldier who failed to save a woman from rape and who carried her tortured spirit until he lost his reason.

In World War I for over two years the soldiers on the Western Front hammered at each other in battles that cost millions of lives but moved the front line, at most, a mile or so in either direction. At Verdun, the Somme and Passchendaele, the nature of Western civilization changed.

The word Passchendaele sounds in English like a setting of natural beauty that is sacrificed to the ravages of human chaos – passion dale – it becomes a moving name in the emotional aftermath of this century of destruction. What seems to have been destroyed, beyond human lives and centuries old towns and cities is something less tangible – but nonetheless conspicuous in its absence today – and that is the ability to feel. We are numb from the violence of the century – not that violence is new – but never before has it been documented in such detail.

Mike Moore, Darryl Hoskins and I have spent the past year reading accounts of the World Wars from all angles. We are trying to bring the reality of the past's tragic mistakes to the attention of those too young to remember, and to bring healing to those affected personally. This theatre of war that seems so far away in time and space has touched every community in this country.

THREE WINTER PRAYERS

(1999)

Composer: Alfred Schnittke
Music Title: Requiem, Lacrimosa,
Sanctus
Costume Designer: Ainslie Cyopik
Premiere Date: February 10, 1999.
Arts Umbrella Dance Company
Premiere Location: Norman Rothstein
Theatre, Vancouver
Cast: Arts Umbrella Dance Company
Senior Ensemble – Lara Brecht,
Meaghen Buckley-Pearson, Katherine
Cowie, Kimberley de Jong, Annika
Olner, Kirsten Pankratz, Ashley
Sanderson. Ballet British Columbia
Mentor Program – Tiffany Antoniuk,
Erin Murphy, Jennifer Nichols, Tara
Shirley, Acacia Schachte.

SUMMARY NOTE

Three Winter Prayers was a restructured
working of *In Memoriam* set on women.
It was commissioned by Artemis
Gordon for Arts Umbrella Dance
Company and Graduate Program,
which is affiliated with the Ballet British
Columbia Mentor Program.

IMAGINED MEMORIES

(1999)

Composers: (1) J.S. Bach, Ron Carter;
(2) Peteris Plakidis; (3) Malcolm
Forsyth; (4) Glenn Buhr; (5) Gyorgy
Kurtag
Lighting Designer: Aisling Sampson
Premiere Date: April 15, 1999.
Dancetheatre David Earle
Premiere Location: Betty Oliphant
Theatre, Toronto
Cast: Suzette Sherman with David Earle,
Edmond Kilpatrick and Mike Moore

SUMMARY NOTE

Imagined Memories premiered at Spring
Rites '99. Each duet portrayed Suzette
Sherman with a lover of a different age:
a lover of the same age – Edmond
Kilpatrick; an older lover/husband –
David Earle; a younger lover – Mike
Moore. The duet with the younger
lover is often performed alone.

PROGRAMME NOTE

This work was created as a tribute to
twenty years of collaboration with
Suzette Sherman – companion,
constant support and muse, with love.

JOURNAL: APRIL 14, 1999

I wanted to create a piece for Suzette
Sherman that would contain a variety
of contrasting sections. With each duet
she would change and shed some of
her clothing. Yesterday Suzette and I
discussed the emotions in her
undressing scene. She is in her room.
She has three photographs: her
husband (a role I danced) who provides
a base for her experience; a playmate
lover (Edmond Kilpatrick) when love
seemed light and full of constant
desire; and a young lover (Mike Moore)
who needed her support, who touched
her soul. The opening is a dance after
her young lover's funeral. She tears off
her mourning clothes unwilling to see
it as an end and recalls each of the men
in her life, returning to a simpler, purer
state of mourning. After the final duet
– when her younger lover dies – she
walks off into the future. I follow
behind, picking up the clothing. It is
clear that I am in the relationship for
the duration.

Suzette is a perfect example of
someone who was tenacious about
achieving what she wanted to achieve
and never gave up despite many
obstacles. Early on, when I was
persuading her to court her demons,
she was resistant because it was
terrifying. I like to think that madness
retreats as you walk towards it and gains
ground when you turn your back and
I'm always encouraging people to walk
towards it – but that takes courage.

Suzette strikes me now as a diva without the trimmings. I remember Martha Graham saying that the results of years of labour sculpt a dancer's face and you can see that in Suzette's face at rest – she doesn't have to do much to hold your attention. Her physical stamina, her unequalled knowledge of my body of work and her teaching skills are unique.

"a ritual for Toronto dance watchers"

SPRING RITES
1999

A DanceWorks CoWorks Event

new choreography by
DAVID EARLE   D.A. HOSKINS
NENAGH LEIGH   JANE TOWNSEND

guest artists
DOGS IN SPACE
DANCETHEATRE DAVID EARLE

April 15, 16, 17, 1999, 8pm
BOX OFFICE (416) 973 4000

Betty Oliphant Theatre, 404 Jarvis Street
Tickets $20; Students, Seniors, CADA $12

Produced with the support of the City of Toronto through the Toronto Arts Council and the Laidlaw Foundation. Design: Deborah Torr Photo: Cylla Von Tiedemann Dancer: Grace Miyagawa

FLYER FOR SPRING RITES 1999, PREMIERE OF *IMAGINED MEMORIES*
DANCER: GRACE MIYAGAWA
PHOTO: CYLLA VON TIEDEMANN
DESIGN: DEBORAH TORR

DANIELLE BASKERVILLE, MICHAEL ENGLISH, NAOKO MURAKOSHI, D.A. HOSKINS, MIKE MOORE, HELEN JONES
IN *EX VOTO*
PHOTO MONTAGE: DAVID EARLE

EX VOTO

(1999)

Duration: 12 minutes, 15 seconds
Composer: Alfred Schnittke
Music Title: Hymn #1
Costume Designer: Cheryl Lalonde
Set Designer: Roelof [Ron] Peter Snippe
Premiere Date: May 20, 1999
Premiere Location: Toronto
Cast: Marie-Joseé Dubois, Naoko
Murakoshi, Graham McKelvie,
Pascal Desrosiers, Gérald Michaud,
David Earle, Valerie Calam

SUMMARY NOTE

Ex Voto was commissioned by Gérald
Michaud of the Danny Grossman
Dance Company, who independently
produced a show called 7 for 7 with
seven choreographers and seven
dancers.

PROGRAMME NOTE

You are never entirely a prisoner as
long as your imagination survives.

JOURNAL: APRIL 18, 1999

I'm reading the book *Pilgrim Among the
Shadows* by Boris Parker … memories
of the prison camps. I also bought a
book of Joseph Sudek's Prague and
surrounding landscapes photographs. I
am wandering down roads shrouded in
mists, bare trees, birds in silhouette
against grey skies. But there are details
on the black branches – tiny knots
ornamenting the skeletons that will one
day bring colour back to this black and
white world. The sun has returned. I've
been out taking photos of the last light
on birch trees. The scent of hope is
unmistakable. My book is so wounding
that I can't take too much at a time.
"Mankind given its inclination to
murder, given our delight in the
suffering and blood of others …" Boris
Parker! One of my current themes –
confessing to the cruelty in our nature.

JOURNAL: TUESDAY, MAY 4, 1999

I ran the work for the first time, fitting
the last piece into the puzzle – a short
duet for Gérald Michaud and me. It
made me sad. Is philosophical
pessimism and existential disgust
visible? Certainly it is a dark work.

INTERVIEW: MARCH 26, 2002

The imagery in *Ex Voto* is of people as
prisoners trying to find an ecstatic
possibility within the boundaries of
what they have. There is elation, and
flights of energy, and Eros. It opens
with a tongue-in-cheek acrobatic
burlesque act, and moves into darker
material. I appear as a sort of corporate
monster wearing a suit and tie, and do
a ritual repetitive walking pattern that
is repeated by the others, dressed in
drab grey clothing, as if they were
obliged to follow my prescribed routine
of conformity. I felt quite cynical and
isolated in the role. Gérald Michaud
was a kind of angel that came to rescue
me from my isolation, but he taught
me resignation not hope. At the end I
am denied release and become one of
them wearing the same drab clothes.
The closing is a reverse lift from the
acrobatic section representing a life
cycle. Graham McKelvie's role, as the
man in red shorts, is meant to suggest
the fascist ideal – military power and
brutality – all fists and flexed feet. It is a
bitter piece although it has ecstatic
healing moments. It suggests that the
prisoners have found some kind of
peace in their condition. Perhaps the
final phase of existence is when you
surrender hope and allow yourself to
be comfortable with acceptance.

lost all sense of human

Human requires humanity

I looked at the people around me in church and felt there was little hope for change in this world. And I thought if all these people would just allow themselves to return to physical and emotional awareness and experience the miracle of the body through movement they would be more apt to discover the sacred in themselves. I danced the day my mother died, and ten years later when my father died. I was grateful for the ritual that allowed my full range of feelings to pass through me.

ARTIST'S STATEMENT: SEPTEMBER 22, 1999

and so ——— It is over

REUNION

(1999)

Composer: Paul Hindemith
Premiere Date: November 11, 1999.
Dancetheatre David Earle
Premiere Location: Waterloo Community
Arts Centre
Cast: Suzette Sherman, Michael
English, Danielle Baskerville,
Mike Moore, Stephen Filipowicz,
Sonny Dickson, David Earle

SUMMARY NOTE

Reunion was presented as part of the
Passchendaele 1999 performance, a
collaboration with Mike Moore and
the Waterloo Dance Frontier.

A short opening companion piece to
set the stage for the duet from *Imagined
Memories*, *Reunion* was a constant
exchange of images of the living and
the dead, the sleeping and the waking
and the wounded returning from war
alive or dead.

ENDANGERED WORLDS

(1999)

Composer: Peter Hatch
Music Title: Endangered Worlds
Premiere Date: November 11, 1999.
Dancetheatre David Earle
Premiere Location: University of
Waterloo
Cast: Suzette Sherman, Michael
English, Danielle Baskerville, Mike
Moore, Stephen Filipowicz, Sonny
Dickson, David Earle, Janet Johnson

SUMMARY NOTE

Endangered Worlds was presented as part
of the Passchendaele 1999 performance,
a collaboration with Mike Moore and
the Waterloo Dance Frontier. It
consisted of seven sections: War, Peace,
Messenger, Youth, Maturity, Magician
and Mystic.

FLYER FOR PASSCHENDAELE, PREMIERES OF *REUNION* AND *ENDANGERED WORLDS*
DANCERS: DANIELLE BASKERVILLE, MIKE MOORE
PHOTO: DAVID EARLE

L'HISTOIRE DU SOLDAT

(2000)

Choreographers: David Earle and
D.A. Hoskins
Duration: 60 minutes
Composer: Igor Stravinsky
Music performed by: Kitchener-Waterloo
Symphony, Canadian Chamber
Ensemble
Narrator: Peter Duschenes speaking
"The Soldier's Tale"
Premiere Date: May 5, 2000.
Dancetheatre David Earle
Premiere Location: River Run Centre,
Guelph
Cast: Devil – Todd Durling; Soldier –
Mike Moore; Princess – Suzette
Sherman; with Danielle Baskerville,
Alison Denham, Ron Stewart,
Michael English, Evadne Fulton

SUMMARY NOTE

L'Histoire du Soldat was part of the
River Run Centre's Guelph Recital
series. It is divided into eleven sections:
The Soldier's March; Airs by a Stream;
Pastorale; The Royal March; The Little
Concert; Three Dances – Tango, Waltz,
Ragtime; The Devil's Dance; Little
Chorale; The Devil's Song; The Great
Chorale; Triumphal March of the
Devil. It is based on the premise that
"the rich man will not go to heaven".

INTERVIEW: MARCH 26, 2003

Stravinsky's *L'Histoire* is some of the
most beautiful music written in the
twentieth century, but I think it
overwhelms the story with its
complexity. I would like some day to
try to present the story in a much more
humble way with something like a
gypsy band. It was a *pièce d'occasion* –
a music concert with dance, not a
dance concert with music – and I think
it worked well.

HORIZON

(2000)

Duration: 15 minutes
Composer: Peter Hatch
Music Title: What is a Country?
Music performed by: Kitchener-Waterloo
Symphony, Canadian Chamber Ensemble
Premiere Date: May 5, 2000.
Dancetheatre David Earle
Premiere Location: River Run Centre,
Guelph
Cast: Suzette Sherman, Todd Durling,
Danielle Baskerville, Ron Stewart,
Alison Denham, Mike Moore, Evadne
Fulton, Michael English

SUMMARY NOTE

Horizon was part of the River Run
Centre's Guelph Recital series. The
choreographic process began in
Vancouver with Ballet British
Columbia's mentor programme and
several Dancetheatre David Earle
dancers.

PROGRAMME NOTE

What is a Country? was written in 1992
while I was spending a sabbatical year
in Europe. During this period
constitutional talks were proceeding
(and failing) in Canada. The work
reflects my concern for the possible
breakup of my country. It is completely
based on a truncation of the last
two phrases of our national anthem
O Canada (although there is only one
point in the piece where this is
obvious). The piece is composed of
small fragments, which seem not so
much to belong to each other as to co-
exist through sheer association and
repetition. *What is a Country?* was
commissioned by Vancouver New
Music through the assistance of the
Canada Council.   – Peter Hatch

INTERVIEW: MARCH 26, 2003

The music was beautiful and powerful
and I heard it as completely abstract
and somewhat Asian, although Peter
Hatch said it was based on themes from
O Canada. *Horizon* was quite dark and
very austere with some dramatic
moments and the dancers found it
technically ruinous.

NIGHT/SUMMER

(2000)

Duration: 10 minutes, 26 seconds
Composer: Alfred Schnittke
Music Title: Hymn #2
Lighting Designer: Aisling Sampson
Premiere Date: June 1, 2000.
Dancetheatre David Earle
Premiere Location: Premiere Dance
Theatre, Toronto
Cast: Helen Jones, Grace Miyagawa,
Suzette Sherman, Danielle Baskerville,
Mike Moore

SUMMARY NOTE

night/Summer was commissioned by
Nenagh Leigh for Spring Rites 2000.
This work was presented in memory of
Craig Baldwin, a youth who drowned
in Elora. In contrast to many of David
Earle's works, *night/Summer* was
photographic, ritualistic and minimal.

PROGRAMME NOTE

Those who feel eternity are above all
fear. They see in every night the place
where daybreak will occur, and are
assured. Summer requires fearlessness.

– Rainer Maria Rilke,
The Florentine Diary

INTERVIEW: MARCH 26, 2003

Shortly after I moved to Elora I heard
about a young boy – sixteen or
seventeen years old – who had drowned
in the local health club whirlpool. His
bizarre and untimely death at the peak
of his beauty and physical power struck
me as mythic. It was as if the Gods
were playing another painful trick on
humanity.

I started the piece with everyone
backing away from a blinding light,
which could represent death; Danielle
Baskerville, as a fate figure, was
backing away in the opposite direction.
There were a series of tableaux for
three woman, like the three Marys,
holding Mike Moore in a variety of
poses that related to diving and
swimming. At the end, Michael and
Danielle made their first contact and
she partnered him in a dive from which
he ended up in her protection – and he
was gone from the world, leaving the
three women in mourning.

Although it was a small cast, the
imagery demanded a large space; it's
not necessarily the space you use that
matters – it's the space you are seen in.

HELEN JONES, GRACE MIYAGAWA, DANIELLE BASKERVILLE, SUZETTE SHERMAN, MIKE MOORE
IN *NIGHT/SUMMER*

III

THE CREATURES OF PROMETHEUS, OP. 43

(2000)

Choreographers: David Earle and D.A. Hoskins
Composer: Ludwig von Beethoven
Music Title: The Creatures of Prometheus, Op. 43
Conductor: Raffi Armenian, guest conductor
Music performed by: Kitchener-Waterloo Symphony
Premiere Date: September 16, 2000. Dancetheatre David Earle
Premiere Location: The Raffi Armenian Theatre, Kitchener
Cast: Kate Alton, Danielle Baskerville, D.A. Hoskins, Michael Sean Marye, Stephanie Mendoza, Mike Moore, Suzette Sherman, Ron Stewart

SUMMARY NOTE

The Creatures of Prometheus was commissioned by the Kitchener-Waterloo Symphony for the Mad About Beethoven Festival and was a collaboration with D.A. Hoskins and the Waterloo Dance Frontier. It consisted predominantly of duets with opening and closing group numbers.

INTERVIEW: MARCH 26, 2003

I couldn't afford not to do this commission to Beethoven's work of the same name, because I lacked income and I could not turn down the opportunity to perform in a large hall with Raffi Armenian conducting. But when I first heard the music I thought it was completely undanceable and yet, in the end I learned a great deal.

Darryl Hoskins injured himself the day before the performance and I had to re-work the last section for seven dancers. After the performance someone told me how brilliant and unpredictable that section was and that only a true genius would think of using seven instead of eight dancers. I cite that story constantly when I realize that I'm losing control – maybe the outcome will be better than what I had planned.

As usual we had no costume budget so the women wore black leotards with semi-transparent pastel skirts and the men wore our much-used black pants and black T-shirts. They looked just formal enough and just casual enough to put the audience at ease.

Although I lost sleep and sweated over this work, wondering if it would be the end of my career, it was very successful in every way and made what I felt was not Beethoven's best music into a pleasant experience for the audience.

DANIELLE BASKERVILLE AND MICHAEL SEAN MARYE IN *THE CREATURES OF PROMETHEUS, OP. 43*
PHOTO: *THE RECORD* STAFF PHOTOGRAPHER
© 2000 *THE RECORD*, WATERLOO REGION, ONTARIO CANADA

DAVID EARLE: A CHOREOGRAPHIC BIOGRAPHY

THERE WAS A SONG

(2000)

Duration: 30 minutes
Composers: Dancehall – Jaubert-Gremillon-Clair; Dada Ballet – Antonio Russolo; Streetscene – Guillaume Apollinaire; Military Parade – Joseph Kosma; Modern Dance War – Luigi Grandi; Fear – Ingram Marshall; Dancehall II – Jaubert-Gremillon-Clair (reprise); Monuments – Antonio Russolo
Premiere Date: November 11, 2000. Dancetheatre David Earle
Premiere Location: University of Waterloo
Cast: Evadne Fulton, Danielle Baskerville, Suzette Sherman, Nicole Fougere, D.A. Hoskins, David Earle, Mike Moore, Stephen Filipowicz, Michelle Mummery

SUMMARY NOTE

There Was A Song was presented as part of Passchendaele 2000 in collaboration with Mike Moore and the Waterloo Dance Frontier. The sections portrayed civilian life during wartime: (1) A Dancehall (I); (2) Café Voltaire; (3) Street Scene; (4) A Parade; (5) A War Dance; (6) Fear; (7) A Dancehall (II); (8) Monuments.

INTERVIEW: MARCH 26, 2003

I had presented work in the Passchendaele collaborations with Mike Moore since 1998, and having read continuously about the wars during those years did not feel I could do another piece about soldiers. I decided I would do something about wartime's social and artistic manifestations. The Dada movement – a kind of cultural disintegration – was happening between the wars and I had a recording of Dada voices and electronic music selections so I pieced together a collage of scenes.

The Street Scene was a kind of Giacomettiesque creation, everyone standing at angles with their legs apart – pictures being made by constantly changing positions and diagonals. They wore trench coats and, if I were to do the piece again, I would have cones made for their heads so they would look more like triangular forms.

JOURNAL: PASSCHENDAELE 2000

On Tuesday we spoke in rehearsal of a basic costume, adding layers for different scenes. We considered having the clothes in piles around the edge of the performance space and I thought immediately of photographer Christian Boltanski saying that clothes, like photographs, can connote death. People today live in such excess we are drowning in possessions. Even in my own home I sometimes can't get to the bed for the mountain of discarded clothing covering the floor.

Journal: Friday, October 27, 2000

Reconsidering my title. Originally *Layers of Darkness*, then *Shades of Darkness* which may seem too facile ... *There was a Song* occurred to me. It seems less about the horror and more about the absurdity of war.

Journal: Wednesday, November 8, 2000

Two school performances yesterday – in a cinderblock studio at the University of Waterloo. Considering the opera houses and theatres all over the world where we've played ... there we were, before a handful of students, fluorescent lights, a white sheet taped up to hide our costume changes; full circle to my childhood. But everyone dancing to his or her soul's limit. Then the question-and-answer session, which I suggested we should not be doing. Audiences should be left with their feelings. And out of the two performances only one question, despite all of the issues involved in an hour of war-inspired theatre: "How many hours did you rehearse for this?"

EVADNE FULTON, MIKE MOORE, DANIELLE BASKERVILLE, D.A. HOSKINS, SUZETTE SHERMAN IN REHEARSAL FOR *THERE WAS A SONG*
PHOTO: DAVID EARLE

DAVID EARLE: A CHOREOGRAPHIC BIOGRAPHY

RICHOT MASS

(2001)

GRAHAM MCKELVIE AND THE TACTUS VOCAL ENSEMBLE IN *RICHOT MASS*
PHOTO: *THE RECORD* STAFF PHOTOGRAPHER
© 2002 *THE RECORD*, WATERLOO REGION, ONTARIO CANADA

Duration: 15 minutes
Composer: Glenn Buhr
Music Title: Richot Mass
Music performed by: Penderecki String Quartet and TACTUS Vocal Ensemble
Premiere Date: February 2, 2001. Dancetheatre David Earle
Premiere Location: Registry Theatre, Kitchener
Cast: Kyrie – Suzette Sherman, Graham McKelvie; Gloria – Danielle Baskerville, Barbara Baltus (Pallomina), D.A. Hoskins, Mike Moore; Sanctus – Suzette Sherman, Danielle Baskerville, Barbara Baltus (Pallomina), Michael English; Agnus Dei – The Company

SUMMARY NOTE

David Earle dedicated this performance of the *Richot Mass* to the memory of Michael Conway. It was commissioned by Jenny Shantz, director of the Schoolhouse Theatre in St. Jacobs, for the NUMUS production The Sacred and the Profane.

TANGO FOR STRING QUARTET

(2001)

INTERVIEW: MARCH 28, 2003

This seemed like a very integrated performance piece for music and dance. A special factor to consider when you're working with great musicians is that we are not producing a dance concert with live music, we are producing a music concert with dancers. I have a bias for creating movement to illustrate music (sometimes excessively so) and I always feel, in these instances, that it's very important the dancers, singers and musicians are equally present in the experience. All participants agree that the commissions are something they respect and enjoy.

JOURNAL: SUNDAY, JANUARY 14, 2001

Night. Listening repeatedly to Glenn Buhr's mass. I have images in my mind. The Kyrie … I have a plan written out, a processional entrance on the diagonal, single file. The most difficult section musically is the Gloria. The rhythms are so complex I can't count it at all. I've listened at least several hundred times, literally all day. The Sanctus summons a vision of women turning and turning in a constantly revolving line. Three women, or should it be three Marys and Christ? The Agnus Dei could have duets in the stunning instrumental passage.

Duration: 15 minutes
Composer: Randolph Peters
Music Title: Tango from Smoked Lizard Lips
Music performed by: Penderecki String Quartet and TACTUS Vocal Ensemble
Premiere Date: February 2, 2001. Dancetheatre David Earle
Premiere Location: Registry Theatre, Kitchener
Cast: Suzette Sherman, Graham McKelvie, Danielle Baskerville, Barbara Baltus (Pallomina), D.A. Hoskins, Mike Moore, Michael English, Janet Johnson

SUMMARY NOTE

Tango was commissioned by Jenny Shantz for the NUMUS production The Sacred and the Profane.

Experience a unique marriage
of dancers and musicians.

THE SACRED AND THE PROFANE

Saturday, February 24, 2001
8:00 p.m.

River Run Centre

When Randolph Peters' music was given to me as a commission I found it daunting, dissonant and tough to listen to but, as so often has happened, I learned to hear the music through working with it.

Originally it was to be a collaboration with Mike Moore – he choreographing some sections in Toronto, and me choreographing in Elora. When I first saw Mike's work I found it too confrontational and graphic for inclusion in this sacred music programme. I knew it would work very well in the Toronto dance arena but not with a music audience. It was a tough bridge to cross with Mike but I felt he was on the track of something powerful that should be realized independently and not diluted by having another person's vision incorporated into it.

So I choreographed the piece myself and, oddly enough, ended up with something that worked incredibly well.

This morning I had an idea as a context for the dancing, although not a highly original one – the dancers as audience, like in Jerome Robbins' *The Concert* and Peter Randazzo's *Recital*. But parts of the music should be without movement so the dancing wouldn't dominate the entire programme. A chamber concert, perhaps elegant chairs facing diagonally upstage towards the string quartet, and dancers dressed formally. I imagined a woman opening a man's shirt and taking out her lipstick and writing I Love You on his chest.

PROGRAMME COVER FOR PREMIERE
OF *TANGO FOR STRING QUARTET*

MERIDIAN

(2001)

Duration: 5 minutes, 13 seconds
Composer: Alfred Schnittke
Music Title: Hymn #3
Music performed by: Kitchener-Waterloo
Symphony
Premiere Date: April 2001.
Dancetheatre David Earle
Premiere Location: Registry Theatre,
Kitchener
Cast: Michael English, Naoko Murakoshi,
D.A. Hoskins, Suzette Sherman

SUMMARY NOTE

Meridian was commissioned by
composer Peter Hatch for the Open
Ears Festival. It began as two back-to-
back duets and later became a single
duet. The theme came from a book,
Midday in Italian Literature, and the title
was intended to suggest the zenith of
passion that meets the music at its
climax.

**MICHAEL ENGLISH AND NAOKO MURAKOSHI
IN REHEARSAL FOR *MERIDIAN*
PHOTO: DAVID EARLE**

DIRAIT-ON

(2001)

Composer: Morten Lauridsen
Music Title: Dirait-on
Words: Rainer Maria Rilke
Conductor: John Ford, Conductor
Emeritus
Music performed by: The Oriana Singers
– William Brown, Artistic Director;
Claire Preston – piano; Ruth Watson
Henderson – organ
Premiere Date: May 12, 2001.
Dancetheatre David Earle
Premiere Location: Grace Church on-the-
Hill, Toronto
Cast: Suzette Sherman, Danielle
Baskerville, Michael English, Evadne
Fulton, D.A. Hoskins, Mike Moore

SUMMARY NOTE

Dirait-on was commissioned for the
Oriana Singers' Psalm and Dance
presentation.

PROGRAMME NOTE

The Oriana Singers, one of the first all-
female choirs in Canada, was formed in
1972. The choir endeavours to achieve
and maintain high levels of vocal and
musical excellence. Great care is taken
to choose music suited to the female
voice, to present music that has already
earned its lasting position in the
repertoire, and to introduce audiences
to contemporary music, including new
works by Canadian composers, some
of which have been commissioned by
The Oriana Singers.

**PROGRAMME COVER FOR PREMIERE
OF *DIRAIT-ON***

IN SPITE OF AND BECAUSE

(2001)

Duration: 15 minutes
Composer: Krzysztof Penderecki
Music Title: Quartet for Clarinet and String Trio
Premiere Date: July 19, 2001.
Dancetheatre David Earle
Premiere Location: Gambrel Barn, Guelph
Cast: Michael English, Suzette Sherman

SUMMARY NOTE

In Spite of and Because was commissioned by the Elora Festival Chamber Branch. The piece follows a long relationship through its constantly changing moods and power shifts.

PROGRAMME NOTE

I love you in spite of everything and because of everything.

— Vladimir Mayakovsky to Lili Brik, 1923

INTERVIEW: MARCH 28, 2003

In Spite of and Because was the first piece I choreographed in Dancetheatre David Earle's new Guelph studio. Although it is an abstract piece of music, the narrative we drew from it seems to be what it was written for. Even a commissioned score could not have been more complementary. People told me that the piece made them reflect on the stress of long-term relationships and how much strength of character it requires to surmount the challenges of staying together. Neither partner is right or wrong, they're just two unique individuals attempting to find common ground. You follow each of them into their own private space and the resolution that they do stay together is very moving.

It gave Suzette a wonderful vehicle to display all aspects of her personality; there's the devilish little girl as well as the responsible, mature person. Michael English is the perfect balance, because he is very Hamlet-like and self-absorbed.

SUZETTE SHERMAN AND MICHAEL ENGLISH IN *IN SPITE OF AND BECAUSE*
PHOTO: DAVID EARLE

This is not dance for dance's sake, for an audience of dancers, for the little kingdom to which contemporary dance has been relegated. This is dance for people who are curious, who love architecture, who need beauty, who wish to feel.

I am not interested in what is considered new as I am in the discovery of what is true. My work is neither traditional nor avant-garde. This is where I believe any self-respecting artist would want to be. As for being contemporary, what could be more radical in these times than expressing an appetite for existence? When birth and death and love have lost their meaning then I'll know that my work is no longer relevant.

My dancers have always been individuals, powerful and clear, and they have touched people profoundly on every continent. I honour my role as teacher, and have spent my lifetime collaborating in the creation of dance instruments that are open, strong and honest.

I would like to preserve some of my works on film or videotape, and to continue to create, because I care deeply about being a continuing presence in an art form that offers affirmative training, encourages uniqueness, and allows new creators to emerge.

ARTIST'S STATEMENT: OCTOBER 2002, DANCETHEATRE DAVID EARLE WEBSITE

LE MINOTAUR

(2001)

Duration: 1 hour, 30 minutes
Composer: A chronological multi-media collage created by Jeremy Bell. Composers were Maryan Mozetich, Yves Gigon, Steve Reich, Zack Browning, Marc Tremblay, Alexina Louie, Eric Schwindt, Sofia Gubaidulina, Peter Eotvos, R. Murray Schafer and the I.C.E. (Improvisation Concert Ensemble, Wilfrid Laurier University)
Music performed by: Lori Gemmel, Jeremy Bell, Julie Baumgartel, Jerzy Kaplanek, Kathleen Kajioka, David Rose, Christine Vlajk, John Marchman, Paul Pulford, Paul Camrass, Richard Moore, Carol Bauman, Heather Toews, with the Improvisation Concert Ensemble, Wilfrid Laurier University
Set Designer: Visual Art by Stefan Rose
Technical Director: Michael Duncan
Stage Manager: Chuck Kemp
Premiere Date: September 28, 2001. Dancetheatre David Earle
Premiere Location: Theatre Auditorium, Wilfrid Laurier University, Kitchener
Cast: Pasiphae – Danielle Baskerville; Daedalus – D.A. Hoskins; Minotaur – Michael English; Icarus – Mike Moore; Theseus – Graham McKelvie; Ariadne – Suzette Sherman; and Heather Roy

SUMMARY NOTE

Le Minotaur was presented as part of the NUMUS 2001/02 Concert Series and was divided into ten scenes. (1) Daedalus Helps Pasiphae Seduce the White Bull; (2) Minotaur Born and Loathed, Labyrinth Contemplated; (3) Labyrinth Dance; (4) Virgins Sacrificed to the Minotaur and the Building of the Labyrinth; (5) Hidden Waste Scene; (6) Daedalus and Icarus Fly Away; (7) The Fall of Icarus; (8) Theseus Enters Labyrinth – Ariadne Unwinds Thread; (9) Theseus Kills the Minotaur; (10) Theseus and Ariadne Elope.

MICHAEL ENGLISH AS LE MINOTAUR
PHOTO: DAVID EARLE

PROGRAMME NOTE

The Greek legend of the Minotaur varies a bit from telling to telling. The collage you will witness tonight is based on the essence of this story. The music, dance, and visuals are intended to provoke thoughts and emotions that relate to the themes therein. At times the relation is direct and at others indirect, seeking to find contemporary or universal parallels. The opening scene provides much to contemplate: Pasiphae has an ephemeral experience which brings about a grave result. She then shuns the victim and the accomplice. Another difficult theme stemming from the Minotaur story is the idea that one tends to hide (sometimes in a maze of complexity) what one does not understand or cannot face. By extension, these fears are often replaced with contempt projected onto a scapegoat. And ultimately, the scapegoat tends to become what the society projects. Sometimes this projection can be an addiction, and as Zack Browning (composer of scene 4) suggests, the impact of addiction is structural power. Later, the Fall of Icarus scene extends to thoughts about one's failure to control one's inventions. This created technology becomes fatal. To Eric Schwindt (composer of scene 7), Icarus's daring is akin to a rock star's toying with extremes – his Fall of Icarus alludes to the fall of a rock star. In this collage, the final death scene of the Minotaur has been given a new spin. Theseus resurrects the dead virgins on his way to the centre of the labyrinth and drags them with him. Now confronting the Minotaur for the last time, all struggle with the fate of the Minotaur and with their own salvation.

– Jeremy Bell

INTERVIEW: MARCH 28, 2003

This theme of the half-man, half-animal figure goes back to my childhood. In a way it is still very much a part of my consciousness as a teacher to help people recover their instinct and relate to their identity and their animal selves.

Composer Jeremy Bell's scenario followed the thread of the original Minotaur myth and also included many disparate elements such as commissioned projections of visual artist Stefan Rose – candid shots of parking garage signs, for example. Jeremy chose all the music. It's a major challenge for a choreographer to accept a full evening of contemporary music and attempt to relate the story that was being laid over it. But I admire Jeremy very much and I trust him completely.

Michael English danced the part of the Minotaur. He wore shoulder pads, a jockstrap with a hockey cup in it, a fencing mask with two silver scythes for horns, gloves, boots with five-inch soles and silver rugby pants. It was a great outfit and he was monumental on that stage.

The students of Wilfrid Laurier University who were involved in the performance were creative, inspired and intelligent young people who were good-natured, good-spirited, interested and interesting. Their after-performance parties are perhaps the best I have ever attended.

A PLAY OF LIGHT

(2002)

Composer: J.S. Bach
Premiere Date: February 2, 2002
Premiere Location: River Run Centre, Guelph
Cast: Aleta Crawley, Michelle Mummery, Rachel Ecclestone, Robin Clavert, Neesa Kenemy, Suzette Sherman, Helen Jones, Michael English, Ron Stewart, Mike Moore, Greg Moore

SUMMARY NOTE

A Play of Light was part of Heart Sapphire, a presentation by Sarah Jane Burton. This 'pure dance' work was divided into four sections: (1) The quintet from *Visible Distance*; (2) An energetic quintet of senior students from Temple Studios; (3) A lush quartet of mature dancers; (4) An outpouring of energy from upstage left to downstage right.

PROGRAMME COVER FOR PREMIERE OF *A PLAY OF LIGHT*

KING DAVID

(2002)

Duration: 1 hour
Composer: Arthur Honegger
Music Title: King David
Conductor: Gerald Neufeld
Music performed by: Guelph Chamber Choir, Orchestra London
Narrator: Colin Fox
Premiere Date: April 7, 2002.
Dancetheatre David Earle
Premiere Location: River Run Centre, Guelph
Cast: King David – Gérald Michaud★; Mical / The Witch of Endor – Suzette Sherman; Jonathon – Michael English; Bathsheba – Danielle Baskerville; with Aleta Crawley, Evadne Fulton, Heather Roy, Rachel Ecclestone

★*Appeared courtesy of the Danny Grossman Dance Company*

SUMMARY NOTE

King David, a passionate portrayal of heroism, love and tragedy, was commissioned by the Guelph Chamber Choir.

INTERVIEW: MARCH 28, 2003

This was another very tough commission, from the Guelph Chamber Choir, that I listened to a thousand times and despaired of being able to create anything to this music. Eventually I chose eight sections that seemed most danceable and could tell the story of King David. Along with Colin Fox's clear narration, the sections illustrated through dance added a great deal to the musical performance and made a difficult piece of music more approachable for the audience.

So often the musical soloists are the people who speak to us and appreciate what we are doing. After the dress rehearsal, two sopranos said they couldn't watch the dancers because they found it too moving and were unable to continue singing.

As always there was no costume budget but we were able to find ten pairs of wrap-and-tie pants in a local boutique and these gave the piece a biblical look. Gérald Michaud's performance of King David's dance before the ark was as big and exuberant and muscular and kinetic as anything I ever remember seeing. Suzette Sherman was the Witch of Endor as well as Mical. It was astonishing to see the power of darkness she evoked as the witch and the innocence that was so poignant in the character of the abandoned wife.

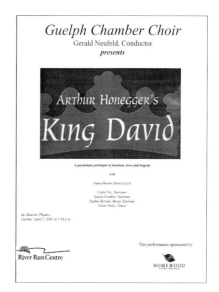

PROGRAMME COVER FOR PREMIERE OF *KING DAVID*

THE REPROACHES

(2002)

Composer: John Sanders
Premiere Date: Spring 2002.
Dancetheatre David Earle
Premiere Location: Fairlawn United
Church, Toronto
Cast: Michael English, Gérald Michaud,
Evadne Fulton, Danielle Baskerville

INTERVIEW: JULY 2003

I believe that dance is perfect in the
architectural setting of a church and I
always like the dancers to look formal
when we perform in those surroundings,
especially because I presume there
might be some resistance in the
congregation.

EVADNE FULTON AND DANIELLE BASKERVILLE
IN *THE REPROACHES*
PHOTO: DAVID EARLE

VANISHING PERSPECTIVES: PARTS ONE AND TWO

(2002)

Duration: 20 minutes
Composer: Rodney Sharman
Music Titles: Four Seasons One Tree,
Cordes Vides
Music performed by: Arraymusic,
Erica Goodman
Costume Designer: Heather Young
Lighting Designer: John Carter
Premiere Date: November 28, 2002.
Dancers Dancing
Premiere Location: Norman Rothstein
Theatre, Vancouver
Cast: Christopher Duban, Desirée
Dunbar, Day Helesic, Lisa Höstman,
Jackie Nel

SUMMARY NOTE

Vanishing Perspectives premiered in a
performance called Elegance + Chaos,
presented by Dancers Dancing, Judith
Garay, Artistic Director. Performance of
the score was donated by Arraymusic.

PROGRAMME NOTE

This piece was created in memory of
Michael J. Baker.

In my search for music for this Vancouver commission, presented by artistic director Judith Garay's group Dancers Dancing, I thought of Rodney Sharman because he is a Canadian composer and more specifically a Vancouver composer. He had sent me a tape of music for dance with one piece in particular I liked, which was played by Arraymusic.

Michael James Baker, a musician who had contributed to many of my works over the years – especially his brilliant musical collage for *Court of Miracles* – had died a year earlier. Because there was a trumpet in the piece and Michael had played the trumpet, I decided I wanted to do something in his memory. It made me feel, in a poignant way, that the piece could be about people offering their gifts to the world and not always having them received. Not that that's necessarily true of Michael – though it's true of many Canadian artists and true of the times, in a way. So I envisioned a band of gypsies – I think a true artist is a kind of gypsy who doesn't belong to any world but his or her own and can adapt creatively to any surroundings.

I used images from some of the first loves of my youth – Chagall's paintings of fanciful, circus-like figures, and Picasso's acrobats – and initially had the five dancers marking acrobatic tricks as if rehearsing for a performance. Each time they would cartwheel forward and arrive at the front of the stage it was as if they had come to a void and they would retreat.

The title *Vanishing Perspectives* was a play on words using the Renaissance discovery of perspective. The dancers' actions were created to establish the sense of a vanishing point but I also wanted to incorporate the intolerable idea of live theatre vanishing from the face of the earth. I choreographed it using the dancers as a visible axis where people kept setting up a perspective, coming and going, and finally vanishing.

The music for the second part was a harp solo and the piece was spatially opposite to part one with all the action moving across the stage instead of moving up and down.

CHRISTOPHER DUBAN AND LISA HÖSTMAN IN REHEARSAL FOR *VANISHING PERSPECTIVES: PARTS ONE AND TWO*
PHOTO: CHRIS RANDLE

STRIP SHOW

(2002)

Composer: A multi-media presentation under the musical direction of Jeremy Bell
Conductor: Evan Mitchell
Music performed by: Julie Baumgartel, Jeremy Bell, Paul Camrass, Omar Daniel, Laurie Gemmel, Amy Hamilton, Cynthia Hiebert, John Marshman, Evan Mitchell, Patricia O'Callaghan, Erika Raum, Mark Thompson, Brandon Valdivia, Noel Webb
Lighting Designer: Peter Carrette
Premiere Date: November 29, 2002. Dancetheatre David Earle
Premiere Location: Humanities Theatre, University of Waterloo
Cast: Danielle Baskerville, Bea Benian, Aleta Crawley, David Earle, Michael English, D.A. Hoskins, Graham McKelvie, Michelle Mummery, Heather Roy, Suzette Sherman

SUMMARY NOTE

Strip Show was part of the NUMUS 2002/03 Concert Series – Jeremy Bell, Artistic Director. Technical direction – Jascha Narveson; Visuals – Ed Video Media Arts; Composers and Videographers – Luciano Berio, Omar Daniel, Louis Dufort, Sofia Gubaidulina, György Ligeti, Kate Monro, Adrian Moore, Jascha Narveson, Kaija Saariaho, Nathan Saliwonchyk, Allen Strange, Sean Varah, Kurt Weill.

PROGRAMME NOTE

On 'Nakedness', Milena Jesenska, the great love of Franz Kafka, said of him, "We all seem able to live because we have at one time or other taken refuge in a lie, in blindness, enthusiasm or optimism, in a belief, in pessimism, or whatever. But he has never fled to a protective refuge, nowhere. He is absolutely incapable of lying. He has no refuge, no home. That is why he is exposed to everything from which we are protected. He is like a naked man." There is not a time in human history in which we were not depicted by artists in our natural nakedness. The range of images, paintings and sculptures, is astonishing in the differing attitudes to God's handiwork. (I like to think that God made many fewer mistakes than are attributed to him.) As a dance artist I have devoted my life to the evolution of the body as an expressive instrument, and as an arena in which character is uncovered. I know of no other experience that engages us mentally, physically, emotionally, and spiritually to the same degree as dance. There have been in our time, images of nakedness of unspeakable horror, and a proliferation of images intended to arouse … there is little mystery left about the way we are made. My definition of sin is making less of something. Our entry into the most significant acts of our existence is marred by prejudice, by guilt, and by fear. I chose the title *Strip Show* for this evening of powerful music and physical imagery to draw attention to the level to which our sacred selves have fallen. "We are always naked. What did we suppose? Our clothes could hide our soul?"

INTERVIEW: MARCH 28, 2003

I had wanted to do something about nakedness for more than ten years because it's been a very big theme in my life. I've always found it bizarre that people put Eros [erotic love] on a level with violence – as a crime. The fact that our sexuality is not introduced to us in a sacred context is very damaging and I don't know if people ever recover from that. I wanted *Strip Show* to sound cheap and vulgar because I think it sums up the place we've reached as a species in our assessment of our physical selves – that the naked body is sort of sideshow material.

NUMUS artistic director Jeremy Bell liked my scenario and was interested in having it happen with live contemporary music. He chose the majority of the music, but I couldn't hear any connection between the music and the scenarios I'd written, so I dropped everything I'd planned and started from scratch. The thing I hadn't considered was that, ironically, the least likely people to disrobe in public are dancers because of their body issues. I realized that, section by section, each piece exposed the dancers so emotionally that having them naked would be redundant and would distract from the real nakedness they were offering.

A serious problem developed over two videotapes that Jeremy had made, one that was very cynical with scraps of pornographic films and highly charged music. It threw into high contrast the two directions we were coming from. I was trying to use nakedness in a way that was moving and humane, and he was pointing out the flaws in our society in its uses of Eros. A very beautiful section I had choreographed for Suzette Sherman was to follow the videotape, but I knew it would look ridiculous. Once you open people up to the cynicism of the present you can't be innocent in front of them a moment later. It was one of the great traumas of my entire professional life that I had to cut Suzette's only section and let the soprano sing it alone.

I created a solo for Danielle Baskerville inspired by a biography about Milena Jesenska, one of Franz Kafka's loves. The account of her existence in a concentration camp related how she retained her elegance and brilliance in the most demeaning circumstances and played a role in helping others. In Danielle's solo to a Sofia Gubaidulina composition, she was continually touching her skin. What would begin as a caress would become an effort to shed her skin as if she could rid herself of the circumstances. Danielle is such an honest dancer that she was concerned she would look too 'healthy' to play such a role, but, of course, dance is never literal. It's taking elements from experience, re-organizing them and juxtaposing them against other elements. In that sense it isn't acting – it's the repetition of gesture and the rhythm of distress. Danielle has

her own extraordinary power and having her as a vehicle for the expression of the greatness of certain individuals provided a profoundly moving performance.

The night before the performance I had great fears that the piece had gotten out of control and the idioms were going to cancel each other out. But it hung together quite well and was another opportunity for the audience to encounter movement imagery while experiencing an evening of very extreme and powerful music.

MICHAEL ENGLISH, DANIELLE BASKERVILLE, MIKE MOORE IN *STRIP SHOW*
PHOTO MONTAGE: DAVID EARLE

Journal: December 16, 1991

This piece has a history with me. The theme is human nakedness in highly contrasting situations – both with humanizing and dehumanizing possibilities.

Journal: September 17, 1993

I have been collecting images and ideas – I think I would have a scrim to lend a little distance, probably very little actual nudity. I imagine a score with completely contrasting sections, from sleazy to sacred – every period of music. When I was a child in the 1940s my parents took me to the Canadian National Exhibition. In the Better Living building, every hour, a woman took a bath in silhouette high overhead in a tower. You saw her enter, drop her bathrobe, breasts in profile – very deco poses – step into the bath, sit down, lift foam up, blow it away, step out, dry herself, wrap a towel around herself. End of show.

As a young boy of that era, starved for naked imagery, I found only magazine pictures of dead men – naked soldiers on the battlefield, slaves that had been captured and tortured by men in white sheets and hung naked from trees. A tragic introduction to sexuality.

Journal: June 28, 1996

Strip Show may happen next December – my farewell season at TDT. I certainly want to face the issue of age in this piece. I've been listening to the Arvo Pärt *Te Deum* and it seems possible to imagine the piece as a continuous unfolding of imagery – a sort of parade toward the audience to this monumental score.

Journal: March 10, 2001

As we drive to Kitchener through the white limbo punctured in places by jet black skeleton trees, we see Mennonites, all in black, in black horse-drawn carriages. I can't help but think how easily people are fooled by the Buck Rogers world and the illusion that we are somehow different than people have been for centuries. *Strip Show* comes up constantly when I describe work I want to do. I have new insights regularly – a modern version of the soldiers dividing Christ's clothing – fighting over it after gambling for it as he hangs suffering overhead. Perfect for this time of acquisitiveness.

Journal: July 10, 2002

Thoughts have been ongoing. Dates have been set! I intend to enjoy this process. *Strip Show* was dropped from Open Ears New Music Festival in Kitchener because it is sponsored by the symphony and the title was too controversial – also banned from the theatre because it is owned by Mennonites. So, NUMUS Concert Series will present it next November.

PICCOLO TEATRO OR SELF PORTRAIT AS A DROWNED MAN

(2003)

Duration: 12 minutes
Composer: Fiorenzo Carpi
Lighting Designers: Ross Manson,
David Earle
Premiere Date: March 1, 2003.
Overall Dance
Premiere Location: St. Jacobs Schoolhouse
Theatre
Cast: Danielle Baskerville, Kate Alton

SUMMARY NOTE

Piccolo Teatro was commissioned by
Overall Dance and Kate Alton. It was
divided into seven duets: Sideshow,
Birds, Dreamwalk, Self Annunciation,
Brides, Mists and Celestial Ballroom.

INTERVIEW: MARCH 28, 2003

The composer, Fiorenzo Carpi, wrote
incidental music for plays at the Piccolo
Teatro de Milano. I choreographed
seven duets for Kate Alton and Danielle
Baskerville – two of the most beautiful
dancers in Canada, if not the world.
They are extraordinary women and of
course known only within our tiny
dance world.

Initially I had the idea to use props,
but in the end it became very minimal.
The Bird duet began with literal
gestures: holding a bird, releasing it,
arm gestures with flared hands, a one-
wing theme. But after seeing it, I kept
just two movement themes – the most
abstract – a hovering shape descending,
and retirés with rises and balances as
long as they can be held … an extreme
contrast to the first Sideshow section.
At rehearsal I showed Kate and
Danielle a photograph of a funeral
monument of two women in a Holland
cemetery, one who is an angel holding
the other in her arms. They reproduced
it so beautifully that I put it at the end
of the Dreamwalk duet. The Self
Annunciation or self-rape section was a
hand touching the self intimately – the
other hand pushing it away, gestures of
adoration, wiping away tears,
overcome, exhausted from resisting,
sensual shocks, acceptance and
beautification.

The costumes, purchased from
Value Village, were ivory coloured.
The performers changed one article of
clothing on stage after each duet.
Suzette Sherman had the interesting
idea to end the number with a costume
change back into the original outfits
and it made a saucy ending.

DANIELLE BASKERVILLE AND KATE ALTON IN *PICCOLO TEATRO OR SELF PORTRAIT AS A DROWNED MAN*
PHOTO: DAVID EARLE

the particulars —

?)

$200 for d———

$250 for the choreog——

Hmmm —

We are working to reaffirm certain values that are threatened in our society, such as dignity, respect and commitment.

It was Martha Graham's intention to create a universal dance language. She was influenced by African dance forms and rhythms, by Asian philosophies and their physical disciplines, and she borrowed elements from European theatre dance. In my classes I acknowledge my inheritance from the artists who have preceded me in modern dance and I trust that in allowing my teaching to be inspired by the great dancers who have illuminated my life's work a new dance language has evolved.

PROGRAMME NOTE FROM ROSEDALE CONCERTS PERFORMANCE,
MARCH 23, 2003

JESU, MEINE FREUDE

(2003)

Duration: 25 minutes
Composer: J.S. Bach
Music Title: Jesu Meine Freude
Conductor: Wayne Strongman
Music performed by: Rosedale Soloists,
Choir and Orchestra
Premiere Date: March 23, 2003.
Dancetheatre David Earle
Premiere Location: Rosedale United
Church, Toronto
Cast: (1) Chorale – Suzette Sherman;
(2) Es ist nun nichts – Suzette Sherman,
Bea Benian, Michael English;
(3) Chorale – Suzette Sherman,
Graham McKelvie, Barbara Baltus
(Pallomina), Evadne Fulton, Ray Hogg;
(4) Denn das Gesetz – Suzette
Sherman, Bea Benian; (5) Chorale –
Suzette Sherman, Gérald Michaud;
(6) Ihr aber seid Nicht Fleischlich –
Suzette Sherman, Ray Hogg, Barbara
Baltus (Pallomina), Evadne Fulton,
Bea Benian, Michael English; (7)
Chorale – Suzette Sherman, Gérald
Michaud, Bea Benian, Ray Hogg;
(8) So aber Christus in euch ist – Suzette
Sherman, Ray Hogg, Evadne Fulton,
Graham McKelvie; (9) Chorale –
Suzette Sherman, Gérald Michaud;
(10) So nun der Geist – Suzette Sherman,
Gérald Michaud, Michael English,
Bea Benian; (11) Chorale – Suzette
Sherman, Gérald Michaud, Michael
English, Bea Benian, Ray Hogg,
Barbara Baltus (Pallomina),
Graham McKelvie, Evadne Fulton

SUMMARY NOTE

Jesu Meine Freude was commissioned
by Rosedale Concerts for Dancetheatre
David Earle through a generous gift by
Jim and Sandra Pitblado.

PROGRAMME NOTE

Johann Sebastian Bach has been a
lifelong companion to me. My first
work for the Toronto Dance Theatre in
its first season in the fall of 1968 was
the Adagio from the *Concerto for Violin
and Oboe in C Minor* (*Mirrors*). Since that
time I have choreographed twelve
more works to his music. I do not hear
an historical period with Bach. The
music is timeless and transcending for
me. Even the darkest texts are a source
of light it seems. If God is a focus of all
human hope, He has the most
luminous messenger in J.S. Bach.

INTERVIEW: MARCH 28, 2003

I felt the first Bach Chorale needed to
be very simple, very human, almost
pedestrian. I used the gesture for
making the sign of the cross, which
turned into an embrace as the opening
and closing of the piece. The floor
pattern was also a cross on the
diagonals so all the Chorales were in
cruciform pattern. I had read the
translated text but, because it was sung
in German, I presumed the audience
would not try to relate what they heard
to what they saw.

I visualized the piece with a large
number of people doing most of the
sections, but the space at Rosedale
Church was twelve feet by thirty-six
feet so I used small groups with Suzette
Sherman remaining in each section as
the through-line.

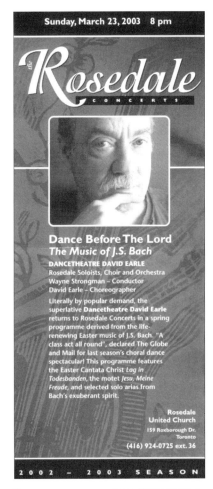

Sunday, March 23, 2003 8 pm

the **Rosedale**
CONCERTS

Dance Before The Lord
The Music of J.S. Bach
DANCETHEATRE DAVID EARLE
Rosedale Soloists, Choir and Orchestra
Wayne Strongman – Conductor
David Earle – Choreographer

Literally by popular demand, the
superlative **Dancetheatre David Earle**
returns to Rosedale Concerts in a spring
programme derived from the life-
renewing Easter music of J.S. Bach. "A
class act all round", declared The Globe
and Mail for last season's choral dance
spectacular! This programme features
the Easter Cantata Christ *Lag in
Todesbanden*, the motet *Jesu, Meine
Freude*, and selected solo arias from
Bach's exuberant spirit.

**Rosedale
United Church**
159 Roxborough Dr.
Toronto
(416) 924-0725 ext. 36

2 0 0 2 – 2 0 0 3 S E A S O N

FLYER FOR PREMIERE OF *JESU, MEINE FREUDE*

SEALEVEL

(2003)

Composer: Morton Feldman
Premiere Date: July 3, 2003.
Dancetheatre David Earle
Premiere Location: 401 Richmond
Street West, Toronto
Cast: Michael English, Bea Benian

SUMMARY NOTE

Sealevel was commissioned for Water, the Ontario Society of Artists' (OSA) 129th Annual Open Juried Exhibition, and performed at the gala reception for The Water Project – a Provincial initiative of the OSA with exhibitions at sixty-seven galleries across Ontario.

INSTALLATION FOR *SEALEVEL*
PHOTO: DAVID EARLE

Madhouse

tableau of inmates

seven solos:

sloth

gluttony

pride

envy

avarice

lust

anger

I feel dancers need to develop their consciousness.
When a dancer, despite wonderful technique, was not
interesting to watch, we would say that they lacked
"psychic density". If a character in a dance work is
completely one-sided it's unacceptable. You need to
show all the dimensions – the good and the bad –
you can't expose only part of yourself. You have to
read, you have to look, you have to listen, and you
have to consume all the other art forms and all of life
as well. You must have substance – everything that
comes out went in, and hopefully emerges
transformed. The more greatness you are able to
absorb the more likely you are to produce something
of meaning and consequence.

INTERVIEW: MARCH 28, 2003

Townspeople steal in and play trio

It is DtDE's belief that dance offers a unique experience, engaging the physical, mental, emotional and spiritual. Dance begins where words end. It is the global language. It is essential in these times to pass on to as many people as possible the solace and empowerment that this, the oldest art form, can confer.

In the age of self, of the computer, I believe that the living arts will experience a renaissance to provide a much needed balance to people's lives. Dance can be the most healing art for those who perform and those who watch. Dancers are not only the athletes of the gods but also their messengers.

There has been a tragic tradition in dance of cruelty, of emotional and physical abuse. We are doing everything in our power to reverse this situation, to bring affirmative values to young dancers that will encourage wholeness and health as well as poetry and personal power in every individual.

THE MERMAN OF ORFORD

(2004)

Composer: Harry Somers
Music Title: The Merman of Orford
Conductor: Les Dala; Music Advisor –
John Hess
Music performed by: Robert Cram – flute;
Bardyhl Gievori – French horn;
Russell Hartenberger – percussion;
Tom Wiebe – cello
Lighting Designer: Paul Mathiesen
Technical Director: Matt Foster
Stage Manager: Kathryn Davies
Assistant Stage Manager: Rachel
Monaghan
Premiere Date: May 26, 2004.
Dancetheatre David Earle
Premiere Location: Jane Mallett Theatre,
St. Lawrence Centre for the Arts,
Toronto
Cast: The Merman – Graham McKelvie;
The Girl Who Loves Him – Karen Rose;
The Prima Ballerina – Suzette Sherman;
The Premier Danseur – Ray Hogg;
The Company – Danielle Baskerville,
Evadne Fulton, Barbara Pallomina,
Roberto Campanella, Gérald Michaud*

**Appeared courtesy of The Danny
Grossman Dance Company*

SUMMARY NOTE

David Earle – Director; Ray Hogg –
Assistant Stage Director.

Soundstreams Canada, Lawrence
Cherney, Artistic Director, presented
Somersfest, a programme of two of
Harry Somers' compositions: *The Merman
of Orford* and *The Death of Enkidu*.

PROGRAMME NOTE

A performance troupe in a seaside town
are preparing a new work based on a
local legend of a curious creature found
in the sea. (1) Prologue; (2) Overture;
(3) A rehearsal; (4) The Merman in his
habitat; (5) The Merman captured;
(6) Training the Merman;
(7) The Merman clothed and shod;
(8) Entr'acte; (9) A ballet class;
(10) The Show Part I, II, III;
(11) The Merman returns to the sea.

CHOREOGRAPHER'S NOTE

Harry Somers' *The Merman of Orford*
was first presented at the Shaw Festival
in 1978 by the Canadian Mime Theatre.
Having a dance company illustrate the
score allows for a new interpretation
of the music, which is very danceable
indeed. And so, I have created my own
story which I hope reflects the curious,
poignant drama I hear in this vital and
mysterious music.

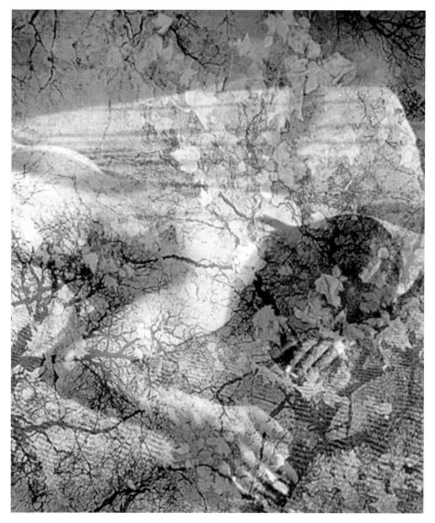

**PUBLICITY ARTWORK FOR *THE MERMAN OF ORFORD*
PHOTO MONTAGE: DAVID EARLE**

THE DEATH OF ENKIDU

(2004)

Composer: Harry Somers
Libretto by: Martin Kinch
Music Title: The Death of Enkidu
Conductor: Les Dala; Music Advisor –
John Hess
Music performed by: Max Christie –
clarinet; Robert Cram – flute; Bardyhl
Gievori, Dan Gress – French horn;
Robin Engleman, Russell Hartenberger,
Bev Johnston – percussion; Erica
Goodman – harp; Andrea Grant –
piano. Singers: Enkidu – David
Pomeroy; Soldier One – Gregory Dahl;
Soldier Two – Doug MacNaughton;
Soldier Three – Alain Coulombe;
Old Woman – Julie Nesrallah; Young
Woman – Amanda Parsons
Lighting Designer: Paul Mathiesen
Technical Director: Matt Foster
Stage Manager: Kathryn Davies
Assistant Stage Manager: Rachel Monaghan
Premiere Date: May 26, 2004.
Dancetheatre David Earle
Premiere Location: Jane Mallet Theatre,
St. Lawrence Centre for the Arts,
Toronto
Cast: Danielle Baskerville, Graham
McKelvie, Ray Hogg, Gérald Michaud*

** Appeared courtesy of The Danny
Grossman Dance Company*

SUMMARY NOTE

The Death of Enkidu was directed by
Ray Hogg. Soundstreams Canada,
Lawrence Cherney, Artistic Director,
presented Somersfest, a programme
of two of Harry Somers' compositions:
The Merman of Orford and *The Death of
Enkidu.*

CHOREOGRAPHER'S NOTE

When I was asked to provide a visual
component to these performances of
Harry Somers' *The Death of Enkidu*,
I was uncertain how much the dramatic
narrative should be illustrated. I
struggled with creating an idiom that
would not seem inappropriately literal
when the text is already so explicit. I
decided to make the dancers spectators
like yourselves, hearing in the music
melodies, rhythms, moods, and
emotions in the text – suggestions for
actions and images. Robert Cram told
me that Harry Somers would have
welcomed more abstraction in the
realization of *Enkidu*. I found in Harry's
writings at the end of the notes on
Enkidu the following statement: "In
short, I feel we're involved with too
much narrative description rather than
allowing for a level of music and
action". This gave me the permission
I needed to take a new approach to this
epic work.

PROGRAMME NOTE

The Death of Enkidu, plot synopsis:
Part 1, Scene 1, of the music drama,
Enkidu, is set in the camp of the
invading army of Chaldea. It is the
seventh year of the war, the enemy is
still undefeated, and Enkidu, Chief
Captain of the King, Gilgamesh, is
dying. It is night. Enkidu is on a litter
and is in a fever. Three soldiers are
engaged in the timeless time-killer of
throwing the dice. After seven years,
two of the soldiers, veterans, are tough,
practical, and unsentimental. The third,
a young soldier, still has some innocence.
Enkidu and the soldiers are living in
two different realities: the former in the
past, the events of his life being relived
as he dies; the latter in the hard reality
of the present, yet now and again
seeing something strange, a foreboding,
a chill whose meaning is beyond their
comprehension. They are in a perilous
situation. They are at odds. They can't
stand this half-savage whose reek of
death makes them only too aware of
their own mortality, yet their own
survival depends on his; he's the only
one who can lead them out of this
barren land. Gilgamesh is away and
they have little faith that he will return.
The central focus, which has been the
soldiers' reality for the opening scene,
moves to Enkidu's for the latter part.
This land, which is so bone-chillingly
desolate to the young soldiers, was
home to the young Enkidu. He recalls
the joy of his life with the wild
creatures, the beauty of the desert,
the swift streams, the running with the
wolf-pack under a clear moonlit sky,
the Wolf-King trapped, his freeing of
the Wolf-King, and finally the hunter's
seeing him and taking the news to
Gilgamesh. The soldiers, in their reality,
only see a rather demented half-man,
half beast, ranting and howling in a
feverish state. Part 1, Scene 2 continues
without interruption. It is cold and
desolate. Words are difficult to utter.
The soldiers try, but can't bring forth
any enthusiasm. An old woman starts
to chant. A courtesan enters, her duty
now to bathe Enkidu's forehead, to
cool the fever. It's sufficiently cooled for
Enkidu to touch the edge of the present
reality of himself and the others before
returning to his own inner reality. He
relives his seduction by the prostitute:
she was like some Ishtar, the divine
personification of the planet Venus,
goddess of love and voluptuousness,
violent and incapable of tolerating the
least obstacle to her wishes. He curses
her for destroying his early days of
peace and joy, yet relives an unfamiliar
passion and lust, which overcame him.
Parallel to his inner reality, the external
reality proceeds as the young soldier is
approached and eventually seduced by
the courtesan, thus not only existing in
the present, but also personifying the
event in Enkidu's past. Enkidu then
relives in his mind the alienation from
his 'brothers' following which we are
brought directly into the present when

the young soldier gets into a fight with the other two over the courtesan. As the fight develops, Enkidu curses his 'civilization'; the adaptation to the ways of men, learning their language, adopting their clothes, learning to use their weapons, training for battle. Finally the young soldier is utterly defeated, his face pushed in the dirt. "Who's a prostitute now!" says the courtesan scornfully. Enkidu has relived the experience – "I touched my forehead to the ground. I called him Master." The scene, and Enkidu: Part 1, concludes with his thrice cry of "Gilgamesh". The old woman intones a last phrase and terminates with a long exhalation of breath into silence.

– Harry Somers, 1977

PUBLICITY ARTWORK FOR *THE DEATH OF ENKIDU*
PHOTO MONTAGE: DAVID EARLE

A FARTHER SHORE

(2004)

Composer: Rabih Abou-Khalil
Premiere Date: November 27, 2004.
Dancetheatre David Earle
Premiere Location: Guelph Youth
Music Centre
Cast: (1) Julia Garlisi, Michael English;
(2) Suzette Sherman, Julia Garlisi;
(3) Suzette Sherman, Michael English

PROGRAMME NOTE

Which is deeper and more impenetrable,
the ocean or the human heart?

— Isadore Ducasse

SUZETTE SHERMAN AND JULIA GARLISI IN *A FARTHER SHORE*
PHOTO: DAVID EARLE

THE HEART AT NIGHT

(2005)

Composer: Dimitri Shostakovich
Music Title: String Quartet #13
Music performed by: Penderecki String
Quartet: Jeremy Bell, Jerzy Kaplanek,
Christine Vlajk, Simon Fryer
Lighting Designer: Aaron Kelly
Premiere Date: April 1, 2005.
Dancetheatre David Earle
Premiere Location: Co-operators Hall,
River Run Centre, Gueiph
Cast: Dancers – Michael English, Evadne
Fulton, Barbara Pallomina, Graham
McKelvie; The Poet – Suzette Sherman;
Her Muse – Danielle Baskerville

SUMMARY NOTE

Full title is *The Heart at Night, A Requiem
for Anna Akhmatova.*

PROGRAMME NOTE

To the heroism of the poet who
continues to speak the truth in times
of cultural control.

ARTIST'S STATEMENT

When I began this work, I did not have
a programme in mind, that is, it wasn't
about anything beyond a physical and
emotional response to the Shostakovich
quartet. I began by making the walking
patterns. After reading *Shostakovich and
Stalin* by Solomon Volkov, to learn
more about the Life that produced this
extraordinary composition, I was
inspired by the great courage of
Dimitri Shostakovich in the face of
alternating encouragement and public
humiliation, and even worse, the threat
of death not only to him but to those
he loved. (It is difficult in these times
when the artist is so marginalized, to
imagine that half a century ago in
Russia artists' powers of influence were
so feared by their government.)

Returning to the studio, to the work
at hand, I came to the moment of
introducing a solo figure. This work is
part of a larger project in which I hope
to create new works for the dancers
who have influenced and embodied my
ongoing quest in this art form. Suzette
Sherman and I have offered each other
inspiration for some twenty-five years.
Initially I found it very difficult to find
the role that she could play amongst
these people who walk the streets with
no destination and who are constantly
threatened by unseen danger. She could
be, except for gender, the composer
himself, who constantly produced
music in which his true feelings were
concealed, risking everything. But then
I thought of Anna Akhmatova, another
hero of that time. In her youth she was
dark and slender, not unlike Suzette. I
don't believe in one human being
actually representing another … so
Suzette is not Anna Akhmatova, she is
the poet in an arena of control and

DANIELLE BASKERVILLE, GRAHAM MCKELVIE, SUZETTE SHERMAN
IN *THE HEART AT NIGHT*
PHOTO MONTAGE: DAVID EARLE

persecution. Akhmatova became the
spokesperson for the Russian people.
Her most famous work is entitled
"Poem Without a Hero".

When I first went to Russia with Bill
Coleman, as rehearsal director for his
magnificent work *Convoy PQ-17*, on the
very first morning I went to see the
little apartment in which Akhmatova
lived and wrote. It is in the servants'
quarters of a vast baroque palace and
has become a museum. Seeing her
photographs, her pens and papers, her
desk and chair were moving enough,
but hearing her poetry declaimed in the
next room to a group of Russian
tourists brought me to tears. Her life
was fraught with challenges and
tragedies. Her former husband, the
poet Nikolai Guliev, was executed on
Stalin's orders, her dear friend and
fellow poet Osip Mandelstam died in a
prison camp, and her son Lev was
constantly arrested and imprisoned.

The great poets Vladimir Mayakovsky,
Sergei Essenin and Marina Tsvetaeva
took their own lives, but Akhmatova
and Pasternak survived. I have added a
layer of imagery over a piece of music
that has no need of it. It will still be
played, hopefully for centuries, without
my interpretation in dance. I have
responded as the music dictated to me,
after listening to it for months. It is a
very rich creation, full of darkness and
light. In one of my many books on
Anna Akhmatova I read that during the
siege of Leningrad she was evacuated
by plane "clutching the score of
Shostakovich's Seventh Symphony".
Choreographing this quartet was
suggested to me by Jeremy Bell. I'm
very grateful for his constant support
and to all of the Penderecki Quartet for
their courage in embarking on so risky
a project, this foray into the unknown,
with their formidable artistry and
generous spirits.

Dance is perhaps the oldest art – when you walk in rhythm with your heartbeat you are close to dance. Choreography is the art of arranging movement in time and space. Even if a work is performed in silence, it is only dance when it contains the elements of music, particularly rhythm.

The most essential element is the dancer. Sometimes a creator in dance may envy a writer or a painter, who can work in solitude with materials that don't have changes of mood or fluctuations of interest or energy … or do the colours on a palette begin to argue amongst themselves from time to time? Although the human instrument is fragile, it offers qualities that artists in other mediums would envy, because each performer in modern dance is trained to offer creative possibilities to the choreographer.

Often, the creator of a work needs only to suggest feelings, ideas, or style and the dancers begin to produce physical vocabulary that, with organization and revision, generates a work from the inside out. Not all choreographers avail themselves of this method – some prefer to prepare movement phrases privately and teach them to the dancers.

So, the choreographer's tools are the highly evolved living instruments entrusted to them, an awareness of the elements of music and an ability to arrange bodies in motion in space. There is something of the sculptor that is needed, and something of the architect.

My way is to drown myself in the music. I listen all my waking hours, and sometimes beyond, to the music I am to visualize. My goal is to find the exact complement to the sound in movement – something which does not distract from it, but illuminates it so that someone discovering the music for the first time, with the addition of physical images, absorbs it as they would on the third or fourth hearing.

All creation requires a leap of faith. There is no direct connection between reason and art. This is undoubtedly why it is so often held in such suspicion. This is also where art connects with the sacred. We were given all the materials and the imagination to enhance paradise. Perhaps because we have denied the fact that every individual is born with a unique gift to deliver, we have destroyed that garden into which we were born. The suppression of expression is the root of anger. We have never seen a world in which every human gift was received and nurtured.

I like to go into the process of creation like a blank page, a white canvas, with few concrete ideas but with a flood of energy from the music, waiting for the impending release through the collaboration with my dancers.

I've worked with my current company for six years, and they are my muses. Desire is an essential part of all creation, and I have been in love with the precious, fragile, powerful individuals through whom I speak, and whose voices I seek to realize and liberate.

Sometimes I have to face the realization that most of my works are lost – even those few that were videotaped have disappeared. I cannot wait for the time when the arts are appreciated and embraced, and for dance to be recorded in print by our writers of substance. But despite these challenges, because of the life element unique to dance, I am grateful to have been chosen by it.

The writer, the painter, the sculptor, the architect, the musician and the composer have all left lasting achievements. But they did not embrace their materials of creation as I have done after a performance, feeling their pounding hearts and knowing they have survived an arena where their honesty, their hard-earned physical and psychic powers have entered directly into people's lives as surely as blood can be passed from one living being to another.

DAVID EARLE, ELORA FESTIVAL PROGRAMME NOTE, 2001

INDEX TO CATALOGUE OF WORKS

David Earle's choreographic works are shown below in alphabetical order. The numbers in parentheses represent the date the work was choreographed followed by the opus number for that year. The final number is the page reference.

AUTHOR'S BIOGRAPHY

MICHELE (PRESLY) GREEN

Michele Green is a freelance writer who has enjoyed a successful career as a dancer, dance teacher and director.

Born in Saskatoon in 1952, Michele began her dance training with Saskatchewan teacher Lusia Pavlychenko. From 1968–1971, while working toward her R.A.D. Intermediate and Advanced exams, she also directed a studio in the town of Unity. Michele attended summer dance programmes in Nelson, Edmonton, Elliot Lake, Toronto, and in Winnipeg on a Royal Winnipeg Ballet scholarship. She trained with distinguished teachers to include Arnold Spohr, Earl Kraul, Eva von Gencsy and David Moroni, and was introduced to modern dance by Toronto Dance Theatre Co-founder Patricia Beatty.

Michele's professional dance career began in 1971 with Winnipeg Contemporary Dancers where she worked with notable choreographers including Paul Sanasardo, James Waring, Sophie Maslow and Rachel Browne. In 1973, she and fellow dancer Jim Green left Contemporary Dancers to marry and, with Lusia Pavlychenko, co-founded Saskatchewan Dance Theatre. The company of eight dancers toured the province offering rural communities their first exposure to live dance performance.

In 1980 Michele, Jim and their two children moved to Stouffville, Ontario where she opened her school, The DanceCentre. This was followed by the formation of The DanceCentre Youth Company created for senior students. Many students were later accepted into various professional institutions to include the National Ballet School and the School of Toronto Dance Theatre. Michele also managed to find time to undertake choreographic projects for outside companies.

In June 2000, after nineteen seasons, Michele sold The DanceCentre and set her sights on a writing career. Her work has since appeared in publications including *Quill & Quire*, *In the Hills* magazine, *Sideroads of Caledon & Erin*, *Dance Collection Danse Magazine* and *Canadian Writer's Journal*. She has also completed her first novel.

Currently, Michele and Jim live in the picturesque countryside of Caledon, Ontario where Michele continues to write and is an active volunteer at The Headwaters Health Care Centre in Orangeville. Together they enjoy following the careers of their children Stephanie and Joel.

CREDITS

Dance Collection Danse is grateful to those who have contributed their time and efforts, writings, photographs and archival materials to assist in building this book.

Jean-Philippe Alepins, Les Grands Ballets Canadiens de Montréal

Carol Anderson, Ontario Society of Artists

Nir Bareket

Danielle Baskerville

William Brown, Oriana Singers

Heather Campbell, Canadian Children's Dance Theatre

Dawn Cattapan, Ballet Creole

Rudi Christl

David Cooper

Michael Cooper

Dave Davis

Rhodnie Désir, Les Grands Ballets Canadiens de Montréal

Eric Dzenis

Michael English

David Ferguson, Suddenly Dance Theatre

Kathe Gray, *id* magazine

Monte Greenshields

Chan Hon Goh

Lori Hamar, Suddenly Dance Theatre

Leica Hardy

Graham Jackson

Nenagh Leigh, Spring Rites

Susan Macpherson

Ken Mimura

Jack Mitchell

Mike Moore

Adrienne Nevile, National Ballet of Canada Archives

Jean Orr, Vancouver Ballet Society

Andrew Oxenham

Jane Parkinson, The Banff Centre Archives

Caitlin Pencarrick, Judith Marcuse Projects

Sylvie Pinard, Université du Québec à Montréal

Michelle Proulx, Les Grands Ballets Canadiens de Montréal

Chris Randle

The Record

Victoria Reilly, *Toronto Daily Star*

Frank Richards

Lutzen Riedstra, Stratford-Perth Archives

Andrea Roberts, School of Toronto Dance Theatre

Germaine Salsberg

Jill Sawyer, The Banff Centre, Media and Communications

Suzette Sherman

Alan Shisko

Michael Slobodian

Peter Sloman

Artis Smith

Ena E. Spalding, The Banff Centre *Centre Letter*

Dawn Suzuki, *The New Canadian*

Iro Valaskakis Tembeck Archives, Université du Québec à Montréal

Cylla von Tiedemann

Ken Townend

Vincent Wong

A HISTORY OF DANCE COLLECTION DANSE PRESS/ES

Publications 1989–2005

Spotlight Newsletters 1951-1956 by Bernadette Carpenter, 1989 (electronic publication)

Dancing for de Basil – Letters to her Parents from Rosemary Deveson edited by Leland Windreich, 1989 (e-publication)

Just Off Stage # 1, 2: Selected stories from Canadian dance history by multiple authors, 1990 (e-publication)

Encyclopedia of Theatre Dance in Canada by Jill Officer, 1990 (e-publication)

Did She Dance: Maud Allan in Performance by Felix Cherniavsky, 1991 (e-publication)

From the Point: National Ballet of Canada Newsletters 1950's -1970, 1991 (e-publication)

Jean-Pierre Perreault Choreographer edited by Aline Gélinas, 1992

Moon Magic: Gail Grant and the 1920's Dance in Regina by Karen Rennie, 1992

Judy Jarvis Dance Artist: A Portrait by Carol Anderson, 1993

Form Without Formula: A concise guide to the choreographic process by Patricia Beatty, 1994

Cecchetti: A Ballet Dynasty by Livia Brillarelli, 1995

Spotlight Newsletters, 1951-1956 by Bernadette Carpenter, 1995

Toronto Dance Teachers 1825-1925 by Mary Jane Warner, 1995

Dictionary of Dance: Words, Terms and Phrases edited by Susan Macpherson, 1996

Dancing for de Basil – Letters to her Parents from Rosemary Deveson edited by Leland Windreich, 1996

Guide to Career Training in the Dance Arts by Grant Strate, 1996

101 from the Encyclopedia of Theatre Dance in Canada edited by Susan Macpherson, 1997

China Dance Journal by Grant Strate, 1997

This Passion: for the love of dance compiled and edited by Carol Anderson, 1998

Dictionary of Classical Ballet Terms: Cecchetti by Rhonda Ryman, 1998

Dance Encounters: Leland Windreich Writing on Dance by Leland Windreich, 1998

Chasing the Tale of Contemporary Dance Parts 1 & 2 by Carol Anderson, 1999 & 2002

Maud Allan and Her Art by Felix Cherniavsky, 1999

June Roper: Ballet Starmaker by Leland Windreich, 1999

The Encyclopedia of Theatre Dance in Canada/Encyclopédie de la Danse Théâtrale au Canada edited by Susan Macpherson, 2000

Theatrical Dance in Vancouver, 1880's- 1920's by Kaija Pepper, 2000

Express Dance: Educators' Resource for Teaching Dance – Grades 4-12 by Carol Oriold, Allen Kaeja and Karen Kaeja, 2000

Revealing Dance by Max Wyman, 2001

The Dance Teacher: A Biography of Kay Armstrong by Kaija Pepper, 2001

Estivale 2000: Canadian Dancing Bodies Then and Now/Estivale 2000: Les Corps dansants d'hier à aujourd'hui edited by Iro Valaskakis Tembeck, 2002

Grant Strate: A Memoir by Grant Strate, 2002

An Instinct for Success: Arnold Spohr and the Royal Winnipeg Ballet by Michael Crabb, 2002

From Automatism to Modern Dance: Françoise Sullivan with Franziska Boas in New York by Allana Lindgren, 2003

DanceForms 1.0 Software for Visualizing and Chronicling Choreography: A Practical Guide by Rhonda Ryman with Lawrence Adams, 2003

Building Your Legacy: An Archiving Handbook for Dance by Lawrence Adams, 2004

Canadian Dance: Visions and Stories by Selma Landen Odom and Mary Jane Warner, 2004